Jerry Flemmons'
TEXAS
SIFTINGS

Jerry Flemmons'
TEXAS SIFTINGS

A BOLD AND
UNCOMMON
CELEBRATION
OF THE
LONE STAR
STATE
★

TEXAS CHRISTIAN UNIVERSITY PRESS ★ FORT WORTH

Acknowledgments

Original *Fort Worth Star–Telegram* illustrations and design by
Don Cook, Dean Eubank, Broc Sears and Drew White.

Computer documentation transfer by Mike Gerst.

Book/cover design by Margie Adkins

Library of Congress Cataloging–in–Publication Data

Flemmons, Jerry.
    [Texas Siftings]
    Jerry Flemmons' Texas Siftings : a bold and uncommon
celebration of the Lone Star state / by Jerry Flemmons.
    p. cm.
    ISBN 0–87565–138–0 (paper) : $10.95
    1. Texas -- Miscellanea. I. Title
    F386.5.F58 1995
    976.4 -- dc20   94–30505
                                                     CIP

CONTENTS

INTRODUCTION

As everything else here, the title is a piece out of Texas' rather formidable literary past. The original *Texas Siftings* was an eight-page magazine begun in 1881 at Austin by Alexander Edwin Sweet. It became America's most successful humor publication, largely because of Sweet's sardonic writing style, but perhaps as much for his subject. Texas always has interested outsiders.

Sweet wrote short pieces – "sketches" was the term in vogue then – on whatever interested him, like the sociability of horned frogs ("a lizard traveling incognito") and what he could invent, such as Texans' inalienable right to be robbed on stagecoach trips.

Anyone curious about this seminal Texas author may track down *Alex Sweet's Texas* (University of Texas Press, 1986) or read him in the original by examining the full set of *Texas Siftings* available in archives of the library of the University of Texas at Arlington.

That's where I began: in libraries, browsing – "sifting"– through old Texas books and publications. I would find something I liked and make a note of it. In one book would be a short, cogent anecdote by a cowboy remembering his cattle drive days; in another, an English lady traveler decrying Texas frontier wives' penchant for dipping snuff. Here was an abandoned Texas slang word worth rescuing; there, a frontier recipe needing a fresh audience, or a clever criticism ripe for resurrection – "Texas is an Elysium of rogues," a Kentuckian wrote in 1833.

Soon, my little smidgens of Texas history and lore grew into columns, and the *Fort Worth Star -Telegram* has been printing them ever since. Alex Sweet's old title was just lying around, gathering dust on a library shelf, so I put it to work again.

The mass of Texas writings is, to understate, substantial. We are a wordy bunch, always have been, and for almost two centuries outsiders, intrigued by all the commotion down here in the Southwest, have come to inspect, dissect, cuss and praise. From the beginning, there was something about Texas, and Texans, that required the world's attention. Texas is a heroic story, the stuff of dreams and myths. Born of an impossible revolution, settled by peoples from somewhere else, Texas engendered the epic American notion of freedom and independence, of self-sufficiency and derring-do. Texas, above all else, has been a spiritual adventure – and the whole grand chronicle is there on library shelves, in newspaper clippings, old letters, written memories. There's little about Texas that hasn't already been said or written, and *Texas Siftings* is a kind of social catalog to much of it.

What's here is a celebration of Texas and Texans, and there is a seriousness to it– a letter to his mother from a Texas Ranger about to be hanged at a Mexico City prison in 1843; the death of a Frenchman during a West Texas buffalo hunt in 1875; the massacre of Indians at Dove Creek. But there's also much that's less than solemn: if our history includes the name of the first white child born in the Panhandle (Joseph Wood in 1877), then certainly we should know the name of the first mule born in Lampasas County (Mag); why cowboy hat brims are turned up at the sides; the etiquette for going through a barbed wire fence; instructions on rolling a Bull Durham cigarette; and the encounter by traveling Russians with a Sweetwater truck-stop cafe waitress.

One indisputable fact about Texans is that we are the textbook definition of a true culture. That is, we have our own food, music, literature, language, societal mores and mythology. The French and English and Japanese and, I suppose, even the Americans have nothing on us.

Chili and beef barbecue, for example, are Texas inventions, and I've included recipes for both (the BBQ instructions will tell you how to feed 600 for a ranch party). Here's two ways to cook rattlesnakes, and how to turn a twenty-five-pound sack of flour into biscuits with "water from the nearest cattle tank," and four ways to make frontier coffee without coffee (ground sweet potato is one). Shouldn't every cook have a recipe for squirrel dumplings?

Mostly I've let the authors and writers speak for themselves. That is, I've left their words as I found them, often ungrammatical, with inventive spellings and roiling syntax. The Texas language is a rich prairie patois, given to studied disregard for classroom rules and bursting with metaphors and similes, elegantly idiomatic – what else could "booger" be but a Texas slang term? Or "prairie feathers"? Or "greasy sack outfit"? All are samples of Texanese that should be preserved. If nothing else, you'll have the answer to that age-old Texas question: What's a "squat"?

I thought *Texas Siftings* had no real organization, that it was only a collection of inter-related excerpts from old writings. But after reading through the assembled manuscript, I can see a pure plot line of renewal and survival and hope in a rough, often unforgiving country, a story told with humor and bravado and bombast. It's a tale of life in a Panhandle dugout and

in a stick hut of South Texas, of brothel madams and mail-order brides, hangings and births, of cowboys and Indians, tough men, tougher women.

And the story is told by people you know, like Big Foot Wallace, Sam Houston, Lindburgh and Steinbeck and Thomas Jefferson (who believed Texas was "the most luxuriant country on earth"), but more that you've never heard of– a 107-year old women remembering the day she was freed from slavery, an anonymous Comanche brave who rode through a prairie fire to rescue a white girl, Uncle Worthy, who explained the dried ear rattling inside his fiddle when he played for country dances, and a frontier wife writing from a crude log cabin at Comanche County in 1861.

If this story is romanticized, and it often is filtered through our mythology, so be it. Aggrandizement is an old Texas habit, though I, as many others, believe that the state really is larger than life. Texas is myth-sized and deserving of the exaggerations we have bestowed upon it over the years.

Perhaps you'll want to know more than the little bits and pieces you find here. Sources are given for almost everything. If, for example, James Cook's account of lawlessness in the Texas of 1875 perks your interest, read his full tale – it's a thrilling and dramatic story – in *50 Years on the Old Frontier* (Yale University Press, 1923, republished by University of Oklahoma Press, 1980).

Read Teddy Blue's book, and Andy Adams' and ol' Charlie Goodnight's saga of ranching life in the wilderness of the Panhandle. They're good stories, well told. I can show you where to find them, back there on library shelves. Come join me.

Jerry Flemmons
Fort Worth, Texas

Like most passionate nations,
Texas has its own history based on,
but not limited by, facts.

John Steinbeck, *Travels With Charley*, 1962

A TEXAS NORTHER EXPLAINED

A gentleman at Sioux City, Ia., appeals to *The Iconoclast* to inform him "What a Texas norther may be." A Texas norther, my Christian friend, may be, and usually is, very much of a nuisance. It is much like a spring day in Iowa, a cold, dank, windy, water wetness. A norther is a Dakota blizzard that has gotten off the reservation and lost its bearings. It usually comes down on Sioux City first like a wolf on the fold, then makes a Fitzgibbons swipe at Omaha. Then it drops a tear on the pine tombstone of the erstwhile Jesse James and blows into the mouth of the Kaw just to see if it's loaded. It then starts across Kansas, but usually becomes frightened by the female reformers; and it comes achortling down into the Indian Territory and makes Lo the poor Indian yearn for a five-finger snifter of bootleg booze and a new government blanket. If it doesn't break its mainspring crossing Red River, it introduces itself to the people of Denison as a full-fledged Texas norther. The norther is bad enough in all conscience, but is to the blizzard what varioloid is to confluent small-pox, or lager beer to Prohibition booze. It is the thin edge of a northern winter which inserts itself into this earthly Eden semi-occasionally, much to our dissatisfaction. It usually catches a man seven miles from home without his overcoat. Sometimes it wanders as far south as Waco and evokes audible wishes that the Yankee would keep their d_____d weather for their consumption. About the time you get a stove up and trusted for a ton of coal, the norther is dead as Hector, the hokey-pokey man is again on the warpath, the kids are rolling on the grass in the glad sunshine and the *gude* housewife is chasing a marauding hen out of the flower garden. That, my dear sir, is all I know about northers. If you can deliver an able-bodied one at this office during the next ten days you will hear of something to your advantage.

William Cowper Brann, *The Iconoclast*, 1897

It is a source of much astonishment and of considerable severe comment upon the religious character of our city, that while we have a theater, a courthouse, a jail and even a capital in Houston, we have not a single church.

The Morning Star, a Houston newspaper, June 18, 1839

STAMPEDE IN STEPHENVILLE

In the 1870s some of the north-bound [cattle] herds of Central Texas passed through Stephenville. It wasn't much of a village and a few fenced-in fields made going around it inconvenient. There were six or seven log cabins, with shed rooms of rawhide lumber, strung along the trail and out from it. The central and largest structure served as a courthouse. It had a gallery covered with boards made of pin oak. The liveliest place in town was a saloon, where, for two-bits, a purchaser could get a 'fair-sized drink' of wagon-yard whisky drawn in a tin cup from a fifty-gallon barrel. Usually a group of cowboys were congregated here, but the dogs of the village far outnumbered both inhabitants and visitors. Dog fights furnished the chief amusement. The sheriff owned a large parrot that habitually perched on the roof of the courthouse gallery. It had picked up a considerable vocabulary from the cowboys, including a profanity. Its favorite expression was "Ye-oh, sic 'em!" which usually started a dog fight. One day a herd was stringing through town, shying but keeping the middle of the road, when the parrot flapped his wings, gave a cowboy yell, and screeched "Ye-oh, sic 'em!" In a second all the dogs in town charged the steers. They stampeded, knocked down all the galleries, including the one the parrot was perched on, rammed through the sheds, and even demolished some of the shacks. Stephenville looked as if a cyclone had struck it.

Dallas News, February 12, 1939

LOST TEXAS

Gunsight
Established as a village about 1880 in southern Stevens County. Named for nearby Gunsight Mountain. By 1885, Gunsight had two churches, a school, gristmill, cotton gin and post office/general store. Population was 50 in 1890. Gunsight station on the Wichita Falls and Southern Railroad was located two miles southeast of the school, church and cemetery. Post office was discontinued about 1920 and mail delivered from nearby Eastland.

AT LAST. THE TRUTH ABOUT TEXAS.

"Dear Sir,
I have been hearing for a long time what a big place Texas is and what wonderful people Texans are, and I have started to wonder.....is there any such place as Texas?"
"Virginia"

"No, Virginia, there isn't any Texas. Texas is just one of those good-natured myths – like Paul Bunyan, George Washington's cherry tree, or Brooklyn – that has been handed down generation after generation, until many people have come to believe it's true. It would be nice, wouldn't it, if there really were a Texas? ...But you're getting to be a big girl now, Virginia, and the truth must not be kept from you. Figure it out for yourself, Virginia; there couldn't be a Texas. No nation on earth, not even this rich and powerful land of ours, could afford a Texas. If Texas really existed, there wouldn't be room for the rest of us. Before you knew it, the whole country would be overrun by Texans. And that way lies madness.

East Texas: Tales from Behind the Pine Curtain,
Michael Dougan, 1985

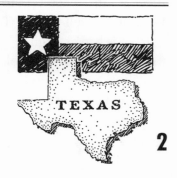

COWMAN'S CLAIM LETTER TO A RAILROAD

Dear Sir:

6:30 this morning in going to the Stockyards to feed at this place another train run in to my stock train. On an open switch. & killed 2 cows & crippled 4. & the rest of the cows in that car is now all over Town. So I got one car less. & few cows in another car is feeling sore & some of them got one horn left.

The Crew of both train jumped off & myself. So it was no one hurt. It was not enough left of the engine & one stock car to tell the Fait [?]. 8 or 10 of the cowboys is all over Town picking up our Cattle — wich you could see them coming down the street driving one or two of them cows - I think they got about 10 of the cows in a Pen (down in Town) & they heard of 5 cows in a corn-field just a little while ago, so I guess they will get most of them back today. I will leave here about 5 p.m. Will make tomorrow market.

Yours truly,

Dock.

P.S. — This R.R. ought to take charge of this whole shipment and Pay for same.

P.S. — The Sheriff shot one cow on the street just a little while ago.

P.S. — The cows down in Town is making the horses run off with buggys and running all the women out of town.

P.S. — I think this will cost the R.R. a good deal in this town.

P.S. — The Rail Road they give me a poor and sorry run.

P.S. — They run my cattle 40 hours before this happened without feed: (how about that).

Jules Verne Allen, *Cowboy Lore,* 1933

RELIGION AT THE GALLUP

I have gone 3/4 of the way around my circuit and find nothing cheering, or encouraging. Many of the members have backslidden, and are spiritually dead– some have been going to dancing school, and some have joined the Baptists.

Reverend Oscar M. Addison, Texas Methodist circuit-riding preacher, 1834 letter

---

TEXAS EATS

Baked Possum

Salt and pepper inside of 1 skinned and gutted possum. Place in a roasting pan with a small amount of water in bottom. Bake for an hour in slow oven. Remove lid and continue to bake until skin is brown.

1840 Texas recipe, quoted in *A Pinch of This and A Handful of That,* 1988

Redeye Gravy

1/3 pound ham per person

1/2 cup of black coffee, very strong, per pound of ham

Ham should be sliced at least 1/4 inches thick. Fry in ungreased skillet – black cast iron is best. When done, remove ham, leave pan drippings.

Add 1/2 cup strong black coffee per pound to the drippings. Bring to a boil and stir constantly. Serve over ham and hot biscuits.

TEXANESE

Round Browns & White Flats

The 19th century Texas Panhandle virtually was without wood or water and families living in sod-roofed dugouts used cow chips for heating and cooking fuel. "Round browns" were considered excellent as a hot-burning fuel and eagerly sought. During droughts, however, the "white flats" were inferior and used only because there was nothing else.

I *want to tell you about a house...* The walls still stand, and part of a rotting roof, from which protrudes part of a rusty stovepipe. Even if I offered explicit directions, many of you would not find it. You'd have to go west from Fort Worth about 225 miles, through Weatherford, Mineral Wells, Breckenridge, Albany, Stamford, Aspermont, Swenson, to Jayton. By now, you'd be into territory from which it costs about fourteen dollars to send a letter to the world, but you'd still not be there yet. Jayton, with a population of about 750, is the last big city before you get there. You drive four or five miles out of Jayton, turn onto a dirt road, and drive deep into what people in the area call the Croton Breaks for seven or eight miles, and after a while you'd come to the little community known as Golden Pond. It's not close to anything. Nobody ever goes there. It's no longer recognizable as a community. The only inhabitants are ghosts, and the southwest wind keens and moans through rotting planks of an occasional ruined shack.

Not far from Golden Pond...is the house I mentioned. It's a little house made of native stone. It measures about ten feet by twelve feet, and there is a small wooden lean-to on the back. You can see through the walls.

[My aunt] lived in that house with a family during the school year of 1933-34... It was her first teaching job, and she made twelve dollars a month with room and board thrown in...

She was far miles from home. There were no telephones in Golden Pond, and she had no transportation save what her feet offered. She was among strangers in a barren, twisty land. That area, the Croton Breaks, is broken, eroded country; dry creeks, ravines, gullies, and canyons break the terrain for thirty miles and more. Even in 1933 it was...nearly forgotten country.

There were no telephones, no electricity, no running water, no way to wash except in a pan or round metal washtub. And the wind whistled and moaned between the rocks.

If you stand on the little rise between ravines where the rock house is, if you stand there even in bright daylight, in every direction you look the distance is blue and far and melancholy. It is the lonesomest country I know. If you stand there at night, imagine what the dark is like when you're far from home and there's only one dingy, smoky kerosene lamp, which for the sake of economy, can't be burned long.

Imagine lying in a narrow bed with the wind coming in between the rocks and across you. How could you possibly imagine a bright future?

Jim Corder, *Lost in West Texas*, 1988

TEXAS POETICAL

Texas

Of all the rich wine
Distilled by sunshine
and mingled with breath of the seas,
With thoughts of full bloom
From Isles of Perfume
Sweet Texas, my star, you have these.

D.S. Landis,
published in *The Bohemian*,
November 1899

T*exas was a new country then...* and certainly an aggressive country. Every brush had its thorn; every animal, reptile, or insect had its horn, tooth, or sting; every male human his revolver; and each was ready to use his weapon of offense on any unfortunate sojourner, on the smallest or even without the smallest provocation...

Richard Irving Dodge,
The Hunting Grounds of the Great West

24 ABSOLUTELY ASTONISHING TEXAS FACTS

1 ★ Texas has one-half of one per cent of all the land area of the world.

2 ★ Texas has seven and two-tenths per cent of the land area of the United States.

3 ★ It's farther around the state of Texas than it is from New York to Liverpool.

4 ★ Texas has a frog ranch, a snake hatchery and a pole cat farm.

5 ★ Texas leads the nation in livestock, land area, wild game, railroad mileage, number of cattle, mules, goats and turkeys, number of cowboys, watermelons, polo ponies, bees, big league ball players, farm laborers, pecans, asses and burros.

6 ★ Texas has: more cotton land than any country on the face of the earth, the longest telephone line in the United States, largest Bermuda onion gardens in the world and the longest reinforced concrete viaduct in the world.

7 ★ The average value of Texas farm land is $14.53 per acre.

8 ★ The Texas farm laborer earns $19.00 per month with board.

9 ★ One year's cotton crop of Texas will clothe 300,000,000 people.

10 ★ There are 17,500 cowboys on Texas ranches.

11 ★ The Texas mule was the predominating class of work animals used in construction of the Panama Canal.

12 ★ Only 3,882 women work in Texas factories.

13 ★ The prevailing hours of labor in Texas factories is 54 hours a week.

14 ★ There are 182 ice factories in Texas.

15 ★ Dallas is the world's largest saddle manufacturing center.

16 ★ Texas ranked fifth with other states in population, having wrested that place from Missouri in the past decade.

17 ★ The 1910 population classifies 3,204,848 whites, 690,049 Negroes, 702 Indians, 595 Chinese, 340 Japanese, 6 Filipinos and 2 Hindus.

18 ★ For every person who leaves Texas and moves to some other State in the Union, we get eight in return.

19 ★ Fifty-eight per cent of our children attend school.

20 ★ There are 10,000 grass widows in Texas and 117,000 of the sod variety.

21 ★ We have 466,562 men in Texas that have never braved the matrimonial seas.

22 ★ There are 20,000 old maids in Texas.

23 ★ One person in every 75 owns an auto in Texas.

24 ★ Texas has 225 buildings five or more stories high.

Five Hundred Texas Facts, compiled by the Texas Business Men's Association, Fort Worth, June 1914

5

Mr. Menasco came into the country when a young man, from Arkansas...

and moved into the northwest part of Denton County, and settled on the head of Clear Creek...

Captain Shegog, who married a sister of Mr. Menasco, lived near him, perhaps a mile and a half from him. One day in the winter of 1868, at a time when Captain Shegog and Menasco were out on the range hunting stock, a large band of [Comanche] Indians, estimated at three hundred, came down through the cross timbers. On this sad and fatal day, the two oldest children of Menasco were at the home of Captain Shegog, where their grandfather, learning that the Indians were in the country, went over to Shegog's to bring them and their aunt, Mrs. Shegog, over to the home of Menasco, where they could be in a safe place.

While they were returning, they were suddenly surrounded by a large number of the Indians. The old man was cruelly murdered and Mrs. Shegog, with her child, a year or more of age, and the two little Menasco girls, four and six years of age, were taken as prisoners. [The Indians] then went to the house of Menasco and began whooping and yelling like infuriated demons...

Mrs. Menasco, taking her stand in the door, with her gun presented, told them that some of them must die, should they attempt to enter there. Just think of this brave woman, standing there all undaunted in the presence of such dreadful danger, seeing her sister-in-law and her own dear children there, captives... Calmly and determinately she stood for home and for fireside and all that was left her there. Those cruel old warriors read in her appearance their fate, so they turned...and left.

They had not taken their prisoners far before they killed Mrs. Shegog's child and, a cold norther blowing and the snow falling, [Mrs. Shegog] slipped off into the darkness and escaped... [The Indians] left both the tender little girls, perhaps frozen to death at the time they were left. The body of one of them was found in about one month afterwards, but that of the other was not found until nearly three months had passed.

"Escape of Mrs. Shegog," *Texas Indian Troubles*, H.G. Bedford, 1905

6

A REPORT OF TEXAS RANGERS IN THE CITY OF THE AZTECS DURING THE U.S.–MEXICAN WAR OF 1847

"There arrived here recently the greatest American curiosities that have as yet entered the City of the Aztecs. They were the observed of all observers, and excited as much lively interest as if President Polk and the American Congress had suddenly set themselves down in front of the Palace to organize a government and laws for the people of this benighted land. Crowds of men flocked to see them (however, always keeping at a respectful distance), and women, affrighted, rushed from the balconies into the houses. Well, they are nothing more or less than Jack Hays and his Texas Rangers, with their old fashioned maple stock rifles lying across their saddles, the butts of two large pistols sticking out of the holsters, and a pair of Colt's six-shooters belted around their waists, making only fifteen shots to the man...

"I have described the entrance of Hays' regiment into this town, and will tell you a little of what took place on their arrival in the City of Mexico. Hays' men entered the city of the Aztecs and approached the Halls of the Montezumas, the objects of universal curiosity. The sides of the streets were lined with spectators of every hue and creed, from the Major General of the North American Army to the Mexican beggar. Quietly they moved along. Not a word was spoken. They seemed unconscious that they were the observed of the observers. The trees in their own native forests would have attracted as much attention as they seemed to bestow upon anything around them. They seemed to say, "We have seen men, and been in cities before..." It is said that a real gentleman is as much at home in one place as in another, the bear dance and the hoe-down, as well as in the King's Palace. In each they acted their part well... After entering the city they had proceeded some distance without being molested; but the temptation at length became too great for a Mexican to withstand, and one standing on the sidewalk threw a stone at the head of one of the Rangers. It was the last stone he ever threw, for quicker than thought, a flash was seen, a report was heard, and the offender fell dead. A flash of lightning from the eternal throne could not have called him more speedily to account. The ranger quickly replaced the pistol in his belt and rode on. Ere long another stone was thrown and another Mexican launched into eternity. During all this time no noise was heard, no disturbance was perceivable, the column never halted, and the ranks were unbroken."

From an unnamed newspaper, December 1847
Reported in *Frontier Times*, May 1931

We are in a helluva fix. Let's go to the saloon, have a stiff drink, and then fight our way out of it.

Said to be the strategy Texians were urged to adopt against Santa Anna and Mexico in 1836. Attributed to Thomas J. Rusk, speaking informally to the cabinet of David Burnet, ad interim governor of the Republic of Texas

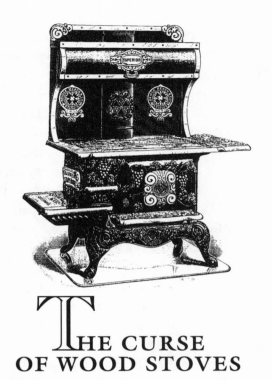

THE CURSE OF WOOD STOVES

The Hill Country farm wife had to haul water, and she had to haul wood.

Because there was no electricity, Hill Country stoves were wood stoves. The spread of the cedar brakes had given the area a plentiful supply of wood, but cedar seared bone-dry by the Hill Country sun burned so fast that the stoves seemed to devour it...

The necessity of hauling the wood was not, however, the principal reason so many farm wives hated their wood stoves. In part, they hated these stoves because they were so hard to 'start up.' The damper that opened into the firebox created only a small draft even on a breezy day, and on a windless day, there was no draft...and a fire would flicker out time after time. 'With an electric stove, you just turned on a switch and you had heat,' said Lucille O'Donnell, but with a wood stove, a woman might have to stuff kindling and wood into the firebox over and over again. And even after the fire was lit, the stove 'didn't heat up in a minute, you know,' Lucille O'Donnell said – it might in fact take an hour. In part, farm wives hated wood stoves because they were so dirty, because the smoke from the wood blackened walls and ceilings, and ashes were always escaping through the grating, and the ashes box had to be emptied twice a day – a dirty job and dirtier if, while the ashes were being carried outside, a gust of wind scattered them around inside the house. They hated the stoves because they could not be left unattended. Without devices to regulate the heat and keep the temperature steady, when the stove was being used for baking or some other cooking in which an even temperature was important, a woman would have to keep a constant watch on the fire, thrusting logs – or corncobs, which ignited quickly – into the firebox every time the heat slackened.

Robert Caro,
The Years of Lyndon Johnson, 1982

★ ★ ★ ★ ★ ★ ★ ★ ★ ★ ★ ★ ★ ★ ★ ★ ★ ★ ★

A traveler who came to Texas in the 1840s described the climate as "tropical between northers." Sandstorms may blow either during the tropical seasons or with the northers. "De rain he vas all vind, and de vind he vas all sand," a German farmer of the Dust Bowl said. The wind out of a cloud will blind the earth with sand, and then the cloud will catch up with the sandstorm and rain mud. "Never mind the weather, just so the wind doesn't blow," is an old saying out where the sandstorms are worst.

J. Frank Dobie,
Tales of Old-Time Texas, 1928

After Texas became an independent nation, a Treaty of Silence was signed with the Indians. According to this compact, everyone agreed to stop making loud noises and go home to bed.

William Gruben, *The Atlantic*, September 1985

★ ★ ★ ★ ★ ★ ★ ★ ★ ★ ★ ★ ★ ★ ★ ★ ★ ★ ★

At the end of the cattle drive in *Abilene, Kansas*...we went into town, tied our ponies, and the first place we visited was a saloon and dance hall. We ordered toddies like we had seen older men do, and drank them down, for we were dry, very dry, as it had been a long way between drinks. I quit my partner, as he had a girl to talk to, so I went out and in a very short time I went into another store and saloon. I got another toddy, my hat begin to stiffen up, but I pushed it up in front, moved my pistol to where it would be handy, then sat down on a box in the saloon and picked up a newspaper and thought I would read a few lines, but my two toddies were at war, so I could not very well understand what I read...

I headed for a place across the street, where I could hear a fiddle. It was a saloon, gambling and dance hall. Here I saw an old, long-haired fellow dealing monte. I went to the bar and called for a toddy, and as I was drinking it a girl came up and put her little hand under my chin, and looked me square in the face and said, "Oh, you pretty Texas boy, give me a drink." I asked her what she wanted and she said anything I took, so I called for two toddies. My, I was getting rich fast – a pretty girl and plenty of whiskey. My old hat now was back on my head. My boss had given me four dollars spending money and I had a five-dollar bill, so I told the girl that she could make herself easy; that I was going to break the monte game, buy out the saloon, and keep her to run it for me when I went back to Texas for my other herd of cattle.

Well, I went to the old, long-haired dealer, and as he was making a new layout I put my five on the first card (a king) and about the third pull I won. I now had ten dollars and I thought I had better go and get another toddy before I played again. As I was getting rich so fast, I put the two bills on the tray and won. Had now twenty dollars, so I moved my hat as far as it would go and went to get a drink – another toddy, but my girl was gone. I wanted to show her that I was not joking about buying out the saloon after I broke the bank. After this drink things did not look so good. I went back and it seemed to me that I did not care whether I broke him or not. I soon lost all I had won and my old original five. When I quit him my hat was becoming more settled, getting more down in front, and I went out, found my partner and left for camp. The next morning, in place of owning a saloon and going back to Texas after my other herds, I felt – Oh! What's the use? You old fellows know how I felt.

J.L. McCaleb
quoted in *The Trail Drivers of Texas,* 1925

The Texan turned out to be good-natured, generous and likable. In three days nobody could stand him.

Catch-22
Joseph Heller, 1961

★ ★

Son-of-a-bitch Stew

(Be aware that without marrow gut it is not a true son-of-a-bitch.)

1 pound beefsteak

1/4 pound beef fat

3/4 pound heart

1/2 pound liver

1 marrow gut

1/2 pound sweetbreads

1 pound brains

Salt, black pepper, cayenne pepper

2 tablespoons flour

1/2 cup water

Cut all beef parts into one-inch cubes. Place everything except brains and seasoning into large stew pot and add water to cover twice over. Cook on low heat for four hours; add water if necessary to keep meat slightly covered. Then add brains, salt, black pepper, and generous dash of cayenne pepper. Simmer for 1/2 hour and then thicken broth with 2 tablespoons flour first mixed in 1/2 cup water. Taste to test, and, if not spicy hot, add more red pepper. Serves 8-10.

(To satisfy any lingering curiosity, marrow gut is the tube connecting the two stomachs of beef cows. It must be obtained fresh since it contains a delicacy very similar to bone marrow. The marrow from this gut is the secret to an authentic sonovabitch stew.)

Western Cooking
Matt Braun, 1988

We emigrated to Texas when I was about four years old...and settled twelve miles from LaGrange. It was in 1852, near as I can remember. We came all the way in house wagons. I don't remember how long we were on the road. We stopped at Little Rock, Ark., quite a while on account of sickness and lost a little sister there....

My father bought cattle and moved to the frontier, Palo Pinto County, where we experienced all the dangers, privations and hardships of a frontier life. We settled on the west side of the Brazos river, one mile from Tom Pollard's place. My father and a hired man made two small cabins in which we lived through the winter. There was no lumber to be had, so we lived on dirt floors and cooked, ate and slept all in the same room....

A neighbor, William Eubank...enclosed his house and yard with tall pickets as a protection against the Indians. One day the men folks were all away when the women discovered a party of Indians approaching the house, so they quickly set a bench by the wall and Miss Mary Eubank put a man's hat on her head and got up on the bench so her hat could be seen by the Indians, then she pointed a gun at them, when they saw the gun they halted, held a consultation, then turned and went away without molesting them. Perhaps she saved the whole family by her brave act. Many other women have been as brave and defended their families from being killed by the Indians....

My mother said she suffered a thousand deaths at that place for fear the Indians would come and kill us or carry off some of the children. Why men would take their families out in such danger I can't understand....

Well, the [Civil] war came up then and our mother died. Her father had lots of slaves and she was raised very tenderly, never having done any work before she was married. The hardships and continuous fear of frontier life was too much for her.

Mrs. Mary A. Nunley of Thorp Spring
quoted in *Pioneers of the Southwest*
John A. Hart, 1909

A MUSICAL DEATH IN SAN SABA

Two San Saba County cowboys, Harkey and Barbee, who had known one another and worked together for years, shot one another to death after Barbee suddenly bawled out a song that started "Dickie dinktum Dick," and Harkey remarked that it was a foolish song.

LeRoy Yarborough, *Canyon of the Eagles*, 1989

THE LAND OF HARD SECRETS

Some of the largest [cattle herds] belonged to great companies operating where the nation's range cattle industry had its origin – along the Rio Grande between the Pecos and Mexico Bay. It was the *brasada*, the brush country, stretching from the Nueces to the Rio Grande. It was profuse in growth – but almost all were thorned. It was either swept with gray dust borne on blistering winds or beaten by deluges that hissed as they first struck the hot ground or raked by blizzards that came whistling out of the north. In the interlocking thickets that enclosed small clearings where grew curly mesquite grass, cattle could graze by thousands and hardly be seen by horsemen who sought them. There cicadas sang of the heat, and sharp-haired peccaries rooted among the thorns and blue quail ran amidst the wire shadows, and rattlesnakes sought the cool and sometimes were drummed to death by wild turkey gobblers at whose destroying wings they struck and struck with no effect on nerveless quill and feather. It was a land of hard secrets, the best kept of which was the location of water. Its few rivers ran in abruptly cut trenches walled with pink or yellow or slate blue limestone, and could not be seen except at their very brinks. In every direction the wilderness looked the same. There were no distant mountains to be seen. The land swelled away toward the white sky in slow rolls and shimmered in the heat that blended the ashen color of the ground with the olive greens of the brush until across the distance there seemed to hang a veil of dusty lilac.

Paul Horgan,
Great River, Vol. II
1954

TEXAS POETICAL	

Fort Worth

Just a few years ago, where there stood
    a small town
That was known as the place where
    "The Panther Lay Down,"
There stands a proud city – a great busy mart –
Where the swift wheels of commerce pulse
    forth from the heart.
A city of churches, of schools and homes,
Of glittering steeples, and towering domes;
And though you may go to the ends
    of the earth,
You'll hear of that city – its name
    is – Fort Worth!

J.P. Brashear, a Fort Worth druggist
printed in *The Bohemian*, November, 1899

Although Texas was always as large as it is now, and even larger, yet somehow or other it was not discovered by Europeans until as late as A.D. 1665. It is a little singular that it was not discovered sooner, particularly as it was always left out of doors after dark. If Texas had been a woodpile or a chicken it would probably have been discovered much earlier.

Alexander Edwin Sweet, *Texas Siftings*, 1882

LOST TEXAS

Gusher
In Hardin County, named by Monroe Edge, who laid out the townsite in 1904 because a nearby oil field was expected to extend in that direction. It did, but barely. At the crescendo of the oil boomlet the town had 3,500 population but it existed only for two years. Post office was discontinued and townsite was abandoned in 1906.

Extracted from *The Handbook of Texas, Vol. I*, 1952

THE CONSTITUTION OF THE STATE OF WEST TEXAS

Texas came into the Union with the right to divide itself into five states, should the need and inclination arise. In the passing century and a half several serious division proposals have been debated. This is one of them. It was advanced at a state Constitutional Convention in January 1869, and argued that West Texas should separate and become a fully self-governed entity of the United States. A Constitution was drafted, bolstered by a Bill of Rights that unequivocally screams for individual freedoms. It is a warning, especially to the government, not to mess with any citizen of the State of West Texas. But the movement failed. The proposal was defeated through administrative strategy and West Texas never became a separate state. Did it?

We, the people of West Texas, acknowledging with gratitude the grace of God in permitting us to make choice of our form of Government, do ordain and establish this Constitution:

ARTICLE I
BILL OF RIGHTS

That the general, great and essential principles of liberty and free government may be recognized and established, we declare:

Section 1. All political power is inherent in the people, and all free governments are founded on their authority, and instituted for their benefit; and the people of this State have at all times the unalienable right to alter or reform their form of government.

Section 2. All freemen, when they form a social compact, have equal rights; and no man, or set of men, is entitled to exclusive separate public emoluments and privileges.

Section 15. No person shall ever be imprisoned for debt.

Section 21. The equality of all persons before the law is herein recognized, and shall ever remain inviolate; nor shall any citizen ever be deprived of any right, privilege, or immunity, nor be exempted from any burden, or duty, on account of race, color, or previous condition.

Section 22. Importations of persons "under the name of coolies," or any other name or designation, or the adoption of any system of "peonage," whereby the helpless and unfortunate may be reduced to practical bondage, shall never be authorized, or tolerated by the laws of this State, and neither slavery nor involuntary servitude...shall ever exist in this State.

Section 23. To guard against transgressions of the high powers herein delegated, we declare that every thing in this "Bill of Rights" is excepted out of the general powers of government, and shall forever remain inviolate...and should any department (either executive, legislative or judicial) attempt, in any manner, to deprive any person or persons of their herein guaranteed civil and political rights, such attempts shall be considered as a violation of the compact under which this State entered the Union.

Authorship is ascribed to E.J. Davis and "six other delegates" at the convention

Weather Report

The weather has been so dry here for the past three weeks that the wells are empty and the fish in the creeks are carrying [toadstools] for parasols to keep the sun from burning their backs. Water is getting so scarce that Baptists and Campbellites are beginning to favor baptism by sprinkling, and they have quit turning up their noses at Presbyterians. A prominent prohibitionist has ordered a case of beer from Decatur – as lather to shave himself. (*Taylor County News*)

Monday morning an individual was seen in town with a long slicker under his arm, and it naturally created intense indignation... [Sheriff] S.C. Hines swore out a warrant against him, charging him with carrying a slicker against the peace and dignity and future prospects of rain. (*Albany News*)

Early Texas humorous news reports during prolonged dry spells, quoted by John Edward Weems in *If You Don't Like The Weather...*, 1986

Hailstone and Damnation in Waco

[An event] in 1920 produced what came to be known as "The Giant Waco Hailstone." The famed Robert L. Ripley reported it in his "Believe It or Not" syndicated newspaper cartoon, declaring that a 10-pound hailstone, the largest ever, fell on a street in front of a downtown Waco hotel before about a dozen or more sober witnesses taking shelter in the hotel's entrance.

So the story goes, one John Fitzhugh, a railroad executive, who was known as "Uncle Johnny" to his friends, was a guest in the hotel that day. His room on the second floor was situated where he could see the people standing under the portico.

Those were Prohibition days and Fitzhugh was having a few illegal cocktails in his room. While sipping along, he chipped away at the big square of ice that the bellboy had brought up in a silver bucket, and the ice soon took the shape of a globe. About that time it started to hail – small pellets (probably pea-sized). Suddenly, forces conspired to inspire "Uncle Johnny," who had a bent for mischief.

He carried the chunk of ice into the bathroom and held it under hot water until its surfaces smoothed out into an almost perfect ball. At the height of the hailstorm, he tossed the ice into the street right in front of the hotel entrance. Cries went up and anxious faces peered skyward. A doorman rushed out, picked up the giant "hailstone" and carried it into the hotel, where the ice was weighed on kitchen scales at 10 pounds.

When a reporter and photographer arrived, Fitzhugh decided things had gone far enough. He called to the reporter, a friend, and told him it was all a joke, that the hailstone was right out of the ice plant. That irked the reporter, who knew he had a good story. He advised Fitzhugh he had half a dozen witnesses who had seen the thing fall right out of the sky.

There was no dissuading the reporter, and the next day there were headlines complete with verification from the doorman and other awe-struck witnesses.

Leon Lyons, *Waco Tribune-Herald*, April 23, 1982

I will say to those who have applied to The Iconoclast *for information that they might do much worse than come to Texas.* They can find here any kind of climate and soil they care to call for. Alpine claims to have had a snow-storm in July, and the musical hum of the mosquito ushers in the glad new year at Galveston, and rises, alike a paean of praise, at Brownsville on Washington's birthday. While the norther in the Panhandle is taking an inventory of every bone in the human body, the Bohemian Club at Houston will be dallying in the shade of magnolia trees and conning its catechism. The soil in some sections is best adapted to the production of mesquite beans and mule-eared rabbits, while in others it is so prolific that an old corset plowed under will develop into a New Woman, and a pair of discarded suspenders if properly planted and "hilled" will produce a candidate for Congress. If he is looking for an urban location he will find Waco a progressive little city, situate on the tawny Brazos at the head of navigation. Its chief institutions are *The Iconoclast* and Baylor University. One can readily see that a city possessing such a combination of purity and genius is bound to progress. The man who has money which is burning in his pockets will find ample opportunity for its investment. We may be far out on the fringes of civilization, but I trust we realize that the gentle stranger, who comes to us in his guileless faith, should be taken in.

William Cowper Brann, *The Iconoclast*, 1898

★ ★

Mankind is one thing; a man's self is another. What that self is tangles itself knottily with what his people were, and what they came out of. Mine came out of Texas, as did I. If those were louts, they were my own louts.

Origin being as it is an accident outside the scope of one's will, I tend not to seek much credit for being a Texan. Often (breathes there a man?) I can work up some proud warmth about the fact that I indubitably am one. A lot of the time, I'd as soon be forty other kinds of men I've known.

It's not necessary to like being a Texan, or a Midwesterner, or a Jew, or an Andalusian, or a Negro, or a hybrid child of the international rich. It is, I think, necessary to know in that crystal chamber of the mind where one speaks straight to oneself that one is or was that thing, and for any understanding of the human condition it's probably necessary to know a little about what that thing consists of.

John Graves, *Goodbye to A River*, 1964

Marshall Hanks was sent to Texas...to run the mining operation at Barringer Hill [in central Texas]....

No Texan has ever been able to resist the possibilities offered by a green Yankee. [The miners] set to work on Hanks and soon they had him convinced they were all unreformed murderers. Their big opportunity came in 1904 when Hanks received word that his company had all the [minerals] it wanted and that he was to shut down the mine and return to Pennsylvania. The miners pretended that they were outraged about the shutdown. They let it be known that they blamed Hanks for it and they put out the word that he would never leave Llano County alive.

Knowing that he would ship the equipment home by rail from Kingsland, they brought the Wells Fargo express agent in on the prank. The agent suggested to Hanks that the only way for him to escape was to hide in one of the shipping crates and mail himself to Pennsylvania. When the agent signaled to the miners, who were loudly pretending to search for Hanks all over town, they congregated at the depot and made all manner of loud threats. Finally, they stomped into the baggage car and one of them called out to the others, "I'll bet he's in one of these crates. Let's shoot into all of them and see." That was the agent's cue to sing out, "You fellows better not mess with Wells Fargo! Get out of this baggage car!"

Hanks mailed himself out of Llano County, and died at the end of a distinguished career fully believing that the miners had meant to murder him.

LeRoy Yarborough, *Canyon of the Eagles*, 1989

Texas is a land of caviar and clabber

Mary Lasswell's description of East Texas in *I'll Take Texas*, 1958

TWO WEST TEXAS WIND JOKES

1. Out at Odessa, a drive-in theater was showing a Western picture and the wind was blowing so strong, it blew Gene Autry out of the saddle.

2. A terrific windstorm was in progress out on the Plains near Lubbock. Houses and barns were sailing by. Finally, here came a hen sailing through the atmosphere — a little hen, brown, with white spots. Somehow she got turned around and was flying backwards and the wind was blowing so strong that she laid the same egg three times before she passed out of sight.

Boyce House, *Texas Laughs*, 1950

TEXAS POETICAL

Cowboy Days

My fancy drifts, as often through the murky,
*   misty maze of the past, to other*
*   seasons, the good ol' cowboy days,*
Where the grass wuz green an' wavin' and the
*   skies were soft and blue,*
An' the men were brave an' loyal an' the women
*   fair an' true.*
The ol' time cowboy – here's to him – from
*   hired hand to the boss.*
His soul wuz free from envy an' his head wuz
*   free from dross.*
An' deep within his nature, which wuz rugged,
*   high and bold,*
There ran a vein of metal, and the metal, men,
*   wuz gold.*

Luther Lawhon, circa 1916

CHRISTMAS COMES TO BLOOMING GROVE, TEXAS. AT LAST.

Once upon a time, meaning the mid-1950s, Jules Loh, who would go on to become a national prize-winning writer in New York for the Associated Press, labored as a young reporter for the Waco News-Tribune. *He was sent to report on a Nativity pageant being staged in the rural community of Blooming Grove. This is the pageant story as seen through his eyes. The* News-Tribune *declined to publish it. We present it now in print for the first time.*

By Jules Loh

BLOOMING GROVE –They held the Nativity pageant here Monday night, and if it had happened in Bethlehem like it happened in Blooming Grove, Christmas would be a day sooner – or maybe not at all.

For a year the good people of Blooming Grove, Barry and Emhouse had prepared for the pageant.

They practiced religiously, as it were, and sacrificed nothing to realism. The women made the costumes; the men gathered their sheep. Somebody even found myrrh.

The Blooming Grove preacher, a former tent show operator called Brother Bill, arranged the setting.

The manger was in an old barn. A milk cow and an old ram were tied to the manger. At the left was the inn, and at the right were the fields where shepherds, costumed and holding long crooks, were watching over their sheep by night.

Brother Bill had put spotlights on both sides, which were to follow the characters as they entered. Miss Alva Taylor was the reader.

As she read the Christmas story from the Bible the characters would enact the passage.

However, some things got enacted that weren't exactly Biblical.

The choir began to sing, the reader began to read, and the pageant was on.

Out of a pasture behind the barn came Mary and Joseph on their way to enroll; Mary riding a donkey, Joseph walking beside.

The donkey was balky. He kept stopping, and Joseph kept yanking at the halter. Finally, right before they got to the inn, the donkey had enough.

With a grand bray, he r'ared back and pitched Mary right on her bundle of swaddling clothes. She lit with both legs up in the air.

The audience gasped. Some of the women thought she was actually pregnant.

The donkey went down on his side. Joseph thought the donkey was hurt. The donkey wouldn't get up. While Mary picked herself up, Joseph inspected the donkey's legs. He finally decided it was a too tight saddle girth that caused him to pitch.

There was Mary brushing straw off her clothes, and Joseph loosening the saddle girth, and Brother Bill hollering, "For Lord's sake, get those spotlights off 'em! Shine 'em on the inn!"

Mary was fixing to mount up again for another try, but the saddle was too loose so she and Joseph decided to walk the rest of the way to Bethlehem.

Joseph stopped at the inn and just as he was about to knock, the door opened with the innkeeper shaking his head. Mary had forgotten about the inn and was already kneeling at the manger.

The ruckus didn't phase Miss Alva a bit. She kept right on reading and managed to stay about four verses ahead of the rest of the pageant.

Then it came to pass for the angels to appear to the shepherds.

16

At about the same time the spotlights shifted to the fields and the choir began with "Angels We Have Heard on High," the sheep spied that ram tied to the manger.

The sheep started for the ram.

The angel popped up from behind some cedar boughs and said, "Fear not!"

And the shepherds were sore afraid. They were running this way and that, swatting the sheep with their crooks, trying to keep the whole flock from charging the manger.

A few got away – about six. They crowded into the barn next to the ram, and began eating the straw out of the manger.

Happy now, the old ram went "Baa, baa" the rest of the night, and it was somewhat disconcerting to Miss Alva. She would look over at that ram disgustedly, lose her place, find it and continue.

Out of the east came the wise men, slowly, following the star. They deposited their gifts before the manger – all except one of them who had a vase and couldn't get it to stand up on the straw.

Finally he got it balanced, stepped back. The old ram stepped up and kicked it over. The wise man shrugged and let it lay.

Now all were in the barn – Mary, Joseph, shepherds, wise men, sheep and cow – for all to watch and meditate while the choir sang.

But there was more excitement.

In the middle of "Adeste Fideles," the loudspeaker went to shrieking.

And during the deathly pause while it was being fixed, the old milk cow raised her tail and let loose right where somebody was sure to step in it.

Then the Blooming Grove Nativity Pageant was over.

"Amen," said Brother Bill, and the audience answered, "Amen."

COWBOYS USED TO TELL A FUNNY STORY ABOUT...

the dainty daughter of old man Tom Drake, Texas cattle rancher. The boys came from far and near to court her and, because of her pa's name, they gave cute little Miss Drake the nickname of Duck. She could stand a lot of masculine teasing, and the whole Drake family enjoyed her popularity. But one cowpuncher by the name of Buck Custer became a bit too serious in his wooing of the girl and, on a fine Sunday afternoon, she ordered him to see what was on the other side of the hill – and not come back.

Buck followed her command, but he swore to revenge himself. He was riding along cursing Miss Drake and the world in general when he suddenly came upon what is known in the cattle areas as a "hatrack," which is an exceedingly bony, tick-covered calf. Buck was inspired. He lifted his lariat rope, twirled his loop, made his catch, and built a fire. Pretty soon he went on his way, his anger somewhat vented.

It wasn't long before the Drake brothers discovered the calf, undoubtedly one of the ugliest and scrawniest in Texas, and saw what Buck Custer had done. There upon its side was branded in huge letters, D U C K .

Oren Arnold and John P. Hale, *Hot Irons*, 1940

John Hendrix, an old-timer friend of mine I'd always visit when in Fort Worth, Texas, before he died, used to tell me a story of a cowhand who declared the best winter he ever put in was when he was sent out to an old abandoned nester shack to make a line camp. The shack was a one-room affair, papered with old newspapers and farm journals. Accordin' to his story, he read the north, south, east and west walls durin' the winter and was jes' startin' in to read the ceilin' when they called 'im to headquarters.

Ramon F. Adams,
The Old-Time Cowhand, 1948

Outsiders never understand that Texas tall talk is not a lie. It is the expression of the larger truth.

Paul Crume, *A Texan at Bay*, 1961

WELL, I NEVER FROZE ON THE TRAIL, BUT...

I did starve for water, and I don't mean maybe either. It was my first drive, too – that was what made it so hard on me. In the spring of '69 we left Pick Duncan's ranch with a bunch of W Cross L's for the head of the Concho to go from there to the Horsehead Crossing on the Pecos River. We left that good, clear Concho with one barrel of water, intending to refill at Hackberry water hole, mid-way the plains. Halting to answer the cook's 'come and git it' at noon, we went on until dusk, when we pitched camp (no where near that water hole) and when supper was finished, so was the water – fourteen men and not a drop, not to mention the stock, and three days to go. We did not bed the cattle as planned but hit the trail all night and at nine o'clock next morning we stopped to rest an hour; then prodded 'em up and on toward that water hole. Finally when within a mile of it the boss said he would ride ahead and reconnoiter. He was back right now with 'It's so confounded dry you could bury a man in the cracks, they're so deep.' That settled it. We kept the herd hoofin' until three o'clock, halting for another hour, then trailing it straight through until the next day noon when we hit the canyon, twelve miles from Horsehead Crossing. The cattle got wind of the water and pulled out plumb pert. It was half an hour by sun when we got there, and when we got to that river not one of the fourteen boys could speak above a whisper and several could not shut their mouths for swollen tongues. If any of you have ever been as thirsty as we were, you know just how good water — just plain, brackish, alkali, Pecos River water — can taste. It was so good we laid up three days drinkin' our fill and enjoyin' ourselves. Water logged, full of good grub, rested and fresh as daisies, we started up the Pecos to the falls.

There the horse wrangler, named Kuykendall, dismounted on herd and stood his gun by a bush. Remounting, he caught it by the barrel, the hammer caught in the brush, pulled back and blew his head off. We buried him and continued on to Hondo, thence to Denver where we delivered the cattle.

Charlie Harmon, a cowboy, quoted in
Texas Monthly, February 1930

★ ★ ★ ★ ★ ★ ★ ★ ★ ★ ★ ★ ★ ★ ★ ★ ★ ★ ★ ★

The prickly pear [cactus] is a few inches to more than 6 feet tall; it sometimes bears beautiful yellow blooms, sometimes a tasty nutritious dark red fruit resembling a fig or pear. Stains clothing. Cows love the plant and eat the leaves, whose juice contains a natural digestive that's also been considered a diabetes treatment. Need little water. Will propagate from small leaf tossed onto the ground.

Rex Z. Howard, *Texas Tourist Travel Guide*, 1948

I must say as to what I have seen of Texas it is the garden spot of the world, the best land and the best prospects for health I ever saw is here. I expect in all probability to settle on Bodark [sic] or Choctaw Bayou of Red River, that I have no doubt is the richest country in the world, good land and plenty of timber, and the best springs and good mill streams, good range, clear water and every appearance of health. Game aplenty. It is the pass where the buffalo passes north to south and back twice a year, and bees and honey plenty.

Davy Crockett, January 1836,
in a letter to his family in Tennessee

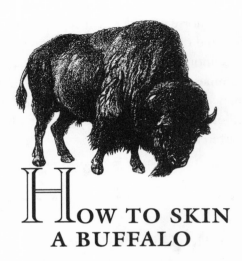

How to Skin a Buffalo

We left the Sweet Water [a Panhandle creek] with enough provisions to last us three months. We had 250 pounds of St. Louis shot-tower lead in bars done up in 25-pound sacks; 4,000 primers, three cans of Dupont powder, and one 6-pound can. We left the Sweet Water a few days after New Year's Day, 1875, starting up Graham Creek; when at its head we veered a little southwest until we crossed the north fork of Red River. Arriving on the breaks of the Salt Fork of the Brazos River, we realized we were in the midst of that vast sea of [buffaloes] that caused us gladness and sorrow, joy, trouble and anxiety, but independence, for the succeeding years. We must have these 3361 hides that this region is to furnish us inside of three months, within a radius of eight miles from this main camp. So at it we went. And [Charlie] Hart started out, and in two hours had killed sixty-three bison.

It was now a busy time. Some days thirty and forty-odd hides, then a good day with eighty-five, and one day in February, one hundred and seventy-one; then again the same month, 203; and these 203 killed on less than ten acres of ground.

We fastened a forked stick to the center of the hind axle-tree of a wagon, letting the end drag on the ground on an incline to say 20 degrees; fastened a chain or rope to the same axle, then we would drive up quartering to the carcass and hook the loose end of the chain over a front leg. After skinning the upper side down, we would start the team up and pull the dead animal up a little, and stop (the stick prevented the wagon from backing up). Then we would skin the belly down mid-sides; start the team again, and pull the carcass over, having rolled the first side of the hide close to the backbone. Then we would skin down to the backbone, and the hide was separated from the carcass. We would then throw the hide in the wagon.

Charlie as a rule did most of his killing from 8 A.M. until noon, but made some good killings in the evening, in which case the carcasses would lie all night before being skinned. These would bloat up and the hide would be tight and stiff, which made the work more tedious. We had to be careful, too, for it was the pride of the skinner to bring in hides free from knife-gashes.

We had good hunting at this camp until the last of February, when all at once the buffaloes were not to be seen.

We then had stacked up and drying 2003 hides; 902 of them I had skinned, and was so accredited. This was an average of 22 buffaloes a day for 41 days. At 25 cents per hide I had earned $225.50.

John R. Cook, *The Border and the Buffalo*, 1907

"Hell," the old-timers used to brag in front of the feed stores in Weatherford and Granbury, "I've done wore out three farms in my time."

John Graves
Goodbye to a River, 1964

A GIRL IS RESCUED FROM A RACING PRAIRIE FIRE BY AN HEROIC COMANCHE BRAVE

As Gus Hartman came back from his Buffalo hunt from up north [about 1878], he come upon emigrant wagon and team, and a middle aged man and woman in great distress. He could see that the plaines from the camp was all burned off. Their camp was where or near where Pampa Texas now stands. The woman told him they were on their way to New Mexico, that they had camped there the day before late in the afternoon, that their daughter, Frances, walked off south of their camp, as she usually took a walk, after riding in the wagon all day. And the woman and her husband had started a fire to prepare their supper. The buffalo grass was about knee high and thick on the ground, and the wind blowing quite hard from the north. Frances had walked off south from the camp. They accidently let the fire catch in the dry grass. They tried to put the fire out but they could do nothing with it. Then they thought of Frances but the black smoke rolling on the ground, and the blaze leaping ten feet high and traviling almost as fast as a horse could run, they were sure Frances had been caught. [They] had been hunting for her since daylight but found no trace of her. They would go to places where they could see something still smoking and burning to find an atelope, deer, wolf or some other animal caught by the raging fire, and burned to death.

[Now], there had been an Indian following the wagon, and as they were up on the staked plains, a levil country, they had not seen this Indian... The Indian saw this girl Frances, running before the fire. He mounted his horse and dashed in to the thick smoke, and a few feet ahead of that awful fire and grabed Frances by one arm lefted her on his horse in front of himself, without slacking his own speed, and turned in the direction the fire was going. He had on only buckskin trousers and mockasons, and an Indian blanket around his body.

Frances did not know what had picked her up, as she had her apron over her face at the time. She said the heat and smoke had about smothered her, but she said she could hear the pounding of the horses feet on the ground, and knew she was on a horse. The Indian was riding a very fast horse & had to let him out to his fastest speed to keep ahead of the fire. The wind whipping the fire this way and that. The fire spread so fast he could not turn to the right or left. They ran south untill they got down off the plaines, then they took it more slowly until they cross a creek, some five miles farther. It was almost dark when the Indian let Frances down on the ground, then he got off of his horse and tied him to a tree that stood near by. He then pulled grass and fixed her a kind of bed in a small ditch, and motioned to Frances to get down in there, and spread his blanket over her. He watched over her through a long cold nite, and next morning took her back to within a half a mile or so of their wagon and pointed to it, and let her down on the ground. Then puting his hand on her head he looked in her eyes a long moment, whirled his coal black steed, and went like the wind back across the burned prairie, leaving only a trail of dust the way he dissapeared.

The Autobiography of Rufe LeFors, 1946

TEXAS EATS

Poke Salad

Leaves of the pokeweed grow abundantly all over East Texas in the spring. Pick only the leaves; the stems are inedible. One resident told us that poke is believed to be a blood thinner.

Pokeweed, leaves only

Enough water to cover the poke leaves

3 to 4 pieces of bacon

salt and pepper to taste

Wash the poke leaves thoroughly two or three times. Place them in a pot with water to cover, then boil them only tender. Drain. Repeat the boiling process. *IT IS IMPORTANT NOT TO EAT THE POKE SALAD AFTER ONLY ONE COOKING.*

Meanwhile, fry the bacon in a skillet until brown, breaking it into small pieces. Add the cooked poke leaves to the bacon and drippings, and heat, adding salt and pepper to taste. Some people prefer to cook the poke and then scramble eggs in with it.

Ellzabeth Davis and
Lauri Strickland-Hays
*Southern Seasons,*1986

TEXANESE

Tin Bellies

Cheap spurs of inferior quality. Prideful cowboys wore more expensive spurs, which carried nicknames like "can openers", "gads", "gut hooks", and "hell rousers."

From the floor of this Senate we have heard many and varied comments upon the magnitude of Texas. Some Senators have expressed a friendly solicitude that we would some day avail ourselves of the privilege accorded us by the resolutions under which we entered the Union, and divide our state into five states. Mr. President, if Texas had contained a population in 1845 sufficient to have justified her admission as five states, it is my opinion that she would have been so admitted… But, sir, Texas is not divided now, and under the providence of God, she will not be divided until the end of time! Her position…excites in her citizens a just and natural pride. She is now the greatest of all the states in area and certain to become the greatest of all in population, wealth and influence…

But, Mr. President, while from her proud eminence today Texas looks upon a future as bright with promise as ever beckoned a people to follow where fate and fortune lead, it is not so much the promise of the future as it is the memory of a glorious past which appeals to her against division. She could partition her fertile valleys and broad prairies; she could distribute her splendid population and wonderful resources; but she could not divide the fadeless glory of those days that are past and gone.

To which of her daughters, Sir, could she assign, without irreparable injustice to all the others, the priceless inheritance of the Alamo, Goliad and San Jacinto? To which could she bequeath the names of Houston, Austin, Fannin, Bowie and Crockett…?

The world has never seen a more sublime courage or a more unselfish patriotism than that which illuminates almost every page in the early history of Texas. Students may know more about other battlefields but none is consecrated with the blood of braver men than those who fell at Goliad. Historians may not record it as one of the decisive battlers of the world, but the victory of the Texans at San Jacinto is destined to exert a greater influence upon the happiness of the human race than all the conflicts that established or subverted the petty kingdoms of the ancient world. Poets have not yet immortalized it with their enduring verse but the Alamo is more resplendent with her heroic sacrifice than was Thermopylae because, while "Thermopylae had her messenger of defeat, the Alamo had none."

Mr. President, if I may be permitted to borrow Webster's well-known apostrophe to Liberty and Union, I would say of Texas: "She is one and inseparable, now and forever."

Speech before the United States Senate
by Texas Senator Joseph W. Bailey, January 1906, during debate over
dividing Texas into five parts

★ ★

THE INSULT

If I owned Texas and all Hell, I would rent out Texas and live in Hell.

General Philip Sheridan, 1866

THE REBUTTAL

Well, damn a man who won't stand up for his own country.

Attributed to a cowboy upon hearing Sheridan's remarks

THE APOLOGY

Speaking so kindly of Texas – and I speak from my heart – probably I ought to explain a remark I once made about it. I had just returned to San Antonio from a hard trip to Chihuahua on some Mexican business when I received an order to proceed at once to New Orleans.

I hired relays and coaches so that I had only to hitch on the wagon and go speedily to get the boat from Galveston. I traveled night and day. It was in August and, need I say, very warm. I arrived here covered with dust, my eyes and ears and throat filled with it. I went to a little hotel in that condition and had just gone up to the register when one of these newspaper men rushed up to me and said, "General, how do you like Texas?"

I was mad and I said, "If I owned Texas and all Hell, I would rent out Texas and live in Hell." Needless to say, that did not represent my true opinion of this magnificent State.

General Philip Sheridan, March 24, 1880 during a speech in Galveston at the Tremont Hotel

---

Mr. Tuttle, a brick mason, fell from the scaffold on which he was working on the new courthouse Monday. He was slightly injured. Mr. John Marening was also injured on the same day standing on the ground. He was shot.

The Lone Star, El Paso, May 6, 1885

TEXAS HOGS

Texas has had an interesting association with the name "hog." Its first native-born governor was James Stephen Hogg. There is a Hog Marsh (Tom Green County), six Hog Mountains (Bell, Brown, Coryell, Llano, Runnels and Stephens counties), and – count 'em – fourteen Hog Creeks in Brown, Concho, Eastland, Ellis, Erath, Falls, Grayson, Hamilton, Houston, Jack, Jasper, Runnels, Shackelford and Upshur counties.

The state is so prosperous it once owned two towns named Hogeye, Texas. One was 16 miles east of Jacksboro on the old Overland Mail route, and had a store, church and school. The other was in Bastrop County near Elgin, and was established before 1858. Only a cemetery remains.

Extracted from *The Handbook of Texas, Vol. I,* 1952

Once I said to a Texas soldier,
   "You're beautiful," and he answered me,
   "Ma'am, you should never say that to a man."
   "And what should I say to a man?"
   "In Texas," he replied, *"The most you can say to a man is that his pants fit him well."*

Marlene Dietrich, *Marlene,* 1989

THE COWBOY

He wears a big hat and big spurs and
    all that,
And leggins of fancy fringed leather;
He takes pride in his boots and the
    pistol he shoots,
And he's happy in all kinds of weather.

He is fond of his horse – 'tis a
    bronco, of course,
For, oh, he can ride like the Devil;
He is old for his years, and he
    always appears
To be foremost at round-up or revel.

He can sing, he can cook, yet his
    eyes have the look
Of a man that to fear is a stranger;
Yes, his cool, quiet nerve will
    always subserve
In his wild life of
    duty and danger.

He gets little to eat and he
    guys tenderfeet,
And for Fashion – oh, well, he's
    'not in it!'
He can rope a gay steer when he gets
    on his ear,
At the rate of two-forty a minute!

His saddle's the best in the wild,
    woolly West,
Sometimes it will cost sixty dollars;
Ah, he knows all the tricks, when
    he brands 'Mavericks,'
But his learning's not gained from
    your scholars.
He is loyal as steel, but demands a
    square deal,
And he hates and despises a coward.
Yet the cowboy you'll find unto
    woman is kind,
Though he'll fight till by death
    overpowered.

Hence I say unto you, give the cowboy
    his due,
And be kinder, my friends, toward
    his folly;
For he's generous and brave, though he
    may not behave
Like your dudes, who are so melancholy.

William Lawrence Chittenden,
Ranch Verses, 1893

26

Texas occupies all
of the North American
continent except the small part set aside
for Canada, Mexico and the 47 less
fortunate states.

Texans are so proud of their state that they
can't sleep at night. If you could examine the
brain of a Texan, you'd find a map of the Lone
Star State printed thereon.

The chief pursuit of Texans used to be
Indians. This was back in the days when our
State was so wild that not even the law of gravitation was obeyed. In fact, the Texas legislature
had not passed the law of gravitation at that
time.

Texas owns the north bank of the Rio
Grande, the only river in the world navigable for
pedestrians.

Texas is so huge that if you used the northern line of the Panhandle for a hinge, you'd flop
Brownsville so close to the Arctic Circle that the
hot tamale peddlers could swap their wares with
the Eskimos for polar bear steaks.

In fact, Texas is so titanic that it is bound-
ed on the north by the Aurora Borealis, on the
south by the invisible lines of equinox, on the
east by primeval chaos and on the west by the
Judgment Day.

If all the bales of cotton produced in our
254 counties in a single season were made into
one stack, you'd have a stairway reaching to the
Pearly Gates.

If all the hogs in Texas were made into one
hog, he could dig the Panama Canal at a single
root of his mighty snoot.

And if all the steers in Texas were made
into one steer, he could stand with his front feet
in the Gulf of Mexico, one hind leg in Lake
Michigan, the other in Hudson's Bay, and with
his tail brush the Northern Lights out of the
Alaskan sky.

And that's no bull!

Traditional Texas chauvinistic boasting

★ ★ ★ ★ ★ ★ ★ ★ ★ ★ ★ ★ ★ ★

The cowboy of the old days is the most misun-
derstood man on earth. Few young people of
the younger generation realize that the western
men – the cowboys – were as brave and
chivalrous as it is possible to be. Bullies and
tyrants were unknown among them. They kept
their places around a herd and under all circumstances; and if they had to fight they were always
ready. Timid men were not known among
them – the life did not fit them. Today many of
the richest and greatest men of Texas were
cowboys. Of the hands I employed there are
now at least three millionaires. Fewer cowboys
have been tried for crimes than any other
class of men.

"Managing a Trail Herd," Charles Goodnight,
printed in *The Southwestern Historical Quarterly*
April 1928

NOT TO MENTION 'HORSE PUCKY'

Texas has immortalized its equine heritage by placing the name 'horse' on all kinds of geographical and natural sites. There is a Horse Mountain (elevation 5,010 feet; Brewster County), which should not be confused with Horse Thief Mountain (not much of a mountain at all in Bell County), which is half a state away from Horse Thief Canyon (Jeff Davis County), which is not the same as Horse Hollow (a stream in Fisher County), which no one should mistake for the bayou called Horse Pen (Harris County), which often is incorrectly taken for Horsepen Creek (Tyler County), which sometimes gets listed for one of the eight tributaries named, simply, Horse Creek (Coleman, Donley, Hansford, Hunt, Lipscomb, Roberts, San Saba and Morris counties), though if you speak Spanish the one in Oldham County more correctly is Agua Caballo and is thought of as Horse Creek by Anglos in spite of the fact that the literal translation is 'horse water,' which might be another thing altogether.

The most famous 'horse' site is Horsehead Crossing in southern Pecos County. The low-water ford was used for centuries by Indians crossing the Pecos River and then in the early 19th century became both a crossing point and water hole for cattle drives heading north (the next water of any consequence was 60 miles), and Butterfield stagecoaches travelling between St. Louis and San Francisco. The crossing received its name because horse skulls were found nearby.

Worth noting were the Texas Horse Marines of the 1836 Revolution. These were a troop of land-locked cavalry which captured three Mexico-bound supply ships at sea off the middle Gulf coast by using phony distress signals. Just using horse sense, of course.

Extracted from *The Handbook of Texas,* 1952

In 1883, Alpine was composed of seven lumber shacks, one general store, and two saloons and dance halls combined. Alpine was in its "wild and woolly" state during this time, and excursions from the East always stopped long enough to give the passengers a chance to view the sights. Most of the passengers were persons who never had been west of New York...

A story is told that on one occasion just before the train departed, one of the passengers, wearing slippers, a smoking jacket, and a monocle, appeared on the rear platform of the last Pullman. One of the cowboys, seeing him, quickly dropped his rope over him, and drew him off the platform, whereupon all of his cowboy companions rushed up shouting, "I saw him first!" "What is it?" "If you can name it, you can have it," "It is mine, I roped it first," and other similar statements were hurled at the head of the scared and helpless prisoner. The westerners, in all good humor among themselves, then began to quarrel over the ownership of the passenger, and guns were brought into play to settle the argument.

The train had gone some distance by this time, but the conductor was implored by the other passengers to back up and recover the man. When it did, there was one frightened tourist who scrambled on board, vowing never to return to the Big Bend.

Carlysle Graham Raht,
Romance of the Davis Mountains and Big Bend, 1919

FOUR WAYS TO SAY YOU'RE TEXAN

1. "I'm the daddy of all the badmen that ever come from Buzzard Hole. I wuz nursed on whisky, cut my teeth on a circular saw, and rattlesnakes wuz my playmates. Us reptiles bit each other to see who's the most piz'nous, and I always win."

2. "I'm a death-dealin' demon from Dead Man's Gulch. The further up you go, the tougher they get, and I hole up a mile past the last camp. I wuz cradled on cholla spines. Grizzlies and catamounts wuz my early playmates, and I'm so hard I kick fire outa flint with my bare toes. I have to put tarantulas and vinegaroons in my whisky to give it flavor, and mix it with strychnine and wolf pizen to give it bite. When I come to town, all the other killers hide under their mammy's aprons. Hide out, little ones, it's my night to drink gore."

3. "I wuz born in an eruptin' volcano and suckled by a lion. I got nine rows of jaw teeth made of iron with holes punched in for more. I'm wild and woolly and full of fleas. Never been curried below the knees. I'm a tornado of destruction, a killer that nourished on blood and it's my night to devour."

4. "I'm shaggy as a bear, wolfish about the head, active as a cougar, and can grin like a hyena until the bark will curl off a gum tree. There's a sprinkling of all sorts in me, from the lion down to the skunk; and before the fight's over you'll pronounce me an entire Zoological Institute, or I miss a figure in my calculation. I could swallow Santa Ann whole, if you will only skewer back his ears, and grease his head a little."

> Traditional early boasting attributed to
> Texas frontiersmen attempting to make others believe
> they were mean; brag No. 4 allegedly was told to
> Davy Crockett and recorded in his diary.

There is an old army story to the effect that, when General [Zachary] Taylor's little army was on the march from Corpus Christi to Matamoras, a soldier on the flank of the column came upon and fired at a [Longhorn] bull. The bull immediately charged, and the soldier, taking to his heels, ran into the column. The bull, undaunted by the numbers of enemies, charged headlong, scattering several regiments like chaff, and finally escaped unhurt, having demoralised and put to flight an army which a few days after covered itself with glory by victoriously encountering five times its numbers of human enemies.

> Richard Irving Dodge,
> *The Hunting Grounds of the Great West,* 1878

TEXAS EATS

Hog Jowl & Turnip Greens

Cook a cured hog jowl in slightly salty water until it is almost tender. Add one or more whole peeled onions, and fresh, crisp, well-washed turnip greens. (To make sure the greens do not retain tiny bugs, soak them for 30 minutes in real salty water and rinse well before adding to the cooking water.) A few sliced turnips should be included with the greens, and added about 30 minutes before the greens are to be removed from the fire. Cook the greens from 1 to 2 hours or until they are very tender. Drain them and serve on a hot platter with the cut-up jowl and the sliced turnips. The pot likker may be served in a separate dish – or how about as a gravy over hot cornbread?

Sarah Morgan,
The Saga of Texas Cookery, 1973

TEXANESE

Wohaw

A word used by plains Indians to indicate cattle when asking for paid tribute from herds crossing tribal lands. Probable origin is that Indians heard cowboys using the English words "whoa" and "haw" and applied them to all of the white man's animals.

TAMING THE WILD MUSTANG

We each bought a horse, or mustang as they call them there, which animals were selling at Brazoria for next to nothing, and rode out into the prairie to look for a convenient spot to settle.

These mustangs are small horses, rarely above fourteen hands high, and are descended from the Spanish breed introduced by the original conquerors of the country. During the three centuries that have elapsed since the conquest of Mexico, they have increased and multiplied to an extraordinary extent and are to be found in vast droves in the Texas prairies, although they are now beginning to become somewhat scarcer. They are taken with the lasso, concerning which instrument or weapon I will say a word or two, notwithstanding that it has often been described.

The lasso is usually from twenty to thirty feet long, very flexible, and composed of strips of twisted ox-hide. One end is fastened to the saddle, and the other, which forms a running noose, held in the hand of the hunter who thus equipped rides out into the prairie. When he discovers a troop of wild horses, he maneuvers to get to windward of them and then to approach as near as possible. If he is an experienced hand, the horses seldom or never escape him, and soon as he finds himself within twenty or thirty feet of them, he throws the noose with unerring aim over the neck of the one he has selected for his prey. This done, he turns his own horse sharp round, gives him the spur, and gallops away, dragging his unfortunate captive after him breathless and with his windpipe so compressed by the noose that he is unable to make the smallest resistance. After a few yards, the mustang falls headlong to the ground and lies motionless and almost lifeless, sometimes badly hurt and disabled. From this day forward, the horse which has been thus caught never forgets the lasso; the mere sight of it makes him tremble in every limb, and, however wild he may be, it is sufficient to show it to him or lay it on his neck to render him as tame and docile as a lamb.

The horse taken, next comes the breaking in, which is effected in no less brutal manner than his capture. The eyes of the unfortunate animal are covered with a bandage, and a tremendous bit, a pound weight or more, clapped into his mouth; the horse breaker puts on a pair of spurs six inches long and with rowels like penknives, and jumping on his back urges him to his very utmost speed. If the horse tries to rear or turns restive, one pull, and not a very hard one either, at the instrument of torture they call a bit is sufficient to tear his mouth to shreds and cause the blood to flow in streams. I have myself seen horses' teeth broken with these barbarous bits. The poor beast whinnies and groans with pain and terror; but there is no help for him, the spurs are at his flanks, and on he goes full gallop till he is ready to sink from fatigue and exhaustion. He then has a quarter of an hour's rest allowed him; but scarcely does he begin to recover breath, which has been ridden or spurred out of his body, when he is again mounted, and has to go through the same violent process as before. If he breaks down during this rude trial, he is either knocked on the head or driven away as useless; but if he holds out, he is marked with a hot iron and left to graze on the prairie. Henceforward, there is no particular difficulty in catching him when wanted. The wildness of the horse is completely punished out of him.

Charles Sealsfield, "Adventures in Texas" printed in *Spirit of the Times*, December 9, 1843

COLONEL TRAVIS SPEAKS TO HIS DOOMED MEN AND DRAWS A LINE IN THE DIRT

Moses Rose, a native of France, was an early immigrant to Texas, and resided in Nacogdoches. Rose was a warm friend of Colonel James Bowie and accompanied him to the Alamo in the fall of 1835. About two hours before sunset, on the third day of March 1836, the bombardment of the Alamo suddenly ceased and during the momentary peace, Colonel Travis gathered his men and spoke to them:

"My brave companions – Necessity compels me to employ the few moments now afforded to make known to you a most solemn and melancholy situation. Be prepared for the worst! Our fate is sealed – within a few days, perhaps a few hours, we must all be in eternity. It is our destiny – we cannot avoid it. It is our certain doom. I have kept you in ignorance of this, in hopes of receiving re-enforcements. I ask your pardon for it. In deceiving you, I also deceived myself. I have all along received assurances of help. Every letter I have received, and every person I have seen, has represented that our people were ready, willing and anxious to come to our relief; and that we might expect enough help to enable us to repulse our foes. The help has not come, and our hopes are dashed to earth. My calls on Colonel Fannin remain unanswered, and the messengers have not returned. It is my belief that his whole force has been cut off, and our couriers have perished. The worst has now come near us. We are surrounded by an army large enough to annihilate us at a blow, from whose arms we are sheltered for the time by these walls. We must not surrender; for should we do so, that black flag waving in our sight admonishes us as to our doom. We can not cut our way through the ranks of the foe. There is no alternative but to remain here and struggle to the last. Santa Anna is, I am convinced, determined to storm and take this fort at whatever cost. Then, let us in this emergency be men and brothers. Let us withstand our adversaries to the last: and should they, as they will, scale the walls, let us meet them as they come, and never cease to oppose and combat them hand to hand while life remains. Thus, though we perish, we shall weaken our enemies and strengthen our friends; and our memories will be cherished by posterity till history shall be erased and all noble deeds forgotten. My determination is taken: but I leave every man to his choice. Mine is to stay in this fort, and to die fighting for my country. This will I do, if left alone."

Colonel Travis then drew his sword, and with its point traced a line upon the ground from right to left. Then, resuming his position in front, he said,

"I now call upon every man who is determined to stay here and die with me, to come across this line. Who will be first? March!" The first was Tapley Holland, who leaped across the line with a bound, exclaiming, *"I am ready to die for my country!"* He was instantly followed by every man in the line.

This account of the famous, and possibly mythical, show of courage at the Alamo was printed in the 1873 edition of the *Texas Almanac*. Moses Rose, by his own account, was the only man who did not cross the line. He scaled the wall, escaped and related this version of Travis' challenge to a friend in Nacogdoches, who told his son, who wrote the remembrance for the *Almanac*.

The "Big Bend Country" of Texas

is like no other place on earth. The air is as clear as glass; the water is fit for a queen to drink; the climate is the best there is outside; there just ain't nothing wrong with it that a little rain won't fix. The people will look you square in the eye when they talk to you. They will give you the shirt off their backs and do something to you if you steal it. They are sensitive to misery; they recognize hard luck. They appreciate prosperity and know how to cope with hard times. They measure a man by what he is, not who he is.

The country is big, unspoiled and lonesome, and the scenery is second to none. I was setting on [my horse] 'Old Red' on the south rim of the Chisos Mountains talking to Ventura Gamboa, a Mexican that worked for me. We were enjoying the view of the Rio Grande which we could see for 107 miles from Santa Elena Canyon to Boquillas, and I asked Ventura how far we were looking across the river into Mexico. He said, "Senor, como ocho dias a caballo." Sir, about 8 days horseback.

I was coming out of the Castalon Country several years ago, and a fellow waved me down a few miles south of Alpine, Texas, and wanted to know if I knew Polk Hinson. I told him I did. He wanted to know where he lived. I told him that Polk lived in the first house on the left, down the road. He thanked me and started to drive off. He stopped and said, "By the way, how far is it?"

"I said, 'About a hundred miles.' "

C.M. "Buck" Newsome, *Shod With Iron*, 1975

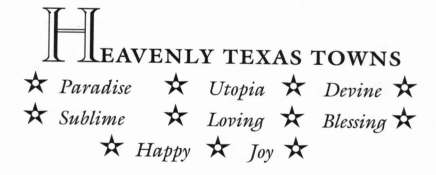

HEAVENLY TEXAS TOWNS
★ *Paradise* ★ *Utopia* ★ *Devine* ★
★ *Sublime* ★ *Loving* ★ *Blessing* ★
★ *Happy* ★ *Joy* ★

Had one stood on the Capote Mountain and viewed the surroundings, he would most likely have been impressed with the thought that the country was just as God had made it.

Lucas C. Brite, circa 1920, recalling the time he had
worked as a cowboy in the Big Bend

THE KILLING OF BONNIE AND CLYDE: MAY 23, 1934

The fact that I was after Barrow [and Bonnie] was known to only a few people before we caught him. On February 10, I took the trail and followed it for exactly 102 days. Like Clyde Barrow I used a Ford V8, and like Clyde I lived in the car most of the time. I decided that Barrow could be most easily caught in Louisiana.

Before the chase ended, I not only knew the general appearance and mental habits of the pair, but I had learned the kind of whiskey they drank, what they ate, and the color, size and texture of their clothes. I first struck their trail at Texarkana. At Logansport [Louisiana] they bought a half-gallon of whiskey; near Keechi they bought gasoline and then went in the night to a negro house and had the negroes cook them some cornbread and fry a chicken. In Shreveport they bought pants, underwear, gloves and an automatic shotgun. In their camp on the Wichita River, near Wichita Falls, they lost or threw away some bills for goods bought in Dallas. From the clerk I learned the size, color and pattern of one of Bonnie's dresses, and the kind of Ascot tie and belt buckle she wore. But the trail always led back to Louisiana, where I located their hideout...

I learned that Clyde had his "post office" on a side road about eight miles from Plain Dealing, Louisiana. It was under a board which lay on the ground near a large stump of a pine tree. The point selected was on a knoll from which Bonnie in the car could command a view of the road while Clyde went into the forest for his mail. By the night of May 22, we had good reason to believe that Clyde would visit this mail box.

[Hamer and five deputies concealed themselves in bushes opposite the "post office" at 2 A.M. and waited for morning. The men were armed with pistols, automatic shotguns, three Winchester rifles and one Browning Machine Gun. At 9:10 A.M. they heard a car. It was, Hamer recalled, ".humming like a sewing machine."]

We first recognized the color of the car, a gray Ford sedan, then the license number; we saw two persons, a small black-headed man and a small red-haired woman. We recognized Clyde and Bonnie... The speed continued to slacken under the brakes and the car came to a full stop at the exact spot that we had previously decided it would.

At the command, "stick 'em up!" both turned, but instead of obeying the order as we had hoped, they clutched the weapons which they either held in their hands or in their laps. When the firing began, Barrow's foot released the clutch and the car, in low gear, moved forward on the decline and turned into the ditch on the left. I looked at my watch and it was 9:20.

There can be no question raised as to who fired the first or the fatal shots. All fired as we had agreed to do and every man in the squad did everything that he was supposed to do. It was not a pleasant duty, but it was a duty which no one shirked.

An examination of the car revealed [it] was nothing but an arsenal on wheels. The inventory included:

3 Browning automatic rifles
1 sawed-off shotgun, Gauge 20
1 sawed-off shotgun, Gauge 16
1 Colt automatic pistol, Cal. 32
1 Colt automatic pistol, Cal. 380
7 Colt automatic pistols, Cal. 45
100 machine gun clips of 20 cartridges each
3000 rounds of ammunition scattered all over the car.

Remembered by Captain Frank Hamer to Walter Prescott Webb in *The Texas Rangers,* 1935

*I*n any group of nineteenth century cow boys, more were bearded than clean-shaven. Their costumes were much alike, though with individual variations. But all their garments were "coarse and substantial, few in number and often of the gaudy pattern." The cow boy wore a wide-brimmed hat with its crown dented into a pyramid or flattened. If the brim in front was sometimes turned up at the face, it could be turned down to protect him from the pressing light of the sky under which he spent all day. Around his neck he wore a bandana of tough silk. It served many purposes. Tied over his face it filtered dust before his breath. It served to blindfold a calf or tie its legs. It was a towel, a napkin, a bandage, a handkerchief, or simply an ornament. His shirt was of stout cotton flannel, in a bright color or loud design of checks or stripes or plaids. Over it he sometimes wore a cloth or leather vest but rarely a jacket. His trousers were either of heavy denim, dyed dark blue, sewn with coarse yellow thread, and reinforced at points of great wear with copper rivets; or were of odd colors and materials, mostly dark, that could stand tough use. They fitted tightly. The trouser legs were stuffed into boots that reached almost to the knee. At work, the cow boy often wore leggings of thick cowhide. They were made after the pattern of Indian leggings of thick cowhide – two long tubes, with wide flaps at each side cut into fringes or studded with silver disks that reached from ankle to groin, and were tied to a belt as though to the string of a breechclout. Their purpose was to shield him against thorns in the brush he rode through, and the violent rub of haired animal hides, and the burn of rope when he pulled it against his leg as he turned his horse to control a lasso'd creature. On his boots he wore large spurs, of silver or iron. He wore gloves to work in, and around his tight hips he wore a cartridge belt from which depended his

pistol – most often a Colt's single-action, .45 caliber revolver called the Peacemaker. He had no change of clothing. He went unwashed and unbathed unless he camped by a stream or pond. "I wash," he said in his multiple anonymity:

> *"I wash in a pool and wipe on a sack,*
> *I carry my wardrobe all on my back."*

Paul Horgan, *Great River, Vol. II,* 1954

Most cowmen wanted hosses of solid colors, browns, bays, sorrels and duns, but no paints. The latter found little more favor in the average remuda than did a mare. Paints were the favorite hosses of the western story writers, but they didn't meet with any favor in the cattle country. It was a rare thing to find one that developed into a cuttin' hoss, or a hoss fitted for any quick close work. They were mostly for show, and got to be pop'lar with town folks. A cowboy didn't mind havin' one in his string to use for a Sunday, or "gallin'" hoss, but when it came to workin' a herd, he'd rather have a solid color hoss with some breedin'. Like the old sayin': "All a paint's fit for is to ride 'im down the road."

Ramon F. Adams, *The Old-Time Cowhand,* 1948

TWO VIEWS OF MR. BAILEY, A STAND-UP GUY

The late B. Bailey, one of the earliest settlers in Texas, was a man of singular habits, but of strong and energetic mind. He was a great hunter and a successful Indian fighter. He always went armed with a rifle, pistols, and large hunting knife and loved the solitude of the woods far better than the conventional usages of society. His death happened, as near as I recollect, in 1832, and he was buried, according to request, near Brazoria in a standing position – with his rifle by his side – his pouch (with a hundred and fifty bullets) slung over his shoulder, and his favorite pistols (a beautiful pair) belted around him.

I have been told by a gentleman of strict veracity that as early as twelve years ago he saw in the Bible of Mr. B. a written request to be buried in this manner. This gentleman had the curiosity to ask him the reason of this singular whim. Bailey merely remarked, "You know I never yet was caught unarmed by Indian or wild beast. I am a rude man and know not whom I may meet in another world. I wish to be prepared, as usual, for all enemies."

Anonymous writer, *New Orleans Picayune*, September 23, 1838

A noted member of Austin's colony was Captain James B. Bailey, better known as "Brit" Bailey, his arrival even antedating that of Austin himself... When he was in his last sickness, realizing that the end was near, he said to his wife:

"I have never stooped to any man, and when I am in my grave I don't want it said, 'There lies old Brit Bailey.' Bury me so that the world must say, 'There stands Bailey.' And bury me with my face to the setting sun. I have been all my life traveling westward and I want to face that way when I die."

His widow, in compliance with his request, had a deep hole dug like a well, into which the coffin was lowered, feet first, facing the setting sun.

Noah Smithwick, *The Evolution of A State*, or *Recollections of Old Texas Days*, 1900

☆　　☆　　☆　　☆　　☆　　☆　　☆　　☆

I shall remain in Mexico with my rangers as long as the situation – in my judgment – seems to warrant it, and I shall recross the Rio Grande at my own discretion. Give my compliments to the Secretary of War and tell him the United States troops may go to hell.

Texas Ranger Captain L.H. McNelly's written reply to an order from the U.S. Army to stop chasing cattle rustlers in Mexico, 1875

WEST TEXAS

Where you go farther and see less,
Where there are more creeks and less water,
Where there are more cows and less milk,
Where there is more climate and less rain,
Where there is more horizon and fewer trees,
Than any other place in the Union.

Beautiful West Texas, what do you think,
Plenty of grapes and nothing to drink;
Plenty of creeks and no water on hand,
Plenty of ponies, none fit to ride;
Plenty of poverty, and some little pride.

Plenty of hides and no leather tanned,
Through the scabby mesquite encumbers
 the land;
Plenty of cattle, no butter or milk,
No dress for the garden, but plenty of silk.
Plenty of rain when it comes down at all,
Enough and to spare, would it come at
 your call.

Plenty of bacon, year before last,
Will be plenty again when comes a good mast;
Hide-bottom chairs not plenty, and all so low
When a fellow eats, he has to hang on his elbow.
Plenty to eat such as corn bread and bacon,
Which reminds of the home long since
 forsaken.

Plenty of wind, no drawback on that,
When talking of stock, is plenty of that;
They never find time to do it at all.
What a great country this might be, if the
 people willed!
With corn bread and bacon men have enough,
And the women get happy over some snuff.

Written about 1922 by Leona Mae Austin, age 14
of Childress, Texas

A TALE OF THIRST

Here's a story I was told 'bout Bud Puryear, an old cowhand of the Texas Panhandle. The ranch had sent several cowboys south to drive a small bunch of cattle to the home ranch. They had to drive them cattle through a dry desert section nearly all day before reachin' the ranch, and both cattle and men suffered extremely from thirst. By the time they reached the southern edge of the ranch where there was a surface tank [man-made pond], the cattle were frantic and the men's tongues were swollen. When the cattle smelled the water of the tank they made a run for it, and the men followed.

Bud rode right in among the cattle, lay down on his belly, and stuck his muzzle in the water. The other boys rode to the other side of the tank where the water wasn't muddied.

"Hey, Bud!", one of 'em called over to the other side. "Why don't you come over here where the water's clear?"

"Hell," answered Bud, "what difference does it make? I'm goin' to drink it all anyway."

Ramon F. Adams, *The Old-Time Cowhand*, 1948

The most-used name for streams in Texas appears to be "Live Oak." There are at least 20 Live Oak Creeks. Longest is in Zavala County and runs 32 miles before joining the Frio River in Frio County. Shortest is in DeWitt County, flowing east into McCoy Creek, a distance of only three miles.

TEXAS-STYLE BED & BREAKFAST IN 1846

We were ferried across the San Marcos a few miles beyond Gonzales [and] came to the farm of Mr. King, an old gentleman with a huge paunch (by the way, in Texas a rather rare attribute). He had come here as one of the first settlers and in the course of years had developed his place into a thriving farm. When immigration into Western Texas had increased rapidly, especially among the Germans, he had found further profitable income by maintaining an inn. All that is needed are a few beds for the guests. When the guest arrives in the evening, usually on horseback, his horse is immediately unsaddled by negroes, or, in the absence of them, by the traveler himself with the aid of the host. Thereupon he enters the hall where a bucket of water, a gourd used as a dipper, and a tin basin are found. After washing face and hands, the traveler seats himself on a rather uncomfortable chair, with a seat made of calfskin stretched tight across it, and chats with the host about politics or the crops. In the meantime supper is being served in the living room. In some houses, the host asks his guests in a sly manner to follow him into an adjoining room, and here offers them a drink of whiskey or cognac diluted with water and with sugar added, to stimulate the appetite.

Supper consists of tea or coffee, warm cornbread and fried bacon. These articles of food are always found, but in the better inns biscuits are served hot in addition to eggs, butter, honey and canned fruits. The hostess, or at least some feminine member of the family, sits at one end of the table and serves the tea. This is done in the most dignified and solemn manner. The cups are passed in silence, and later repassed in the same manner to be refilled. No sound is uttered by her except the necessary question, asked in a quiet, indifferent tone of voice: "You take tea or coffee, sir?" "Do you take milk and sugar in your coffee?" In explanation of the latter question, I wish to remark that the milk and sugar are added to the tea or coffee by the hostess serving it.

The host urges his guests now and then to partake of this or that food, but a conversation to his part does not take place during the meal. In eight to ten minutes the whole "operation" of eating is finished and the guests assemble on the porch for an hour, in order to enjoy the cool breezes and to chat before retiring. The sleeping quarters are usually confined to one room where two or three beds are found. Each guest selects his bed and if there is not a sufficient number to go around, the guests must share beds. On the following morning breakfast is served. It is a duplication of supper in every detail, as far as the food is concerned. The journey is then resumed immediately after breakfast.

A lodging of this kind, including corn and fodder for the horses, can be had for $1.00 to $1.25.

Dr. Ferdinand Roemer, *Roemer's Texas*, translated from German, 1935

☆ ☆ ☆ ☆ ☆ ☆ ☆ ☆ ☆ ☆ ☆ ☆ ☆

This country isn't bad. It's just worse. Worse the moment you set foot from the train, and then, after that, just worser and worser.

Anonymous cameraman, in Big Bend to film U.S. Army pursuit of Mexican bandits, 1916

In 1881, cattle herds passing through the Panhandle spread "Texas fever" to range animals there and ranchers gathered together to force drives around their area. This is a warning letter sent in 1883 to an Albany rancher with a large passing herd by the legendary Charles Goodnight:

Que Ti Que Ranch, Aug. 20.
Geo. T. Reynolds, Esq.,

Dear Sir:

I send Mr. Smith to turn your cattle so they will not pass through our range. He will show you around and guide you until you strike the head of this stream and then you will have a road. The way he will show you is nearer and there are shorter drives to water than any route you can take. Should you come by here you will have a drive of 35 miles to make.

I hope you will take this advice as yourself and I have always been good friends, but even friendship will not protect you in the drive through here, and should you attempt to pass

through, be kind enough to tell your men what they will have to face as I do not wish to hurt men that do not understand what they will be very sure to meet.

I hope you will not treat this as idle talk, for I mean every word of this, and if you have any feeling for me as a friend or acquaintance, you will not put me to any desperate actions. I will not perhaps see you myself, but take this advice from one that is and always has been your friend.

My cattle are now dying of the fever contracted from cattle driven from Fort Worth, therefore do not have any hope that you can convince me that your cattle will not give mine the fever, this we will not speak of. I simply say to you that you will never pass through here in good health.

Yours truly,

C. GOODNIGHT.

Printed in the *Fort Griffin Echo,* November 8, 1881

*I*t was not long after 1867, before trail-driving became a science, if not an art. The details were worked out by the trial and error method with scientific precision. In time, the drovers discovered the number of cattle making the most manageable, as well as the most economical unit for trail driving, the number of cowboys necessary to manage it, the number of mounts required for each man, the best way to manage the remuda, the kind of "chuck-wagon" to use, the type of goods to carry, the best routine for the cook, how to direct the daily movements of the herd, how to bed-down and control the herd at night, what to do in time of stampedes and storms, how to swim the herd across swollen streams, and how to treat other trail outfits – the etiquette of the trail.

The technique of the cowboy, or his ability to manage the "critters" under his care, his capacity to tame a wild bunch of rangy longhorns and to reduce them within a few days' time to a "trail-broke," almost gentle, herd; his power to soothe the animals when restless and panicky at night by singing to them; and his skill in controlling a stampede on a dark, blustering, storming night by getting the leaders of a fleeing herd to run in a circle until eventually the whole herd was "milling," – these phases of trail driving were an art.

It has been estimated, that between 1867 and 1890 approximately 10,000,000 went up the various trails. Each year there were from 150 to 200 herds of about 2500 head each. A herd required about twelve men, at least six saddle horses for each man, and a mess wagon and team. The cattle traveled on an average of fifteen miles or more a day, or 450 to 500 miles a month. Each year the cattle movement up the trail required an army of approximately 2400 cowboys and 14,000 saddle horses. From first to last, between 45,000 and 50,000 cowboys using almost 300,000 saddle horses, took part in the drives. The cost of operating a trail unit was about $500 a month. It cost the drover between fifty and sixty cents to transport a cow from Southern Texas to the Kansas railroad stations.

Alkali Trails, William Curry Holden, 1930

As Justice of the Peace and leading saloon keeper

[Judge] Roy Bean gradually became a sort of alcalde to the neighborhood, performing wedding ceremonies, christening babies and arbitrating family troubles.

Marriages constituted a steady source of revenue.

Even Bean himself appreciated the humor of the situation, especially in the days when he was not a legal justice of the peace and thus had no lawful right to perform marriage ceremonies. "Juan," he said in a typical ceremony, "do you take this woman for your lawful wife? The answer is 'Si, Senor.' " Obtaining the befuddled promise from Juan, he turned to the girl. "Maria, you want to marry this sorry maverick?"

With the proper answer extracted from the participating parties, he dismissed them with, "And Lord have mercy on your pore souls! Five dollars!" When the young husband did not have the five dollars, as was frequently the case, Justice Bean would permit him to work out the fee.

"Judge," a downhearted cowboy bemoaned one day, "that weddin' you give me shore didn't take. I caint get along with that gal atall!"

Bean stroked his beard. His face brightened. "By gobs!" he exclaimed. "I guarantee all my weddin's. If yores ain't satisfactory, why, I'll just divorce you; but it'll cost you ten dollars." He reasoned that it was worth twice as much to get out of a bad bargain as to get into it; and he found the cowboy willing enough to pay.

Vinegarroon, The Saga of Judge Roy Bean,
By Ruel McDaniel, 1936

Dancin'

The Texans cannot be described as graceful dancers, although they have some power of expressing the poetry of motion; their figures are supple, and they swing and sway a great deal, with much facial by-play.

Cowboys are not exactly light-footed, but they are very springy, and make fun with their high action, which they pirouette on their high-heeled shoes. They are extremely particular about their shoes, which are always of the best make and fitting to perfection, whilst most of them possess the distinguishing mark of small, shapely feet. A cowboy's garments may be sometimes rather dilapidated, but he would go without a coat or deny himself luxuries rather than wear a boot that had not a fine upper to its sole, or that did not fit like a glove. The boot is to the cowboy what the sombrero is to the Mexican; its extraordinary high heels being partly to prevent the foot from slipping through the large wooden stirrup. Their boots are certainly not made to walk in. Spurs are now dispensed with at dances, except in the case of "rangers" or under-sheriffs in uniform. These men display their six-shooters, and are occasionally required to keep the peace. Sometimes the exuberant cowboy becomes uproarious, when he begins to shoot at the lamps and windows – a signal for the company to make a general stampede.

Texas Ranch Life, Mary Jaques, 1893

★　　★　　★　　★　　★　　★　　★

A SAMPLING OF COWBOY NICKNAMES

Alkali Hunter • Rawhide Crow • Shanks Hogg • Pieface Greely • Muley Johnson • Joggy Barnes • Bar Dog Powell • Shotgun Collins • Cold Chuck Johnny Howe Wild Horse Jerry Morris

I was taking a herd of cattle East and it was an awful wet year. We'd been having plenty of trouble. We had to pull twenty or thirty out of a bog they got into in a cut at the Colorado River. Then the Brazos was up on a toot, and the herd got into a mill when they were swimming in the middle of it. We'd sweated at some of the little creeks, and I shore was a-dreading the San Jacinto.

But when we got to it, the sun was right for crossing – back behind us instead of in the cattles' eyes – and I told the boys to pop their leggins and bring 'em a-stringing. I was back a little from the point, and when I got to the bank I never was more surprised in my life. Them cattle was a-walking across dry-shod, like the children of Israel a-crossing the Red Sea. They was a-stepping on alligators' backs. Seemed like the alligators had all congregated to sun their backs or something like that. They didn't seem to mind the weight. I guess being so thick that way they kinder supported each other.

When I come to cross, my horse give a snort, but he took the bridge all right. Still, I didn't feel easy. I knowed if one of them alligators give a flip of his tail so's to hit the nose of some snuffy steer, there'd be a stompede would shake their ancestors. But nothing like that happened.

The biggest alligator I ever see was in the Mission River, right here in Refugio County. I was riding up it one day looking out for bogged animals, and before I knowed it, the bed was practically dry. Thinks I, 'This is mighty peculiar. I was up above here about three miles day before yesterday and the river was bank-full – fuller'n I ever see it except after a big rain. Now down here there ain't no water at all.'

Well, I kept a-riding on upstream, my curiosity getting more and more het up. Then I comed to the answer of all my curiosity. It was an alligator, a regular giant of an alligator, the Goliath of all alligators that ever lived. His tail had got tangled up in a lot of willer roots on one side of the bank and in pawing and struggling he had evidently hung his snout and forelegs in the roots on the opposite bank. There he was stretched out damming the whole river up, so the water was about to make Refugio a deep-sea port up above and the bed drying up down below.

I could have killed the critter easy, but I wasn't going to destroy a specimen like that. I just took my axe and cut the roots. But when the alligator got loose, danged if he didn't have to crawl out on the prairie to turn around. The river was just too little for him to operate in.

Attributed to storyteller/cowboy Findlay Simpson, in *Cow People*, J. Frank Dobie, 1964

LOST TEXAS

Lobo

In southwest Culberson County, originally as a station on the San Antonio-San Diego stage route in the 1850s. Later became a stop on the Southern Pacific Railroad. Named for packs of wolves that marauded the surrounding prairies.

Grit

Six miles from Mason in Mason County. Formed in 1901 around a few stores and post office and was little more after five decades. Name claimed as derived from (1) the texture of area soil, or (2) the determination and perseverance of early settlers.

HIGH PLAINS DRIFTER

I had not seen anything that would lead me to any startling new assessment of Texas. The long, sloping fall sunlight fell beautifully on the green winter wheatfields east of Dalhart; in the gullies and breaks of the rougher country I saw seedling mesquite spreading up out of the draws in irregular lines. The persistent mesquite. When my father was a boy there were none in Archer County, almost four hundred miles to the south – by the time my son is old there will probably be mesquite on the slopes of Pikes Peak.

When I passed through Dalhart the sun was not more than ten minutes above the wheatfields. I had forty miles to go, into a clear Panhandle sunset. When I drove through Texline and out to the marker at the border, the sun had been down twenty minutes and afterglow circled the entire horizon with pink and rose. The sky, which had seemed clear, really held a thin, almost invisible glaze of cloud, and streamers of afterglow reddened the clouds as far east as one could see. I got out and stood by the marker a minute in the biting north wind, 1,073 miles from the Rio Grande bridge in Brownsville. It was only thirty-five degrees, a warm evening for the plains. You cannot see the Rockies from Texline, but you can sense them.

I drove slowly into Texline, rather dreading the forty-mile return trip to Dalhart. As soon as I got rolling the dread fell away: the plains were lovely as they darkened, and I cannot but love the plains, nor cross them without the sense that I am crossing my own past. I curved back down to Dalhart through the wind the trail herders bucked, and the last few miles, with the lights twinkling ahead of me on the plain, were among the best of the trip. It only remained to perform some acte symbolistique to give the drive coherence, tie the present to the past. I stopped at a cafe in Dalhart and ordered a chicken fried steak. Only a rank degenerate would drive 1,500 miles across Texas without eating a chicken fried steak. The cafe was full of boys in football jackets, and the jukebox was playing an odious number called "Billy Broke My Heart in Walgreen's and I Cried All the Way to Sears."

The waitress was a thin, sad-eyed woman with hands that looked like she had used them to twist barbed-wire all her life. She set the steak in front of me and went wearily back to the counter to get a bottle of ketchup. The meat looked like a piece of old wood that had had perhaps one coat of white paint in the thirties and then had had that sanded off by thirty years of Panhandle sandstorms.

"Here," the waitress said, setting the ketchup bottle down. "I hope that steak's done enough. There ain't nothin' like steak when you're hungry, is there, son?"

"No, Ma'am, there ain't," I said.

Larry McMurtry, *In a Narrow Grave*, 1968

THE BLUEBONNET

[N]o other flower – for me at least – brings such upsurging of the spirit and at the same time restfulness.

J. Frank Dobie, 1944

Bluebonnet time is a time when the sky falls on Texas.

A.L. Morgan, 1958

THE RIO GRANDE

The Devil was granted permission one day
To make him a land for his special sway;
He hunted around for a month or more,
And ripp'd, and snorted, and terribly swore.
But at last was delighted a country to view,
Where the prickly-pear and the
        muskeet-tree grew;
After very brief survey, he took up his stand
On the eastern bank of the Rio Grande.

Some little improvement he wished to make,
For his own reputation he felt was at stake.
An idea struck him; he swore by his horns
To make a complete vegetation of thorns.
So he studded the land with the prickly-pear,
And scatter'd muskeet trees every where;
"Spanish bayonets," still, sharp-pointed,
        and tall,
Were spread around to outstick them all.
He imported Camaches direct from Hell,
The tide of his sweet-scented train to swell;
A legion of skunks, whose loud, loud smell,
Perfumed the region he loved so well.
And as, for his life, he couldn't see why
The river did not enough water supply;
So he swore, if he gave it another drop,
They might take his head and horns for a mop.

And he thought Rio Grande not
        crooked enough,
He twisted it up about "quantum stuff";
So the birds when they seek to fly over its tide,
He fixed the least heat at one hundred
        and seven.
And banished forever the moisture of Heaven;
Though none must think (by his tail he swore)

He wish'd he'd be d____d if potatoes
        should grow,
Or anything else that was fodder, by Jo!
And when he had fix'd things, all thorny
        and well,
He said, "By the Lord! It's a joy to Hell!"

He was satisfied now; he'd done all that
        he knew;
And vanish'd from earth in a blaze of blue;
And no doubt, now, in a corner of Hell,
Gloats over the work he accomplish'd so well;
And vows that on earth is no hellisher land
Than the eastern bank of the Rio Grande.

Attributed to an unnamed military officer stationed in
deep South Texas beside the Rio Grande
Spirit of the Times, April 1, 1854

Time will pass and seasons will come and go; Spring with its wavin' green grass and heaps of sweet-smellin' flowers on every hill and in every dale. Then will come sultry Summer, with her shimmerin' heat-waves on the baked horizon; and Fall, with her yeller harvest-moon and the hills growin' brown and golden under a sinkin' sun; and finally Winter, with its bitin', whinin' wind, and all the land will be mantled with snow. But you won't be here to see any of 'em, Carlos Robles; not by a dam' sight, because it's the order of this court that you be took to the nearest tree and hanged by the neck till you're dead, dead, dead.

Trial decision by Judge Roy Bean
cited in *Vinegarroon, "Law West of the Pecos,"*
by Ruel McDaniel, 1936

---

*I can do it neater, sweeter
and more completer than
anybody else in Lometer.*

Attributed to a 19th century cedar chopper in the
Hill Country town of Lometa

Chow-Chow

One gallon green tomatoes
One-half dozen peppers
  (green or ripe)
Two large onions
One small head of cabbage
One teaspoon of ground cloves
One teaspoon of ground
  cinnamon
One tablespoonful of mustard
One cup of sugar

Chop tomatoes and cabbage
and sprinkle with 1/2 cup of
salt; mix well; let stand over
night. Next morning drain off
the water; then add onions,
peppers and seasoning, and run
through a meat mill. Put in a
granite vessel, cover with
vinegar, and boil about 1 hour.
Put in Mason jars, and seal.

Attributed to
Mrs. Sue E. Vannoy of Tehuacana
The Capitol Cookbook, 1899

Toasted Pecans

1 cup pecans
2 tablespoons vinegar
1 tablespoon sugar
 tablespoon melted butter

Measure pecans into a small
bowl. Mix vinegar and sugar,
pour over pecans and stir to
coat thoroughly. Let stand for 15
minutes, stirring every 5 minutes.
Place pecans in shallow baking
dish and bake in 300 degree
oven for 10 minutes. Add melted
butter to pecans, stir and allow
to bake for another 5 minutes.

Tastes & Tales from Texas, Peg Hein,
1984

It was the town of Clarendon, a *devout community,* which furnished the courts of Tascosa, the near-by cattle boom town, with a means of punishment for thorough recalcitrants. When an offender went too far at Tascosa, he was sentenced to ten days in Clarendon. That was the nearest thing to solitary confinement for a cowhand who liked his likker.

[Before the Clarendon rule was established] Law violators were tied in Jack Ryan's saloon. One such prisoner was Jack Martin, who was bound tightly on a December evening in 1881. However, Jack's arms were left free and during the night he tore his blanket into shreds and formed a rope. With this improvised "lariat" he lassoed whiskey bottles from the shelf behind the bar and enjoyed his night's imprisonment very well, thank you.

[Tascosa] was some place. The fiddler in Tascosa was named "Snake" Thompson, and he had another claim to fame besides his prowess with the bow. He brewed his own whiskey and got his nickname because he claimed he put snake heads in it to make it strong.

Curtis Bishop, *Lots of Land,* 1949

When one of the first windmills in the Texas Panhandle was installed and put into operation, the owner took his crew of riders out to see how it worked before acceptin' it from the contractor. When he saw the little trickle of water flowin' out he was as tickled as a cub bear with a honeycomb, and declared that the windmill would revolutionize the cow business. One skeptical cowhand eyed the small stream, and said, "Hell, Boss, I could get behind a bush and do a better job than that."

Ramon F. Adams, *The Old-Time Cowhand,* 1948

THE TEXAS RANGER EXPLAINED

As a mounted soldier he has no counterpart in any age or country. Neither Cavalier nor Cossack, Mameluke nor Moss-trooper are like him; and yet, in some respects, he resembles them all. Chivalrous, bold and impetuous in action, he is yet wary and calculating, always impatient of restraint, and sometimes unscrupulous and unmerciful. He is an excellent rider and a dead shot.

Unnamed military officer quoted in
Sketches of the Campaign in Northern Mexico, 1853

It starts in *Ozona with flowers along the roadside* and the desert turning to tree-covered hills. Home territory – that Stephen Vincent Benet-place: "bone of my bone."

I came back to it – from the west, after a month of soaking rains. Through Pecos, Fort Stockton, all the Texas desert towns. I had been content with sunlight and space: I was still pleased by the absence of things. But at Ozona the mesquites began – miles of them, fresh and green and shiny as silk, with the white-ivory blooms of Spanish daggers scattered through them like cannon bursts – and it was there, at the sight of greenery and hills, that I knew I was home.

For home country does not mean relatives, or city streets, or friends of the past. That is something else again: a world made by people, complex and painful. Home country is country – a place of rocks and trees and goats and sheep; of mourning doves and cypress-lined rivers; of hay-fields; of pastures.

(Pastures: To go into them as a boy – into the grass, the scattered flint and limestone rocks, the shadows, the leaves and dirt on the sides of ravines, the bare clearings, the green thickets – was to enter a beautiful clarity, a great sense of what was pure and real. I would walk through tall needlegrass – stumbling now and then over half-buried rocks – and when I rested in the shade of a live oak tree it always seemed that each limb was hugely intimate, like a thought, and the tree itself like a family. I came to love trees – and summer glare, and fence lines, and cedar posts – the same way you come to love people.)

Home country, hill country, the whole stretch of familiar land: I drove past shin oaks standing in the heat like demure tree maidens, heads together, their feet lost in a pool of mid-afternoon shadow; and a rancher in a beat-up hat and faded blue denims, reaching down from his horse to loosen a goat from a wire fence; and a highway workman resting in the roadside shade. Closer and closer, a sweet-sinking into familiar things – and pondering them in the leisure of the passing miles.

A windmill, say: There it was, mounted on its commanding knoll. How many years had it turned like an all-seeing eye above the same clump of ranch house trees – a constant symbol of possessions and home to the rancher riding horseback across the land?

Or rocks. Lying there, white as tombs, they represented all that was timeless and impersonal – geologic upheavals, erosion by wind and water. Yet a rock in a pasture was not like a galaxy suspended in eternal night; it was a human-sized thing fit for both the hand and the mind. A rock, in summertime, was one of the beatitudes of the earth – enduring as the trees, pleasing as grass.

I thought: Now I know why I am not a revolutionary – have never had the desire to kick over old, established things. It's because the hill country does not teach you the need for change. The land is always so satisfying that you want it to remain the same forever as a kind of handy immortality.

This Favored Place, Elroy Bode, 1983

Texas has a timbered track as large as Massachusetts; a cotton patch, in black waxy country, as big as all Ohio; a grazing belt in the Panhandle as large as Pennsylvania; more wheat than either of the Dakotas; and more corn than Illinois can boast. If Arizona should run short of desert, Texas, out of her Staked Plains, could furnish all the desert Arizona could find room for, and never miss what it gave away. At the same time, bananas are ripening in one part of Texas, and blizzards in another.

Irwin Cobb, *Everything the Urban Cowboy Needs to Know about Texas,* 1940

YEARNING FOR TEXAS: THE DEATH OF OLD SLATE

In 1876 I was driving for King and Kennedy. A good many of our cattle were sold in Colorado. In the herd we delivered on the Arkansas loomed Old Slate, the biggest [Longhorn] steer I ever saw. He was what we call a "moss-head," a worthless old thing, as he must have been fifteen years old. His color was a blue-slate, and he looked like he was seven feet tall. We delivered the herd and turned back for South Texas. From the banks of the Arkansas, Old Slate, towering above all the other steers, watched us go.

Then one day during the winter a rider found Old Slate grazing in the brush. Through southern Colorado, across the Panhandle, and down through Texas, Old Slate had trudged the miles away, and now contentedly rubbed his neck against a mesquite, a thousand miles by trail from where the South Texas cowboys had left him.

We kept him on the ranch until we started a herd to Caldwell, Kansas, for shipment to market at St. Louis. Old Slate was thrown in. In the herd was a six-year-old red white-faced steer called Baldy, and a spotted one that the boys called Christ. Both kept wanting to head for South Texas. But Old Slate was the worst. I put a bell on him and roped and hobbled him every night, and we finally got him to Caldwell. His horns were so wide that two men had to twist his head to one side to get him through the car door.

The train pulled out for Kansas City, and Harry Derrick went with it to care for the shipment. At Pierce City, Missouri, the cattle were unloaded to be watered and fed. Old Slate, tired of captivity and mad as he could be, jumped over the high railroad corral fence and went tearing down through a cornfield, scaring the farmers out of their wits. They pulled down their old squirrel rifles and shot and killed him.

Story told by cowboy Jim East
in *The XIT Ranch of Texas*, J. Evetts Haley, 1929

One identification of West Texas is simply that it is dry. Dryness creates a way of life more demanding than the facts of heat or height or abnormal wetness. The too-dry region is hardest to accommodate by man because he is the thirstiest animal. Even when he is trying to adjust to dry living he sometimes consumes more water than he has any right to expect nature to supply. This is one of the ways in which rainfall influenced the history of West Texas. Up to the 1870s even the occasional scientific expert who wandered around it thought most of the area was uninhabitable. It was too dry for crops and humans. As one of the early Army officers reported, "This country will be unsuited to human use for a hundred years, if then anyone wants it."

A Personal Country, A.C. Greene, 1969

Puny Wilson had been a great football player at Texas A&M in the days when the All-American selectors did their picking from the Ivy League. According to local legend, Puny Wilson also had the distinction of being the only football coach in the nation who actually, honestly, had a degree in basket weaving.

When he was in college peach growing was the rage in East Texas towns eager for new income. The peach crops created a demand for baskets in which to ship the fruit. So the Agricultural and Mechanical College of Texas offered an undergraduate certificate in basket weaving, and Coach Puny had one.

Dan Rather, *The Camera Never Blinks*, 1977

46

BRIDE BY PANHANDLE MAIL: POSTAGE & HANDLING INCLUDED

Old Seman Taber was a small, stooped, bewhiskered fellow, unobtrusive and mild mannered, but very industrious. How he happened upon the plains no one knows, for he was a Yankee by birth and a peddler by trade and apparently in no financial difficulty. In spite of his alien temperament and the semi-aridity of the land he set himself to raise fruit and vegetables where heretofore, only mesquite and sagebrush had grown. In a few years his orchard and garden began to bear and in the role of the county's first experimental farmer and the town's only green grocer he prospered greatly.

Previous to that time he had been content as a bachelor but affluence and the needs of his declining years wrought a change and with the assistance of a matrimonial agency he began his quest for a mate. The bride arrived in due time, a nice, little widow by the name of Mrs. Helen Moore. After a few days sojourn at the home of the Combs in which to give herself time to look the situation over, she and Taber were married. Strange as it may seem they lived most happily together until death severed the union.

Their dugout had once belonged to Straight, the buffalo hunter, and like all of those on Carroll Creek had a roof on a level with the hill behind and, in their case, walls of sod. It was, as dugouts go, a commodious dwelling with all three rooms arranged so as to open one into the other. To prevent the untidiness of scaling dirt, gunny sacks were stretched across the surface of the walls, then held in place by a tightly tacked top covering of cheese cloth. On small dry-goods boxes carefully fitted in to serve as shelves were kept the couple's few prized books and knick-knacks. The roof and floor were of wide planks.

The mail order wife was not only a very good woman but neat as a pin and an excellent cook.

Between Sun and Sod, Willie Newbury Lewis, 1938

In no state of the Union does a woman enjoy a higher social status than in Texas. She is really revered. But in few states does she enjoy more limited freedoms.

James Michener, *Texas,* 1986

THE FIRST BABY

My husband and I came to the Panhandle in December 1875 and built us a two-room house on Gagby Creek. Came from Colorado with a hunting party headed by my husband…I would go along and cook for the men, load ammunition, help stake the buffalo hides and sometimes skin them. I enjoyed the camp very much. When the buffalo would get scarce, we would go back to our house…nine miles from Ft. Elliot. My son, Joseph, was born there in 1877, the first child born in the Panhandle. The officers' wives would come out from the fort every week and visit him. They seemed to like the first baby.

Mrs. I.B. Wood, quoted in *Between Sun and Sod,*
by Willie Newbury Lewis, 1938

An easterner was being shown a West Texas ranch. A large colorful bird flew near him and he asked what it was.

"That's a bird of paradise," said his Texan host.

The easterner thought awhile, surveyed the flat, hot, dry desert land all around and said, "Pretty long way from home, isn't he?"

Traditional

Τhe Texas ranch, or house, is generally a rude log structure, frequently with only one compartment, to serve as kitchen, bedroom, and parlour. The rough logs of which it is built are simply nailed together, leaving numerous chinks and crevices. The floor is raised a foot or more from the ground, and rests upon four blocks of stone or timber, with a vacant space beneath, steps to reach the floor, and generally a gallery on one side.

But sometimes ranches are built without this underneath space, when the ground serves as the only floor.

These mansions are any thing but warm during a "norther," a snap of cold which sets in suddenly, and may continue either a few hours, two or three days, or, at the outside, a week.

On these occasions the inmates stuff up the holes in their ranches with bags and old garments, and sit crouching over the wood fire on the hearth.

The toilettes of these people are not very elaborate; the washing utensils consisting of a basin and towel placed in the gallery outside the ranch, where there is always a pail or bucket of drinking water and an enamelled iron or tin cup with a long handle like that of a saucepan.

On the arrival of a visitor, he is greeted with "Take seat!" "Have off your hat!" "Cool yourself down!" On taking his departure the guest is bidden "Good-bye!" and "Come again!" To omit the latter injunction is to betray a shocking defect in manners.

In order to "cool yourself down," you take a seat on the gallery and remain inactive for a considerable time. You are invariably offered water, and expected to drink a vast quantity. I believe it is contrary to the etiquette of the country to refuse it. The men generally help them-selves; any water which remains in the vessel being tossed far away and describing a circle of spray in mid-air. To accomplish this effort neatly requires a dexterous turn of the wrist and twist of the elbow, which can be acquired only by long and frequent practice.

To this "cooling down" process – the prolonged inactivity after exertion, and the great quantity of cold water consumed – may probably be ascribed the constant "chills" and "fever" (a kind of ague) from which so many Texans suffer. Another cause may be their custom of not wearing flannel. Very few Englishmen suffer in this way, though they are troubled with "prickly heat" or "Texas boil," due, probably, to change of diet, excess of salt meat, and deficiency of green food.

Texas Ranch Life, Mary Jaques, 1893

★ ★ ★ ★ ★ ★ ★ ★ ★ ★ ★ ★ ★ ★ ★ ★ ★

[In early West Texas] Cosmetics were unknown but the ingenious female could paint her lips with the juice of a berry or petal, blacken her eyebrows with a burnt match, and whiten her skin by an application of corn-starch or flour. Her hair, however, was a more difficult problem as a hue not desired by the owner was a matter to be grieved over but never changed. The wife of one of the town's leading judges was looked at slightly askance because it was whispered that her beautiful bronze locks were artificially tinted by the use of soda shampoos and the sun's hot rays, an almost immoral procedure in the eyes of the other women.

Between Sun and Sod, Willie Newbury Lewis, 1938

EAST TEXAS EXPLAINED

Hound dogs and blowing horns. Blackeyed peas and hog jowl. Sausage, with a flavor unrivaled, red-pepper-hot, solid pork-meat with some substance. Grits floating in fresh butter or redeye gravy. Hot biscuits and mayhaw jelly. A poky mule turning a syrup mill. The land where The King and I means nothing but an old-time gospel hymn. Gray silvered shacks with bitter oranges and chinaberry trees near them, the yard a bleached sweep of hard-packed earth, an iron washpot turned over near a round white spot on the ground where the suds from strong yellow lye-soap wash water had been emptied for years. The broomstick used to punch the clothes down, boiled to the color and smoothness of old ivory. Grove's Chill Tonic and Slaughterine for Pains. Crisper's Hot Shot Nerve Sedative.

The country where a midwife is a "granny woe-man"; one a 92-year-old mulatto woman with slender steely fingers who was said to have delivered a live baby from a dead mother. "White doctor say she daid, so I don't say she aint." Signs saying "Wheels Spoked." [T]he stomping ground of a blind, toothless guitar player: "Play me some blues," "I don't play no sinful songs, lady." His gigantic wife, Billie, emerging from out back hollerin' "An' me lookin' like Who'd-a-Thunk-It!" Razor-back hogs and hickory nuts. Light-bread and sweet milk. English walnuts and Irish potatoes, and firecrackers at Christmas. The smell of fresh-made lye hominy, and the lacquered cypress beams of the smokehouse. A hint of frost in the air, and the sweet mouth of a coon dog when he trees.

Mary Lasswell, *I'll Take Texas,* 1958

THE TOUGHEST TEXANS

The settlers who have recently opened farms near the source of the San Gabriel and Brushy [creek] find the country well stocked with a singular breed of wild cattle... They differ in form, color and habits from all the varieties of domestic cattle in Texas. They are invariably of a dark-brown color, with a slight tinge of dusky yellow on the tip of the nose and on the belly. Their horns are remarkably large and stand out straight from the head. Although these cattle are generally much larger than the domestic cattle, they are more fleet and nimble and when pursued often outstrip horses that easily outrun the buffalo. Unlike the buffalo, they seldom venture far out into the prairies, but are generally found in or near the forests that skirt the streams in that section. Their meat is of an excellent flavor and is preferred by the settlers to the meat of the domestic cattle. It is said that their fat is so hard and compact that it will not melt in the hottest days of summer, and candles formed with it are far superior to those that are formed with the tallow of other cattle.

Littell's Living Age, January/March 1846

COWBOY CORRESPONDENCE

In order for the foreman to be in close touch with the men at Trujillo and Tombstone [line camps], a camp diary was kept under lock in a small box. The foreman carried one key to the lock, the cowboy keeping the camp kept the other. Daily entries were made. At random, from the Trujillo Diary of 1902 and 1903:

Dec. 29th. I rode the Mexico fence –

Jany – 4th. Frank Cavender came over to have small pox –

Jan. 26. [Foreman] Ira Aten came to camp at dinner today.

Feby. 13th. Bad day sleeted all day, we soaked [loafed].

Feby. 19th Greased mills chopped ice, rode Mexico fence and rounded up bulls!

Jan. the 4th – 1903. Rode to Caps dam then to Holy dam then to the Mohairs & to Chalkey and down the Mohairs to Henry the first, from their to camp found the cow dead that we dipt.

9. Sand Storm done nothing.

Aug. 25. Two wagons loaded with chickens & Kids passed Camp from Tucumcari.

Aug. 17 Skined – 3 – cows came on to camp found the tombstone mill out of whack. Fraters [freighters] past by.

April 23 – 1903 rode Phone line then rode bog Skined – 4 – cows one with ticks Came back found that an unnoen friend had been at camp prised into grane house taken one sack of grane.

Ma 30 1903 One man past Camp driving to black asses with a long whip in Buggy Concord Springs on it he looked suspicious he came and watered and went to feed and just got up and drug it [left abruptly].

June 22 – 1903 Three men passed here on foot back, going from Rag Town to Hereford at the rate of 3 miles an hr They looked kinder lank in the sinch [through the girth] and week in the hine legs.

27. Sept. Old Dynimite was bitten by rattle snake.

The XIT Ranch of Texas, J. Evetts Haley, 1929

★ ★ ★ ★ ★ ★ ★ ★ ★ ★ ★ ★ ★ ★ ★

I f on a clear day in October there is a single dark puff of cloud on the northwestern horizon, a man sees it within moments of coming outside (that swift eye-sweep of the sky that you find in all old rurals, even those ending their days in rest homes and wheeled onto a terrace for air) and gauges its probable meaning. Bouncing through a pasture in a pickup and passing a cow on her left side, he somehow discerns a wire cut on her right shoulder and checks it out for screwworms, hemorrhage, or infection. At supper he may rise from the table in response to sounds that others have not heard, and go to the porch to learn where a pack of marauding dogs is running or a family of coyotes has its base. On a dusty path in the hills he can tell you, if asked, what creatures meek or fierce have trotted and slithered and shuffled there the night before. Distant columns of smoke have messages for him, as do neighbors' tractor sounds, shots, the urgent cries of jaybirds and crows, the alarm coughs of unseen deer, hillside seeps, and the tinge of blooming sweetclover on damp evening air. All these things lodge in him and combine into understanding, for they are a part of his world, and so integrally is he.

John Graves, *From a Limestone Ledge*, 1980

ONE'S FEELINGS IN TEXAS ARE UNIQUE AND ORIGINAL....

[A]nd very like a dream or youthful vision realized. Here, as in Eden, man feels alone with the God of nature, and seems, in a peculiar manner to enjoy the rich bounties of heaven, in common with all created things. The animals, which do not fly from him; the profound stillness; the genial sun and soft air, – all are impressive, and are calculated, both to delight the imagination, and to fill the heart.

With regard to the state of society here, as is natural to expect, there are many incongruities. It will take some time for people gathered from the north, and from the south, from the east, and from the west, to assimilate, and adapt themselves to new situations. The people are universally kind and hospitable, which are redeeming qualities. Every body's house is open, and table spread, to accommodate the traveler. There are no poor people here, and none rich; that is, none who have much money. The poor and the rich, to use the correlatives, where distinction there is none, get the same quantity of land on arrival, and if they do not continue equal, it is for want of good management on the one part, or superior industry and sagacity on the other. All are happy, because busy; and none meddle with the affairs of their neighbors, because they have enough to do to take care of their own. They are bound together by a common interest, by sameness of purpose, and hopes. As far as I could learn, they have no envying, no jealousies, no bickerings, through politics or fanaticism.

The common concerns of life are sufficiently exciting to keep the spirits buoyant, and prevent every thing like ennui.

Mary Austin Holley,
letter written from Bolivar, 1831

THE WINTER OF '99

...was an awful winter on everything, but I don't know as if it was any worse on animals in general than the drouth of '86. The creeks all dried up that year and what waterholes were left got so boggy the buzzards were scared to fly over them for fear their shadders would bog down. The country was full of razorback hogs then, and most of them got such big balls of mud on their tails that the weight would draw back everything on the animal clear up to the snout. When you met a razorback face to face, he'd be grinning at you like a Cheshire cat, 'cause his lips were pulled back. Why, the mudballs on their tails drew their eyelids back so tight the razorbacks couldn't sleep.

Then the critters drunk so much mud they all got pot-bellied. I've seen one of them just a-rocking and a-teetering and a-seesawing on his belly, unable to get his hind feet or his forefeet either on the ground. There he'd be up in the air, on top of his own belly, his eyelids pulled back by the weight of mud on his tail, and his eyes bugged out till you could have roped 'em with a grapevine. It was a sight, I tell you.

Attributed to storyteller/cowboy Findlay Simpson in
Cow People, J. Frank Dobie, 1964

The earliest known play about Texans, *The Triumph of Texas,* or, *The Siege of San Antonio de Bexar,* greeted New York audiences on December 31, 1835, three years before the appearance of the first Texas novel, Anthony Ganilh's *Mexico Versus Texas.* The theater was packed, and receipts for the evening totaled the unusual sum of $1,700. A large crowd, unable to find seats elsewhere, sat on the stage, and hundreds were turned away at the box office.

The Typical Texan, Joseph Leach, 1952

✪ ✪ ✪ ✪ ✪ ✪ ✪ ✪ ✪ ✪ ✪ ✪ ✪

DID I EVER TELL YOU ABOUT BROTHER FOSTER'S THANKSGIVING PRAYER?

Long ago, out in that West Cross Timbers country beyond Fort Worth, Brother Foster was famous for prayers that showed scope and style. I once heard him send up a Thanksgiving prayer that was major league in all respects, and he did it standing in the kitchen door on Grandma Hale's farm.

This old fellow was not really a preacher. But in rural regions at the time I am talking about, purebred and registered preachers were scarce and people made do with the nearest they had to the real article.

Brother Foster taught Sunday school, and did funerals, and went around comforting the sick and sorrowful, and generally made a satisfactory substitute for a pastor. My father used to say you could put a black hat on Brother Foster and hand him a Bible and a collection plate and he could pass for a preacher at a Baptist convention.

There were whispered stories that Brother Foster would even do you a quiet and slightly invalid wedding, in case of an emergency where the need for quick nuptials were beginning to show. But I don't know if that was true and even if it was, then I figure the old gent was simply rending a public service, so let it go.

His speciality was prayers on special occasions, like at Forth of July picnics, ice cream suppers, Christmas gatherings, and other holiday affairs. It must have been in '31 or '32 that Brother Foster came to Grandma Hale's farm for Thanksgiving dinner. All the women, especially, counted it a social triumph to have Brother Foster for Thanksgiving. I don't know how we got him, as he was spread pretty thin over that region.

The meal was the occasion for the prayer, so it was delivered as the blessing. Or asking the blessing, as we said, or returning thanks.

When the formal invitation was issued – "Brother Foster, will you return thanks for us?" – that luminary backed away from the table and took up position in the doorway that led into Grandma's kitchen. Evidently he felt a need to be isolated from the general bunch...

He started out quietly, and built volume as he went along. He began with the food and the blessed hands that prepared it. He called Grandma by name, and I learned later that this was a high blessing, to get your name sent up in a prayer by Brother Foster, and on Thanksgiving day, at that.

From the women he went to the men who tilled the land and brought forth its fruits. He went on to thank the Lord for the beasts that pulled the plows, and those who sacrificed their lives to give us sustenance.

Then he took up the children and asked the Lord to bless their little hearts and keep them safe. (It didn't occur to me that he seemed to rank children behind mules and poultry, since this was before the age of child worship.)

He went into the field of medicine and thanked the Lord for protecting those of us who hadn't caught terrible diseases or suffered crippling injuries. He got into agriculture and mentioned the good corn crop, and the cotton crop which was fair. Went then to meteorology and pointed out to God that the rains came a little too late in the season but were appreciated anyhow. He called the names of people who had died during the year, people we knew, and he gave thanks for their lives. He gave thanks for breezes that turned windmills, for pretty music, for the love of friends and kinfolks, for the very roof over our heads, for feather mattresses on cold winter nights.

This litany went on until the dressing was cold and I thought it was more a sermon than a prayer. Not until a good many years later did I understand why Brother Foster's long prayers were sought and appreciated.

Life in that country was hard, and those folks needed somebody to remind them that they had a lot to be thankful for.

Leon Hale, *Texas Chronicles*, 1989

A small circus once came to stage a one-night show for the people of the Big Thicket living in the Kountze-Saratoga area, before moving on to the cities nearby. Overnight an old baboon in the circus died. Instead of burying him, the circus owners, anxious to be on their way, put the body of the animal in a ditch.

The story goes that the men who discovered the body didn't know what it was, but they figured Lance Rosier, a self-taught naturalist who lived in Saratoga, could identify it. He was forever finding out things about animals and plants. They got word to him to come on over and put the right name to the discovery.

Rosier looked at the carcass, rubbed his chin, and intoned in a serious voice:

"Considering his stooped posture, the frown on his face, and the calluses on his rump, I'd say he was a big thicket domino player."

The Big Thicket of Texas, Howard Peacock, 1984

In America, the Bostonian looks down upon the Virginian – the Virginian on the Tennesseeian – the Tennesseeian on the Alabamian – the Alabamian on the Mississippian – the Mississippian on the Louisianian – the Louisianian on the Texian – the Texian on New Mexico, and we suppose, New Mexico on Pandemonium.

The Flush Times of Alabama and Mississippi, Joseph Baldwin, 1853

After the turn of the century the oil boom brought fatigue to Texas in epidemic proportions. After fourteen hours on a drilling rig many oil-field roughnecks suffered from insomnia. The price of a sleeping pill jumped to ten dollars, and a glass of water to wash it down cost three dollars. Some roughnecks would pool their money, break up a pill and just get drowsy together. Others got religion. Denominations with long sermons on biblical minutiae were popular among roughnecks who otherwise would have had to count sheep.

These measures did not work for everyone, though, and not a few roughnecks took to drinking all night and shooting each other with horse pistols. In response one town council secretly legalized the eight-minute hour and hired Pinkerton detectives to break into homes and adjust watches and clocks to comply with the law. The idea was that if roughnecks worked fourteen eight-minute hours, they would have to go back to work as soon as they got off, and couldn't cause any mischief. The ruse was discovered the next morning, however, when the sun came up at 3 a.m.

William C. Gruben, *The Atlantic* magazine, September 1985

TEXAS IS. . .

An Eldorado of modern hope.
The New York Mirror, 1836

★ ★ ★ ★ ★ ★ ★ ★ ★ ★ ★ ★

An Elysium of rogues.
James Pattie, a Kentuckian, 1833

★ ★ ★ ★ ★ ★ ★ ★ ★ ★ ★ ★

A valley of rascals.
Whig campaign paper, 1844

★ ★ ★ ★ ★ ★ ★ ★ ★ ★ ★ ★

*The dark abode of barbarism
and vice.*
Texas and the Texans, H.S. Foot, 1841

★ ★ ★ ★ ★ ★ ★ ★ ★ ★ ★ ★

Utterly depraved.
The Travels and Adventures of
Monsieur Violet in Western Texas, 1843

★ ★ ★ ★ ★ ★ ★ ★ ★ ★ ★ ★

*The green corner of Mrs.
Liberty's garden.*
The Squatters Almanac, 1845

★ ★ ★ ★ ★ ★ ★ ★ ★ ★ ★ ★

*A den of thieves...a rendezvous
of rascals for all the continent.*
Newspaper publisher Horace Greeley,
circa 1850

★ ★ ★ ★ ★ ★ ★ ★ ★ ★ ★ ★

*The 'Old Man River' of states.
No matter who runs it or what
happens to it politically, it just
keeps rolling along.*
Will Rogers, circa 1930

★ ★ ★ ★ ★ ★ ★ ★ ★ ★ ★ ★

A blend of valor and swagger.
Carl Sandburg, circa 1940

★ ★ ★ ★ ★ ★ ★ ★ ★ ★ ★ ★

*A most delicious country; fertile,
bountiful prairies covered with
grass and flowers.*
Senator Thomas Benton, 1829

★ ★ ★ ★ ★ ★ ★ ★ ★ ★ ★ ★

*The finest portion of the globe that has
ever blessed my vision.*
Sam Houston, in a letter, circa Spring 1833

It was strange, leaving Texas. I had no plans to leave it, and didn't know how I felt... Then I really felt Texas. It was all behind me, north to south, not lying there exactly, but more like looming there over the car, not a state or a stretch of land but some giant, some genie, some god, towering over the road. I really felt it. Its vengeance might fall on me from behind. I had left without asking permission, or earning my freedom. Texas let me go, ominously quiet. It hadn't gone away. It was there behind me.

Larry McMurtry,
All My Friends Are Going to Be Strangers, 1972

Texans are the only 'race of people' known to anthropologists who do not depend on breeding for propagation. Like princes and lords, they can be made by breath; plus a big hat – which comparatively few Texans wear.

J. Frank Dobie in an undated
weekly newspaper column, 1952

I've come to believe that the morons, thieves and cutthroats who with their women settled Texas have passed on genetically a spirit of independence, courage and tenacity which has given me an edge over these defeated, pessimistic and cynical Easterners.

Attributed to Betty Dooley, a Washington
lobbyist, quoted in *Range Wars,* edited by
Craig Clifford and Tom Pilkington, 1989

In those days Houston was filled with soldiers of the Revolution who were waiting for their pay in military script and bounty land, as the Republic possessed no cash. These veterans of the war fully made up for the long-sustained privations by often patronizing Kessler's Round Tent, which was so famous at the time. Kessler was a native Silesian, who had come over from Kentucky with one of the volunteer companies. He had the soldiers pawn their script certificates to him for his brandy cocktails, gin toddies, claret punches, cherry-brandy de la foret noire, etc., and thus became a rich man in a very few years.

At that time fifteen hundred to two thousand people, mostly men, were living together in Houston in the most dissimilar manner. The President, the whole personnel of the government, many lawyers who found ample means of support in those new regions, a large number of gamblers, tradesmen, artisans, former soldiers, adventurers, curious travelers from the United States, about a hundred Mexican prisoners who made suitable servants, daily new troops of Indians – all associated like chums on an equal footing.

Crimes, the desire for adventure, unfortunate circumstances of all sorts, love of freedom, and the fair prospect of gain had formed this quaint gathering. It was everyone's wish to be somebody in the general company, and therefore everyone threw the veil of oblivion over past deeds. Everyone stood on his own merit.

Houston Journal: Adventures in North America and Texas, 1837-1841, Gustav Dresel, 1954

Any person caught monkeying with any of my cattle without permission will catch h—l.
Yours in Christ,
Grizzley Caleen

The Tascosa Pioneer, June 12, 1886

ANOTHER VIEW OF SAM HOUSTON

The "Hero of San Jacinto" is not much troubled with mauvaise honte. He is a fine look-ing man and would not be taken for more than fifty years of age although he must be near sixty. In his rollicking speech on Friday night in the park [Washington D.C.], he told some capital stories and laid bait for complimentary notices with singular adroitness. "I have come to this city," said he, "the companion of men far more distinguished in the history of my country than myself."

Here, of course, there were loud cries of "No!" "No!" "No!"

"Well, gentlemen," said the Senator from Texas, "as you please. There was once a boy who came home drunk to his mother, and when she scolded him, he vowed that 'they had forced it down me.' 'Pshaw!' said his mother, 'I don't believe it.' 'Well, mother,' said he, 'they were going to force it down me, and so, seeing that, I took it freely.'

"Now, gentlemen," said Gen. Houston, "seeing that you will force this distinction down me, I'll take it freely!"

The story was admirably eked out with staggering and hiccoughing, as "natural as life." Gen. Houston would make a first rate comedian, should all other trades fail.

New Orleans Picayune, June 29, 1848

Brandy, Whiskey, and Accommodation for Man and Beast

Sign above entry door of a Galveston saloon, 1832

55

*...for all purposes of human
habitation — except it might be for
a penal colony — these wilds
are totally unfit.*

An assessment of West Texas by W.B. Parker
Expedition Through Unexplored Texas, 1856

***P**ampa was a Texas oil boom town and wilder than a woodchuck.* It traveled fast and traveled light. Oil boom towns come that way and they go that way. Houses aren't built to last very long, because the big majority of the working folks will walk into town, work like a horse for awhile, put the oil wells in, drill the holes down fifteen thousand feet, bring in the black gushers, case off the hot flow, cap the high pressure, put valves on them, get the oil to flowing steady and easy into the rich people's tanks, then the field, a big thick forest of drilling rigs, just sets there pumping oil all over the world to run limousines, factories, war machines, and fast trains. There's not much work left to do in the oilfields once the boys have developed it by hard work and hot sweat, and so they move along down the road, as broke, as down and out, as tough, as hard hitting, as hard working, as the day they come to town.

The town was mainly a scattering of little old shacks. They was built to last a few months; built out of old rotten boards, flattened oil barrels, buckets, sheet iron, crates of all kinds, and gunny sacks. Some were lucky enough to have a floor, others just the dusty old dirt. The rent was high on these shacks. A common price was five dollars a week for a three roomer. That meant one room cut three ways.

Women folks worked hard trying to make their little shacks look like something, but with the dry weather, hot sun, high wind, and the dust piling in, they could clean and wipe and mop and scrub their shanty twenty-four hours a day and never get caught up. Their floors always was warped and crooked. The old linoleum rugs had raised six families and put eighteen kids through school. The walls were made out of thin boards, one inch thick and covered over with whatever the women could nail on them: old blue wallpaper, wrapping paper from the box cars along the tracks, once in a while a layer of beaver board painted with whitewash, or some haywire color ranging from deep-sea blue through all the midnight blues to a blazing red that would drive a Jersey bull crazy. Each family usually nailed together some sort of a chair or bench out of junk materials and left it in the house when they moved away, so that after an even thirty-five cents worth of hand-made wash benches, or an old chair, or table had been left behind, the land-lord hired a sign painter to write the word "Furnished" on the "For Rent" sign.

Woody Guthrie, *Bound for Glory*, 1943

The Chili Prayer

Lord God, You know us old cowhands is forgetful. Sometimes I can't even recollect what happened yestiddy. We is forgetful. We just know daylight and dark, summer, fall, winter, and spring. But I sure hope we don't ever forget to thank You before we is about to eat a mess of good chili.

We don't know why, in Your wisdom, You been so doggone good to us. The heathen Chinee don't have no chili, ever. The Frenchmens is left out. The Rooshians don't know no more about chili than a hog does about a side saddle. Even the Meskins don't get a good whiff of it unless they stay around here.

Chili eaters is some of Your chosen people. We don't know why You so doggone good to us. But Lord, God, don't ever think we ain't grateful for this chili we about to eat.

Amen.

Attributed to Bones Hooks, a black cowboy cook at a ranch reunion, in *A Bowl of Red*, Frank X. Tolbert, 1972

When I started...I knew that sooner or later I would have to have a go at Texas, and I dreaded it. I could have bypassed Texas about as easily as a space traveler can avoid the Milky Way. It sticks its big old Panhandle up north and it slops and slouches along the Rio Grande. Once you are in Texas it seems to take forever to get out, and some people never make it.

...[I]f I wanted to avoid Texas I could not, for I am wived in Texas and mother-in-lawed and uncled and aunted and cousined within an inch of my life. Staying away from Texas geographically is no help whatever, for Texas moves through our house in New York, our fishing cottage at Sag Harbour, and when we had a flat in Paris, Texas was there, too. It permeates the world to a ridiculous degree. Once, in Florence, on seeing a lovely little Italian princess, I said to her father, "But she doesn't look Italian. It may seem strange, but she looks like an American Indian." To which her father replied, "Why shouldn't she? Her grandfather married a Cherokee in Texas."

Writers facing the problem of Texas find themselves floundering in generalities, and I am no exception. Texas is a state of mind. Texas is an obsession. Above all, Texas is a nation in every sense of the word. And there's an opening covey of generalities. A Texan outside of Texas is a foreigner. My wife refers to herself as the Texan that got away, but that is only partly true. She has virtually no accent until she talks to a Texan, when she instantly reverts.

I've studied the Texas problem from many angles and for many years. And of course one of my truths is inevitably canceled by another. Outside their state I think Texans are a little frightened and very tender in their feelings, and these qualities cause boasting, arrogance, and noisy complacency – the outlets of shy children. At home Texans are none of these things. The ones I know are gracious, friendly, generous and quiet. In New York we hear them so often bring up their treasured uniqueness. Texas is the only state that came into the Union by treaty. It retains the right to secede at will. We have heard them threaten to secede so often that I formed an enthusiastic organization – The American Friends for Texas Secession. This stops the subject cold. They want to be able to secede but they don't want anyone to want them to.

Like most passionate nations Texas has its own private history based on, but not limited by, facts. The tradition of the tough and versatile frontiersman is true but not exclusive. It is for the few to know that in the great old days of Virginia there were three punishments for high crimes – death, exile to Texas, and imprisonment, in that order. And some of the deportees must have descendants.

John Steinbeck, *Travels With Charley*, 1962

The English get homesick because they cannot get gooseberries and 'arf-and-arf' and Lea & Perrin's sauce, growing on every mesquite in Texas. They forget to give any credit to the watermelons, the figs, and other good things that they get in Texas, and that they could not raise, even in a hothouse, in England.

On a Mexican Mustang Through Texas
Alex Sweet and J. Armoy Knox, 1905

Increased ranching brought more and more people to northwest Texas, a vast, flat prairie of titanic weather forms. Blasting by tornadoes was one frequent hazard; another was dust storms... Winters could be bitter; the most regular event was the "norther," and nowhere in Texas were they more abrupt than on the treeless plains: [One rancher wrote] "First, a chilly whiff; then a puff, the grass bends flat, and, bang, it is upon us – a blast that would have taken a top-gallant sail smack out of the bolt-ropes, and cold as if blowing across a sea of ice. We gallopped to the nearest ravine, and hurried on all the clothing we could muster. A thermometer...showed a fall of sixty degrees in seven hours."

Texas: An Album of History
James Haley, 1985

CONFESSING AN 1871 WAGON TRAIN MASSACRE

Once the Kiowas were seated, Tatum [the Indian agent] inquired whether they knew anything about the destruction of a wagon train near Fort Richardson. After a silence the man who rose to reply was Satanta (White Bear), who of all the Kiowa leaders was best known to the whites. Satanta looked straight at [Tatum]

and thumped his chest.

"Yes, I led that raid. I have heard that you have stolen a large portion of our annuity goods and given them to the Texans; I have repeatedly asked you for arms and ammunition, which you have not furnished, and made many requests which you have not granted. You do not listen to my talk. The white people are preparing to build a R.R. through our country, which will not be permitted... When Gen. Custer was here two or three years ago, he arrested me & kept me in confinement several days. But arresting Indians is played out now & is never to be repeated. On account of these grievances, I took, a short time ago, about 100 of my warriors, with the chiefs Satank, Eagle, Heart, Big Tree, Bog Bow & Fast Bear. We went to Texas, where we captured a train not far from Fort Richardson, killed 7 of the men, & drove off about 41 mules. Three of my men were killed, but we are willing to call it even. We don't expect to do any raiding around here [Fort Sill, Oklahoma] this summer, but we expect to raid in Texas. If any other Indian comes here and claims the honor of leading the party he will be lieing to you for I did it myself!

"Satanta and Big Tree," unpublished manuscript, Oklahoma Historical Society; Satanta was convicted of the crime and later committed suicide in the Texas prison at Huntsville

★ ★ ★ ★ ★ ★ ★ ★ ★ ★ ★ ★

250 miles to nearest Post Office; 100 miles to wood; 20 miles to water; 6 inches to hell. God bless our home! Gone to live with the wife's folks.

Sign on deserted house in Blanco County, quoted in the *Mason News*, June 18, 1887

LIGHT BREAD

In early Texas, bread made from milled flour and baked into loafs was called "light" bread, denoting its color and to differentiate between it and the courser-grained yellow cornbread. The first pre-sliced loafs of bread also was called "light" bread.

Put one yeast cake in a teacup, pour tepid water on to soften it. Do this half an hour before time to set the bread. Take one quart of water, sweet milk or butter milk, either will make good bread. If water is used, let it be as hot as the hand can bear. Stir in sifted flour until a stiff batter is made; stir in the dissolved yeast cake, and beat thoroughly. This sponge should be set at night, and kept in a warm place until morning; then add one small tablespoonful of salt, one-half a teacup of butter, and, if the weather is very warm, a lump of soda as large as a pea, add flour enough to make it stiff; put on the pastry-board and knead until it no longer sticks to the board; set away to rise, which it ought to do in one and one-half hours; then make into four loaves, working each well, and when light, set in the oven to bake. The proper temperature for the oven is such as will allow the hand to be held to it while you can count thirty. Allow one hour for baking. When taken from the oven, rub over the crust with butter, and wrap in several thicknesses of cloth to soften. If properly made and baked, the crust will be thin, and the bread as white and close-grained as sponge cake.

Attributed to Mrs. J.L. Cunningham in
The First Texas Cook Book,
A Thorough Treatise in the Art of Cookery
The Ladies Association of the First Presbyterian Church
Houston, 1883

Not making the task of the English rancher any easier in Texas was a natural antipathy which existed between the aristocratic English and the democratic Americans. The general American idea of an Englishman was the stale stereotype, a titled fop, vulgarly overdressed, almost invariably wearing white spats, with monocle, walking stick and silk hat. Whatever his class or education he never used his "h's" in his speech, and "Don't you know," "deucedly clever" and "blooming" punctuated every sentence.

On the Texas frontier the genuine article proved at least as exotic. Illustrating the fastidious nature of the English gentleman rancher, the Texas cowboys tell of the blistering summer day when the British manager rode into a line camp complaining of a hellish thirst. "How's that?" asked a hand. "You passed a windmill and forded a creek on the way out."

"Yes, but I didn't have a cup," was the astonished reply.

Ranches and Rolling Hills, Fred Arrington, 1971

When a British journalist remarked about the ragtag uniforms worn by Civil War soldiers of Hood's Texas Brigade, General Robert E. Lee replied:

"Never mind the raggedness.
The enemy never sees the backs
of my Texans."

Texas: An Album of History, James Haley, 1985

Northwest of Van Horn, in the Sierra Diablo, cloudbursts and persistent winds have carved tortuous Victorio Canyon from an uplifted Permian ocean reef that rises steeply to more than six thousand feet above a closed salt basin on the east, then slopes gently westward into the Diablo Plateau.

I went in with a natural area survey team…toward J.V. McAdoo's pioneer home-stead. We rode from the town of Sierra Blanca over the wide, brown Diablo Plateau through a cholla forest blooming head-high in magenta cactus flowers that opened at sunrise, spread at noon, then closed again at dusk. Roaring bees contended with relentless winds as I wandered up a slight rise to the edge of a bleak expanse, unprepared for what lay before me. The earth fell away as if stricken aeons ago by some huge hammer on the side of a gigantic anvil…

An ignominious hollow near the rim marks the final battle site between Texas Rangers and the last of dead Chief Victorio's defeated Mescalero Apaches. It does not look particularly sacred despite the blood shed on that cold January Day in 1881 when native American men, women, and children were shot to end their occupation of West Texas.

Texas West of the Pecos, Jim Bones Jr., 1981

★ ★ ★ ★ ★ ★ ★ ★ ★ ★ ★ ★ ★ ★ ☆

I'm goin' to leave ol' Texas now,
For they've got no use for the
Long-horn cow!
They've plowed and fenced my
cattle range,
And the people there are all so
strange!

Traditional, circa 1900

You can find anything in there, from a cricket to an elephant.

Old saying about the Big Thicket of East Texas

The two-legged hairless ape ought to be mentioned in any [Big] Thicket inventory. Of this species, the most spectacular are those which hide in the deep woods seeking sanctuary from the outer world. The most famous of these is the Nude Man of the Big Thicket, who lived there in the 1950s. Several people had glimpsed the man. Then one fine day, a Mr. Sutton encountered him on a lonely road. The hermit announced that if anyone wanted to come in after him they'd have to come in shooting. He was a large man, deeply tanned and hairy, with a long beard. He had a gun in each hand, and was naked. So far as is known, no one "went in after him" though there are stories of the subsequent capture of an escaped mental patient who had lived for nine years in the Thicket on wild fruits and armadillo. Whether the two hermits are one and the same is – well, as usual, the facts get a little vague on that point.

The Big Thicket, A.Y. Gunter, 1972

"**P**ERT NIGH BUT NOT PLUMB"

Basically, this phrase translates as "almost but not quite," but of course there is more to it. Used correctly it implies a certain character lack and indecision, perhaps even mental strangeness, as in "That ol' boy's pert nigh but not plumb brain-sprung."

Eastland County, Texas, had *its share of certified illiterates in the 1930s* and later, people who could no more read a Clabber Girl Baking Powder billboard than they could translate from the French. I recall witnessing old nesters who made their laborious "marks" should documents require signatures. A neighboring farmer in middle age boasted that his sons had taught him simple long division; on Saturdays he presided from the wooden veranda of Morgan Brothers General Store in Scranton, demonstrating on a brown paper sack exactly how many times 13 went into 39, while whiskered old farmers gathered for their small commerce looked on as if he might be revealing the eternal rules of heaven.

We lived in one of the more remote nooks of Eastland County, in cotton and goober and scrub-oak country. There were no paved roads and precious few tractors among that settlement of marginal farms populated by snuff dippers, their sunbonneted women, and broods of jittery shy kids who might regard unexpected visitors from concealment. We were broken-plow farmers, holding it all together with baling wire, habit, curses, and prayers. Most families were on FDR's relief agency rolls; county agriculture agents taught our parents to card their cotton by hand so they might stuff homemade mattresses. They had less success in teaching crop rotation, farmers feeling that the plot where Daddy and Granddaddy had grown cotton remained a logical place for cotton still. There were many who literally believed in a flat earth and the haunting presence of ghosts; if the community contained any individual who failed to believe that eternal damnation was a fair reward for the sinner, he never came forward to declare it.

Of Outlaws, Con Men, Whores, Politicians, and Other Artists, Larry L. King, 1973

☆ ☆ ☆ ☆ ☆ ☆ ☆ ☆ ☆ ☆ ☆ ☆ ☆ ☆ ☆ ☆ ☆ ☆ ☆ ☆

I have no hesitation in warning any restless, roving spirits who may be attracted by picturesque descriptions of a cowboy's life that, unless they are prepared to toil during the long summer months, both by day and by night, for small pay on scant fare, to be in the saddle from early dawn until sunset both Sundays and weekends, to abstain from comfort and civilization for a greater part of the year, and so to wear themselves out with exposure and manifold fatigues as to be reckoned old and past their work whilst still young men in years, they had better remain at home and leave cowboy life alone.

English cowboy John Baumann in *Fortnightly Review*, April 1, 1886

G*eneral Santa*
Anna escaped from the Texians' carnage on the battlefield of San Jacinto. A day later soldiers found hiding in tall grass a Mexican dressed "in common clothes" but having a "…shirt, which was very splendid…" The man was taken to the Texian camp where he admitted he was Santa Anna and was taken to Sam Houston, who recalled the moment:

"I was lying on a blanket at the root of a tree, with my saddle for a pillow, when Santa Anna approached my tent, studiously inquiring for Houston. I was in a partial slumber and lying, for the sake of an easy position for my wounded ankle, upon my left side, with my face turned from Santa Anna as he approached. The first I knew of Santa Anna's presence was by a squeeze of the hand and the calling of my name; whereupon I looked upon him with a mild expression of countenance, which seemed to inspire him with confidence and hope of life, which evidently he had expected to forfeit. I desired him to be seated upon a medicine chest standing by, upon which accordingly he sat down, much agitated, with his hands pressed against his chest. Presently, he asked for opium, which being given him, he swallowed a considerable quantity, and soon became more composed. He said to me, 'General, you were born, like Wellington, to no ordinary destiny; you have conquered the Napoleon of the West.' He soon desired to know what disposal was to be made of him. Waiving the question, I told him he must order all the Mexican troops in Texas to march beyond the Rio Grande, and then spoke of his late cruelty to the Texans, and first at the Alamo; upon which he said that at the Alamo he had acted according to the laws of war of all nations. I then spoke of the massacre of Fannin and his men…upon which he proceeded to say that their executions were in
obedience to the orders of the Mexican government. 'You are that government,' I retorted.

"Changing the subject in order to return to the point which concerned and tormented him the most, he told me that if the Texans would spare his life, he would repay them by the greatest services, in particular by recognizing their independence. 'How can you make that commitment?' I asked.

'Recognition of Texas can only be granted by an official act of your government.' 'Why, my dear friend,' he fatuously exclaimed, 'that government is myself.' That is exactly what I was trying to say a moment ago concerning the massacre of Goliad!' He turned pale and stammered a few words in an embarrassed attempt to draw a distinction between the two situations.

"Upon this subject, the conversation was waived, and, it being night, I asked him if he would have my camp bed, which being desired, I ordered it to be brought into the tent. He reclined upon it, but did not sleep during the night, being in constant dread of assassination."

Quoted in *History of the Revolution in Texas*
Chester Newell, 1845
Houston's words generally are considered to be paraphrased

✴ ✴ ✴ ✴ ✴ ✴ ✴ ✴ ✴ ✴ ✴ ✴ ✴ ✴ ✴ ✴ ✴ ✴

…The most awful slaughter I ever saw… Texans pursued the retreating Mexicans, killing on all sides, even the wounded.

Moses Austin Bryant, after the Battle of San Jacinto
April 21, 1836

THE BULL DURHAM GUIDE TO MAKING READY-ROLLS

Smoking, while universal, was practically restricted to cigarettes, which were pronounced cig-a-reets, and were made by the smoker. Although in fact the great majority of cowboys had to use both hands in the operation of rolling and lighting, consummate elegance dictated that but a single hand should be employed; and that the rolling should be effected by the finger-tips of this single hand, or better still, through a method which was successfully followed by some of the cowboys and was studiously attempted by all of them.

In this later method, the paper, laid above the knee, received a charge of tobacco, and then, without change of position, was rolled into shape with a quick sweep of the ball of the thumb. Next, with the finished cigarette held between the fourth and fifth fingers of the rolling hand, the thumb and forefinger of that hand grasped one loop of the tobacco-sack's draw-string, the puncher's teeth seized the other loop, and a whirling of the sack like a windmill closed its aperture. A dab by the tongue along the papered cylinder, a match drawn by that same rolling hand across tightened trousers, and the cigarette was "working." The performance of this feat was one of the conventional ways of exhibiting ostensible nonchalance when on the back of a bucking horse.

The Cowboy, Phillip Ashton Rollins, 1936

Thirty-five of the most beautiful white stallions were brought into Hollywood for the role of "Silver." None would do until one was found in Texas — perfect for the role.

The Lone Rangers of the Silver Screen and Television
Mario DeMarco, undated book

You might as well try to drive sheep across the Desert of Sahara in mid-summer as over the route between this [New Braunfels] and Matagorda Bay just now [July 1860]. Why, I was told the other day that good drinking water was 50 cents a bucket full at Lavaca, and I suppose it is as dear at Indianola! No rain there for three months! On the route up, the first water is at Victoria, 40 miles – a hard journey with the thermometer at from 115 to 130 in the sun, and ranging at 103 to 105 in the shade! Such blistering weather as we have had this summer was never felt before in Texas – it would be insupportable on the Coast of Guinea. All of today I have been facing a perfect sirocco [wind] in an open wagon, the hot air coming ten times heated over the parched lower plains. Three weeks ago, I paid a man $1.00 per 100 lbs. for bringing up a load of salt for my sheep: today he would not stir a step after another load for $10.00 a 100 – not for $20.00. The trip would inevitably involve the loss of every ox in his team. So it goes. I still hope that we may have a rain…

Letters from A Texas Sheep Ranch
George Wilkins Kendall, 1959

Among the very early cowmen, the long hair was quiet prevalent. This was not worn in a spirit of Wild West showmanship, as really happened in many cases later on after Buffalo Bill, Ned Buntline, and the lurid dime novels created a Wild West type for eastern consumption. In the ante bellum days...the trend in masculine coiffure was for long hair. I do not mean that in all cases it had to drape over the shoulders, but it was for long locks. That was the natural trend in all branches of society, and so it was but natural that on the frontier where a man might go for months and months without even an approach to a barber shop, long-hairs were not an uncommon note. Moustaches were the vogue, and the smooth face was the exception; and that generally due to extreme youth or the inability to raise one. And let me state right here that there were some wonderful handlebars to be found in those days. Goatees were also quite popular, and, as a rule, cowboys looked older than they do today.

Trail Dust and Saddle Leather
Jo Mora, 1946

★ ★ ★ ★ ★ ★ ★ ★ ★ ★ ★ ★ ★ ★

"I guess [my son will] be a cowboy, too," Glenda says. "I hate for him to do it, but that's what Bigun would want, and I know Banty (Bigun's daddy) is going to have it that way. Bigun was never allowed to be a little boy. Banty had him out breaking horses when he was old enough to ride. I mean breaking horses … colts... not riding old nags. Bigun and Banty and all their people, cowboying is all they've ever known or wanted. To be on a horse chasing a cow was what Bigun enjoyed. Kent has already turned that way. Unless I remarry and my husband is so different...but I don't think I'd like any other life except cowboying."

Glenda Bradley, widow of Bigun Bradley,
The Marlboro Man, quoted by Gary Cartwright in
Confessions of a Washed-Up Sportswriter, 1982

A PROGRAM OF DANCIN'

The *Taylor County News*, March 19, 1886 gave a typical program of a western ball:

☆ ☆ *Program for Cowboy's Ball* ☆ ☆

1. Grand circle round-up march
2. Horse hunters' quadrille
3. Catch-horse waltz
4. Saddle-up lancers
5. Broncho racquet
6. Captain's quadrille
7. Circular's gallop
8. Round-up lancers
9. Cut-out schottische
10. Branding quadrille
11. Cow and calf racquet
12. Night-horse lancers
13. First guard waltz
14. Second guard quadrille
15. Third guard Newport
16. Fourth guard quadrille
17. Day herders' waltz
18. Maverick's polka
19. Bull calves' medley
20. Stampede all

No doubt, it takes strong men to live along the Rio Grande, but the women here are uncommonly resourceful. Mrs. [Johnnie] Chambers acknowledges, "The desert is not for everyone. Some grow weary of it quickly, for others, it becomes the only place to find peace. If you are meant to live here, once you drink the river, it always calls you back. But if you don't love it, you can't stay."

Texas West of the Pecos, Jim Bones Jr., 1981

*W*eddings were *grand events.* Although not attended by as many people as the big [cowboy] balls of the year, they had all the attractions of a ball and more – the feasts, the dances… It was a protracted season of festivities, lasting two or three days.

Notwithstanding the fact that people, as a rule, married young, the courtships were usually long, often having their origin in childhood attachments. The engagement was announced several weeks in advance of the wedding. Then the necessary preparations followed. Among the well-to-do these took on elaborate proportions. The exact date of the wedding was determined by the arrival of the preacher, usually a Methodist circuit rider or a Baptist missionary on his regular circuit. A general invitation was sent out, by word of mouth, to all the neighbors. This included everybody within twenty, thirty or forty miles, depending upon how well the country was settled. On the appointed day the guests began assembling hours before the time of the ceremony, which usually occurred about the middle of the afternoon. The wedding often took place on the front porch of the home of the bride's parents, for the simple reason that the crowd could not be conveniently assembled in one room of the house. After the ceremony came the congratulations, the wedding feast, and the dance. Some of the older people with their smaller children would leave after the congratulations, but all were urged to stay.

The matter of feeding from fifty to a hundred people in one small kitchen (the dining room and kitchen were generally one and the same) was no small task. But the food was already prepared. The bride's family and relatives had been cooking cakes, pies, hams, and other appetizing dishes for days. Perchance, a beef had been slaughtered for the occasion. The guests were served in relays. Some eight, ten, or twelve could eat at one time. When they had finished, the dishes were quickly washed and the tables "re-set," and so on until all had eaten. The bride and groom were given the places of honor at the first table and made highly uncomfortable by the jests of the others. For them it was more like an inquisition than wedding feast.

Alkali Trails, William Curry Holden, 1930

LOST TEXAS

Sherry Prairie Cemetery

This lyrical final resting place in Red River County got its name from the Sherry family which owned and was buried in a far corner of their prairie land.

New Fulp

Yes, there was an original Fulp in Fannin County, named for a local resident, Russell Fulp, but Fulp consolidated its school with that of a neighboring community and therefore was forced to become New Fulp.

Dimple

Began as a community named Cravens in Red River County but a family with a cute little girl arrived in 1901. She had dimples. When the Post Office was established, the postmaster submitted the town name as Dimple to honor the small girl.

Mutt And Jeff

Rural community of Wood County, suggested by the comic strip characters because of the contrasting sizes – one short, one tall – of the town's most successful merchants.

Dancin' in West Texas to Bob Wills' Fiddle Music

Though most West Texas dances were held at ranches, they were generally referred to as 'country dances.' Bob Wills, however, often referred to them as 'ranch dances.' The influence of ranch dances on Wills's music was very important. The country or ranch dance was also significant as an institution in the social life of many Americans...

When someone decided to give a dance at his ranch or farm, word was passed from neighbor to neighbor, by people on the streets, or by telephone. On rare occasions the dances were by special invitation, but most of the time everyone who met certain standards of conduct was invited. The 'all night' dances brought people from such a broad geographical area that they could not return home the same night. Entire families came, mainly by wagon or buggy, a few by car, others on horseback.

These were great social events, for some people the biggest social events of their lives. Since the adults did not sleep at these dances, the beds became the 'baby sitters,' [and] little children were put there to sleep until morning... The older children played in a designated area, while the teenagers often danced and socialized; some met and courted their future spouses there. The older men stayed outdoors when they were not dancing. Whiskey stills were quite common, and some of the men consumed the 'good whiskey' they produced. Intoxication, however, was not the norm. It was frowned on by nearly everyone because it led to fighting, which spoiled everybody's fun.

It was at one of these dances that [Bob Wills] first played the fiddle in public. The year was 1915, and he was ten years old... It was an incredible fact that he would provide dance music for the next fifty-five years.

San Antonio Rose, Charles R. Townsend, 1976

In spite of his acknowledged heroism and subsequent martyrdom at the Alamo, William Barrett Travis was something of a twit. He thought Texans were barbaric and in desperate need of heavenly salvation. Because Texas was, in his words, 'destitute of religion,' he wrote in 1833 asking *The New York Christian Advocate & Journal* for its help in providing missionaries. But he warned:

"Texas is composed of the shrewdest and most interesting population of any new country on earth. The people you send to exhort them must be respectable and talented."

CAMPING IN WILD, WILD TEXAS

We have stationed mounted pickets on the summit of a neighboring bare hill whence they can view the country for many miles. This being on the direct path of Indian raids is a dangerous place & demands the above precaution. It is truly a wilderness – no signs of human beings in any direction – it is indeed the limit line of civilization – where the scattered farmers labor with arms in their hands & others are killed or scalped or driven off – their females massacred or carried into captivity. This sad tale I hear from many who have once had homes upon this land [Palo Pinto County] – which is less inhabited than 20 years ago. Is it a humane policy to protect the savage & feed & arm him, whilst such atrocities are of common occurrence? The hardy bold settler thinks not; and the question he will soon settle for himself. "Pleasant Cooley," the young farmer here, is now sitting by me and giving me notes. His father was killed last year by a white boy – and he was killed by some men on the farm as revenge. Cooley opened this farm last winter and the corn crop is finer than anything he ever saw. Corn is worth $2 a bushel at his door. It was he who killed the Indian whose bones graced the tree we passed yesty [yesterday]. He…Cooley…had lost a mare & colt and in hunting the thieves came upon a body of Indians with the horses, among which he recognized his own. A fire commenced between the parties which resulted in the killing of two Indians and capture of two horses. Cooley scalped one – the other was dragged off by his fellows. The scalp was of long black hair, the scalp lock braided in with the beautiful locks of a white woman reaching to the waist. He took the scalp to as proof that Indians were really killed in the region, a thing doubted by legislators.

Texas Journal, M.K. Kellogg, June 27, 1872

Our herd started from near Snyder, Scurry County. We went by the Double Mountains; 2700 was the biggest herd I had ever been on the trail with and they kept us busy. We had cold rains and the herd stampeded several times. Sometimes it would take all day to gather what we had lost the night before. For several nights in succession they ran. On Duck Creek there was lots of dead wood. Our boss decided to try a new scheme. We gathered a lot of wood, had some great big logs that took five boys on horses to drag them up to the fire. As it began to get dark we rounded the cattle up within one hundred yards of this big fire, and kept that fire burning all night. They did not get up off the bed ground all night. So we all got a very good night's sleep. First we had for several nights. After that we got along very well although we had lost some cattle…

We went down Pease River quite a way, went within a few miles of Vernon, Texas. I left the herd and went to Vernon to get some medicine. My horse had fallen with me before we left the ranch and hurt my ankle and Vernon was the first place I could get medicine. Vernon was a very small place then, in 1883. Had a drug store and I suppose a dozen other business houses. We crossed Red River at Doan's Store about fifteen or twenty miles above Vernon. Then we were in Indian Territory where I saw my first Comanche Indians; but from then on we saw them plenty, for they came to our wagon every day.

Cowboy Life, Rufe O'Keefe, 1936

CAMELS IN TEXAS

Just as I entered [San Antonio, June 18], the camels with their Arab attendants were coming in, causing a general excitement among the population, and a general stampede among all the horses within sight of the strange procession. It is not every town in the new world that can boast of having witnessed such a scene, and my own mind was carried away to Cairo and other cities of the East, where a caravan of some forty camels is nothing to stare at. The last I saw of the animals they were browsing about among the mesquite trees near the San Pedro Springs, looking patient, contented, and apparently well reconciled to their new home.

George Wilkins Kendall, on the U.S. Army's ill-timed experience with camels in Texas, in a letter to the *New Orleans Picayune*, July 6, 1856

"Don't bring a wife to Texas,"
Thomas Borden wrote [1835] to
Moses Lapham in Iowa. "Wait to
find one here. Then she'll be
used to the climate."

The Land of Beginning Again, Julien Hye, 1952

CANOEING ALONE THROUGH MARISCAL CANYON

In most of the unfolded canyons, the river travels through similar-aged layers of marine limestone, but at the far end of the great Big Bend, in narrowly compressed Mariscal Canyon, the river penetrates back in time to its dark depositional heart, then flows out again to the present on the other side. I entered quietly in the late afternoon, passed irregular barriers, and found myself in a moist cathedral filled with wildflower incense. Light fell snow-soft on smooth rocks, and a timeless patience pervaded the great hollow from which cubic miles of stone were taken, a work incomprehensible except by being in the consequent void. The shallow river looked so innocent, yet its mercurial essence belied immense forces forever beyond our control. All at once the folded walls soared up and narrowed down to a slender corridor against the Mexican shore, where I stopped as advised, to scout, and frightened a red racer in the dry champagne glass. I went to the edge of the battered block that chokes the whole river to a passage scarcely three yards wide at the Tight Squeeze and stared in disbelief.

It looked mighty tricky, but to portage single-handed over the breakdown was impossible. I drifted on the edge to the throat, turned to barely miss Texas, then pulled hard on the left, ascended a roaring pillow, and dropped down the other side on a breathless rollercoaster ride. I whooped and hollered like a fool...

Texas West of the Pecos, Jim Bones Jr., 1981

Texas is where men are men and the plumbing is improving.

Will Rogers in early movie, *A Texas Steer*, 1915

I have been in the heart of the "Big Thicket" in Polk and Hardin counties, Texas, for ten days. Nothing can be seen except the tangled underbrush and tall trees. In a ride of 150 miles through…there is one continuous dense growth of tall pines, oaks, magnolias and numerous other forest trees. As far as the eye can penetrate, it is the same; the tangled undergrowth and fallen trees block and interpose an almost impassable barrier in the way of any kind of vehicle. In many places we have to get down on our hands and knees to crawl through the thick, close knitted growth of bay, gall bushes and cane-brakes. Not a human being can be seen for miles… Not a voice is heard except our own; and when we pass a grove of pines, the moaning of the wind makes us feel as if Judgment Day was about to come…

The people who live in the pine woods of Eastern Texas are very primitive in their habits. As this was the first part of Texas that was settled by the early pioneers, their descendants form the principal part of the population… You often find grown men and women that have never seen a prairie country, mountain or valley, railroad or steamboat. They grow to manhood and womanhood in the heart of the thick pine woods, and are contented and happy in their log cabins… Their diets would by no means please the stomach of an epicure. Corn-bread, bacon and potatoes, with an occasional treat of venison, give them perfect satisfaction. Nearly all the children born and reared in the pine woods have light hair; it is a rare sight to see a black-haired family.

Very few…own their own land. For the last forty years they have been in the habit of settling upon any land fit for cultivation. After finding a good, rich land, the piney woods settler will commence felling and cutting the trees and underbrush away from where he expects to have his field. When all the space he wants is cut down he informs his neighbors that on a certain day he will have a log-rolling. His wife makes preparations for a big dinner, and all his neighbors, for miles around, come and pile up the logs that have been cut, then put the brush in piles and set them on fire. In a few days his field is all cleared and ready for the plow…

After a hard day's ride I stopped at a house near the road for supper and shelter for the night. About fifteen minutes after arrival my host announced supper was ready. I cast my eyes over the anticipated meal. My digestive organs, after the inspection of the supper spread over me, rebelled and contracted. The following is the bill of fare complete: Corn-bread, very fat bacon, and clabber [curdled milk]. As I am not fond of clabber, I did not eat it. My host called his daughter and said: "Emma Jane, bring this man some water." The girl brought me a cup of water. My heart was sick within me to think I could not get a cup of coffee. I had not missed my evening coffee in ten years, and the result was that I suffered with a raging headache all night; and the next day the fat bacon and corn-bread that I had partaken of could not or would not settle without the coffee. The next time I come along this way I will fill my pockets with ground coffee.

John A. Caplen in Atlanta's *The Sunny South*
November 5, 1887

★ ★ ★ ★ ★ ★ ★ ★ ★ ★ ★

I suppose that Texans can joke about anything. At least there's a story of a lad in Sunday School who was asked to name the birthplace of Jesus. He guessed Gladewater, Mount Pleasant, and Bonham. When told the answer was Palestine, he said, "I knew it was in East Texas somewhere."

The Truth About Texas, Lewis Nordyke, 1957

*O*ne cold, rainy day a gang of old-timers were in a saloon drinking and sitting around the stove telling yarns and getting mighty cheerful. After a while they all agreed to tell why they had come to Texas. One said he'd come because his neighbors all seemed so anxious for him to try another climate. Another one said that he always thought a lot of his horses and that the brands on some he'd got hold of back in Georgia seemed to keep them from resting easy. Another one said he never did want to be tied down to property and had simply refused to inherit a shotgun from a man who wanted to be his father-in-law.

The confessions went on this way until all but one old gray-whiskers had told his story. "Now, Uncle Billy, let's hear why you came to Texas," they said.

Uncle Billy stroked his chin and said: "Back in Kentucky, where I come from, I was a preacher — and a damn good one. One Sunday morning I got up in the pulpit and told my flock how the congregation over in Pleasant Valley had agreed to build a twenty-five hundred dollar church house and were raising the money. I proposed that we go the Pleasant Valley brethren and sistern one better and build a thirty-five hundred dollar church house.

"They all sanctioned the idea. It had been a good year, and right then and there the money was subscribed. They appointed me treasurer. Bright and early next day I started out to collect the pledges. It certainly wasn't blue Monday that week. I got every dollar of the thirty-five hundred. But I was in such a hurry to come to Texas that I didn't have time to stay and build the church house."

My Rambles, Solomon Alexander Wright, 1942

A Texan will think about Texas. It's a given; they always do. I'm one; I do. On Crete I thought about Texas. It was the same in San Francisco and in Les Montils, France. Happens at conventions; happens at the gymnasium; happens when I wait in lines. Now it happens in Iowa City, Iowa.

The secret holding power? The land, el sol, caliche soil, hot wind, creosote smells at the Big Bend, rows of date palms near Edinburg, pine-needle cushions and splashing bass near Caddo Lake, an Orange Julius at the state fair in Dallas; these are a few…

Rogers Killingsworth in a letter to the editor, *The Atlantic*, March 1975

Jackrabbit in Mushroom Gravy

Finding tender little cottontail rabbits is difficult in the Hill Country. The jackrabbits outnumber them 20 to 1. Most folks wouldn't think of eating jackrabbit, but you should try this recipe.

1 jackrabbit, cut into serving pieces

1 quart water

3 tbsp. salt

4 tbsp. vinegar

8 tbsp. butter

2 1/2 cups sliced mushrooms

1 tsp. chopped parsley

1/2 cup dry sherry

2 tsp. Worcestershire sauce

2 cups heavy cream
salt and pepper to taste

Make up a brine from the water, salt, and vinegar. Marinate the rabbit pieces in the brine for 24 hours. Remove the meat, rinse with cold water, and wipe dry. In a heavy skillet, brown the meat in the butter. Cover and continue cooking until tender. Add a little water if necessary while cooking. When tender, remove the meat and add the mushrooms to the butter remaining in the skillet (add a little more butter if necessary). Cover the skillet and simmer the mushrooms in the butter for 15 minutes. Stir the mushrooms frequently while simmering. Add the parsley, sherry and Worcestershire sauce. Simmer for 5 minutes more. Stir in the cream, season to taste, and pour the hot sauce over the rabbit. Serves 6 to 8.

The Broken Arrow Cookbook
Mike Hughes, 1983

In the distant past, a cattle king named R.A. (Bob) Houston (not related to General Sam Houston) operated a vast ranch in the Gonzales country, and his brand was T41, which was registered in 1870. In going up the Chisholm Trail with his herds, Houston noticed weather vanes on houses – chickens, pigs, very small horses, and sometimes miniature buggies. He wanted a weather vane, but the samples he had seen weren't of the breed or size he liked. The greatest thing in Texas was the longhorn steer. Now that ought to make a weather vane a man could be proud of!

Whereupon Houston got in touch with an Eastern metalworks concern that could cast a life-sized steer – an exact likeness of a Houston animal with the Houston brand. He ordered the steer made of copper, which was to weigh the same as a mature Texas steer, something like two thousand pounds.

When the weather vane arrived it was installed on top of Houston's well-supported two-story mansion in Gonzales. The steer was the tallest thing in town and therefore the sole skyline of Gonzales. Houston liked to point to old T41 and say, "He always faces the wind no matter how hard or cold it blows."

After Houston's death, old T41 was a relic around Gonzales. In 1928 the city leased it from the Houston estate for ninety-nine years, and the vane became a fixture on the firehouse. In the spring of 1951, the city had the steer gold-plated but made sure that the brand was not obscured.

While all this information about the Texas-sized weather vane was coming out there in the crowded courthouse office, I could see that a dark-haired lady was just dying to say something, and finally she did:

"Bet you don't know what the T41 stands for," she said.

"No," I said. There was a chuckle around the room.

"Well," the lady continued, "it stands for 'take four and leave one.' You know the story of the old cattle families. They got their start by getting their rope and brand on cattle that belonged to others."

The Truth About Texas, Lewis Nordyke, 1957

Raising cattle in Texas during my boyhood and before that time did not take much trouble, but they were not worth much after a man got them started. My father sold four-year-old steers for as low as six dollars a head, and it wasn't every year that he could sell them even for that much. In some parts of Texas, big fat steers were killed merely for their hides and tallow.

People cooked with tallow. Bread made with it tastes fine while it is fresh and hot, but when cold it gets heavy. Hot tallow used as butter will often congeal in the eater's mouth before he has time to swallow it. The reason there were so many bald-headed men in Texas, the saying went, was because so much hot water had been poured on their heads in order to melt the tallow sticking to the roofs of their mouths.

My Rambles, S.A. Wright, 1942

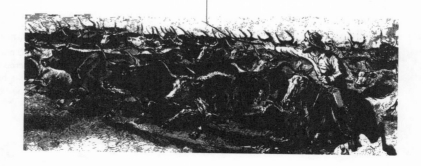

Americans should try to look on Texas in the light of its history. See a people who entered a harsh and dangerous country, fighting desperate, essentially cultural battles when their numbers were still small, who asserted their independence from one civilization while keeping another race in bondage, who conquered all, and who then, over a century, both from war and from forces they could not control, saw their pride humbled in countless ways. See a people, conquerors and conquered, never entirely leaving their soil, with an almost sacred sense of that soil. See the nature of the colonial Texas economy, the continuing, ancient bias against social organization and associations. See a population that remembers where grandparents are buried, and that has changed only superficially, from horse to auto, over a hundred years. Then, perhaps, things fall into place: the pride, the politics, the patriotism – for land and people and symbolic nation, never for ideologies or regimes – the essential conservatism underlying even occasionally radical politics, the deep if unarticulated sense of territoriality, of peoplehood, the eternal feeling for time and place, and above all, for place and people without regard to time.

T.R. Fehrenbach, *The Atlantic*, March 1975

✪ ✪ ✪ ✪ ✪ ✪ ✪ ✪ ✪ ✪ ✪ ✪ ✪

In the whole population of Houston, I doubt whether there were more than sixty or seventy females, both married and single. Some of the immigrants had left their wives behind until the country became more settled, and many had never had any. For the benefit of the ladies, I would mention that speculations are to be made in Texas.

Quoted in *Texas in 1837*, Andrew Forest Muir, 1958

The Texas flag, the Lone Star flag, was not a Texas idea. In November, 1835, a mass meeting took place in Macon, Georgia. It was called to discuss aid for the Texans in their struggle against Mexico. More than three thousand dollars in cash was raised and plans were made for organizing a company of volunteers. One hundred and fifty Georgians enlisted in the company, under command of Colonel Fannin, later to become immortal in the massacre of Goliad.

Johanna Troutman, inspired by the Texas cause, sacrificed a beautiful silk skirt. She converted it into a flag, on which she sewed a large azure star, a Lone Star, since that time the political symbol of Texas. Over the star, she placed the words, "Liberty or Death." Below it was the Latin inscription, *Ubi Libertas Habitat Ibi Patria* – "Where Liberty dwells, there is my country." The flag designed by Miss Troutman was presented to the company of Georgians. At Valasco, Texas, on January 8, 1836, they raised the first Lone Star flag. After Texas had won independence, the government of the Republic honored the designer of the flag by presenting her with a spoon and a fork, of solid silver, that had belonged to Santa Anna, the defeated Mexican general. Later, the state of Texas further paid homage to the memory of Miss Troutman by arranging to move her body from Georgia to the Texas state cemetery in Austin. Her remains now rest in a place of honor, close to those of Stephen F. Austin, the "Father of Texas."

Saddle in the Sky, J.H. Plenn, 1940

TEXAS EATS

Fried Okra

For years I tried to fry okra. The cornmeal would never stay on. It always fell to the bottom of the skillet and quickly burned, ruining the okra as well as the pot. Somebody finally told me how to do it. First, you have to use young okra. The best way to test okra for tenderness is to try to stick your thumbnail into the skin up close to the stem. If you get resistance, the okra is too stringy and won't work. Okra is another of those vegetables that is best picked early and cooked quickly. Pick small, bright green pods that have a tender skin.

Okra

Cornmeal

Small brown bag

Skillet full of very hot oil

Place young okra into a pan full of cold water. Take the okra out one piece at a time, cut into medallions, and drop them in a bag of cornmeal (without shaking off the water). Shake the sack vigorously to coat the okra. When you remove the okra, use your hands to shake off any excess cornmeal (so it won't come off in the oil) and drop into very hot oil. Cook quickly, a little at a time; scoop it out and drain on paper towels. Now that's fried okra. Some people add salt and pepper to the cornmeal.

Last night that crazy fool husband of mine came up with a new invention. Using equal parts of each, he fried okra, onion rings and (you'll never believe this) jalapeno. He simply cut the peppers in half, seeded them, then dipped them in a little beaten egg before coating them with the cornmeal. To tell you the truth it was delicious. Nobody but a Texan would try it.

The Only Texas Cookbook
Linda West Eckhardt, 1981

T*his [stagecoach] line starts from San Antonio* and runs via Boerne, Fredericksburg, Loyal Valley, Fort Quitman, Fort Bliss, to El Paso, a distance of 735 miles, carries the United States mail and passengers weekly…

Entirely along this portion of the line the Comanches and Apaches, the most troublesome and bloodthirsty tribes of Indians, frequently commit severe depredations, not only to the mail line, but to the government trains and droves of cattle passing through the country. They frequently, by their skill (if it may be called such) stampede every hoof of stock belonging to a mail station, and more frequently, by the same means, manage to get possession of a whole [herd of] mules belonging to a government train, thus leaving the train and wagoners at a complete standstill, their train being loaded with stores for different military posts along the lines, and they in a wild Indian country without food or water. As a matter of consequence, great suffering on the part of the train employees is occasioned, as well as for the stores and by the troops for whom such stores are designed.

The Indians, thus far, have only captured three mails since the establishment of this line, the managers using every effort to guard against capture, etc. We are informed and see by various accounts in newspapers, that these Indian depredations are frequently committed by small parties of Indians. Still, while they are small, the United States forces to watch them are much smaller, which the Indians are smart enough to know – hence the casualties.

Texas Almanac, 1870

T he first English-speaking men to come to Texas were filibusters ready to sell their lives in the mad scheme of taking the land from Spain. The Texas colonists fought the Indians for every plot of ground they settled on. Next they fought the Mexican nation for independence, and then fought Mexican raiders for decades over a far-stretched frontier. Finally, having attracted the fighting blood of the nation, Texas became an arena in which the Colt's revolver was law, and blood was commoner than order… It used to be said of these Texians that they "fought for their lives, hunted for their living, and died for their country."

Flavor of Texas, J. Frank Dobie, 1936

In September every year the [Comanche] Honey-Eaters in great numbers went to the Rio Grande and deep into Mexico to take horses. Then the heat of full summer was waning and the rains were over so that no marks of travel would be left in mud for pursuers to follow, and the nights were fragrant and clear, and the grass was still succulent before winter. Because of where they went, and when, they called the month of September the Mexico Moon.

The raid was carefully organized. It began with ceremony – dances and songs and tales in honor of war, around a great fire, at night. Of the men, only the warriors going on the raid took active part. Each had a woman to dance with him. Leaving the firelight some vanished into the trembling shadows to make love, while men too old to accompany the raid told of their great days and struck drums for emphasis. The raid leader was absolute in his command. He said where they would go, who would be the scouts, who would do the camp work, where they would camp…

When September came, the Mexico Moon, the residents of the river lands took their annual precautions. Sentinels were sent out to stations on the highest peaks and crags of the western approaches to the Big Bend. There they set up piles of brush and faggot to light as signal fires when the time came. They stood guard night after night as the moon rose later and fuller, until in its fall of turquoise light the whole fantasy of the rocky night seemed visible in sharpest detail and distance…

And then one night, far across the land, a pinpoint of rosy light would show like a fallen star burning on the ground; and near it another, and another, in the order of campfires; and the farthest sentinels on their cold platforms would know that they saw what they were watching for – the advance elements of the Honey-Eaters. Striking life to their fire high in the sky they gave the signal that was awaited by watchers on the next height, who in turn lighted their wood; and soon the news was taken south all the way to the river by the chain of watchfires, telling men and women on their scattered ranches to gather their children and their animals and go to the river villages for protection.

In another day and a night came the rustling and glittering front of the war party, standing forth in the pour of the moon. The land [the Comanches] crossed was banded with every color, and so were their painted faces and breasts, their arms and bellies. If mystery was suspended in the very landscape of the Big Bend, it also clung around their spirits; and as they contended with a land of the utmost hardness, hardness hung like conviction in their hearts. In oddly stirring ways they seemed like direct expressions of the fantastic lands where they roved.

They approached [the Rio Grande] river whose sandy slopes were made of powdered mountains. There they would camp; water the horses; smoke and rest and ignore the poor settlements upriver and down, at least on the southerly journey, for they were after greater spoils than those huddled about the darkened jacales and earthen huts near-by. At day-break they would cross over the Rio Grande and be on their way, together a living embodiment of the land they called their own.

Paul Horgan, *Great River, Vol. II*

THREE INSIGHTFUL OBSERVATIONS ABOUT TEXAS

1. [W]e have the general rule: once a Texan, always a little goofy, often quarrelsome, fabulously virile, bubbling with grandiose schemes, and funny as hell in an exccentric and not always ingratiating fashion. It does little good to tell the world that the average Texan is a little poorer than most folks, that he has a horror of showing off, and that, far from being vigorous in the grand manner, he is forever seeking a place where he can lie down and get some more rest. The didos of a few rich boys have given the state a reputation which may live forever.

2. Texas talk is an insidious thing, and it is hard to identify. The difficulty is that there are several kinds of Texas talk; speech varies quite as much as the Texas soil or vegetation. It is all mixed up. I have a pretty good ear for talk (I may be deceiving myself), but I wouldn't bet that I could always spot a Texan by his talk. My own way of talking, I have been told, shows traces of many influences, and the principal characteristic is a tendency to mumble. The late Alva Johnston, a New York journalist, once said of my speech, "It is a brand of Texas shorthand, a little baffling at first but intelligible once you get used to it – generally, that is."

3. Part of the confusion in Texas comes from a misinterpretation of the signs. For example, when a woman insists on driving three hundred miles in her Cadillac from her home town on the western plains to hear Maria Callas or Joan Sutherland sing in Dallas – does it mean that Texas is undergoing a tremendous cultural renaissance? Hardly. It may mean many things, including a yearning to show off some new furs.

What Is Texas? Stanley Walker, 1962

IN THE EARLY DAYS OF THE REPUBLIC OF TEXAS

…many of the white men who came to Western Texas from all parts of the United States had strong sanitary reasons for preferring a change of climate. To be more explicit, the most of the invalids had been threatened with throat disease. So sudden and dangerous is this disease that the slightest delay in moving in a new and milder climate is apt to be fatal, the sufferer dying of dislocation of the spinal vertebra at the end of a few minutes and a rope. A great many men, as soon as they heard of Western Texas, left their homes in Arkansas, Indiana and other states – left immediately, between two days – the necessity for their departure being so urgent that they were obliged to borrow the horses they rode to Texas on. All of these invalids recovered on reaching Austin. In fact, they began to feel better, and considered themselves out of danger as soon as they crossed the Brazos River. Some of those who would not have lived twenty-four hours longer if they had not left their old homes lived a green old age in Western Texas, and, by carefully avoiding the causes that led to their former troubles, were never again in any danger of the bronchial affection [sic] already referred to. As soon as it was discovered that the climate of Western Texas was favorably disposed towards invalids, a large number of that class of unfortunates came to Austin. Many well authenticated cases of recoveries are recorded.

Alexander Edwin Sweet, *Alex Sweet's Texas,* 1986

I will now speak of a circumstance

which happened to us while eating supper one evening whilst the [Civil War] Federal soldiers were in town [Matagorda]. These soldiers entered our house by one door and three by another. They said to me, "Are there any of our men here?"

"Who do you mean, sir?" I replied.

"Federal soldiers, Ma'am."

"No, sir, there are not."

"How do you get flour and coffee, Ma'am?"

I replied, "We have a way to get it, sir."

"We have been trying to starve you out for the last two years, but your supper table does not look much like it."

"In this one thing," I said, "you will not find it so easy to do whilst there is a beef in our prairies."

"Are you a Union lady, Ma'am?" one of the men asked.

"No, sir, I am surprised you should take me for one."

"You do not seem to be afraid of us, made me think so."

"That word afraid is not in my vocabulary, sir. I am one of the old Revolutioners of Texas."

"Ah," he replied, "I thought you were something uncommon, you are so spunky."

Asking me if I had any butter or eggs to sell and being told I had not, he departed with his comrades, a little wiser than when he came in about Texas women.

Victorian Lady on the Texas Frontier, ed. by C. Richard King, 1971

★ ★

And who was the heftiest Texas governor? Not Sam Houston? No. James Stephen Hogg at roughly three hundred pounds? Not so. The champ was Governor Richard B. Hubbard, who took office in 1876 and who outweighed Hogg by a hundred pounds... An unsuccessful search was made to find the mammoth zinc bathtub which Hubbard had used while governor.

What Is Texas? Stanley Walker, 1962

★ ★

Well, it is not quite so hot as Death Valley, and, on the other hand, it is not quite so cool as Greenland.

Answer to visitor's inquiry about summer in West Texas, circa 1960

TEXAS EATS

Texas Caviar

1 pound black-eyed peas

2 cups Italian dressing

1 cup diced green pepper

1 1/2 cups chopped onion

1 cup finely chopped green onion

1 small can chopped green chilies

1 2-ounce jar pimento, chopped and drained

1 tablespoon chopped garlic

1/2 teaspoon salt

1/8 teaspoon hot pepper sauce

Wash the peas in several changes of water. Soak them for six or so hours. Cook them until tender. Mix with the remaining ingredients. Refrigerate. This is good with chopped ham added before serving. Place the mixture on lettuce leaves. Serves 10 to 12.

Ernestine Sewell Linck and Joyce Gibson Roach, *Eats,* 1989

★ ★ ★ ★ ★ ★ ★ ★ ★

These Are Some of the Things Texas Barbecue Is Not:

It is not three-day-old shards of overcooked roast beef drenched in catsup, sitting disconsolately in the steam trays of a deli.

It is not a steak grilling over charcoal on a suburban patio.

It is not a side of beef turning on a spit – and most especially with Texans lurching around drinking bourbon and branch water in the noonday sun, a la *Giant.*

It is not shredded pork with peppers of the kind Craig Claiborne [once *New York Times* food editor], bless him, discovered North Carolinians selling by the quart in goldfish cartons. Texas barbecue is never pork.

Griffin Smith, *The Atlantic* March 1975

IT WAS A PRETTY SUNDAY MORNING IN WEST TEXAS THAT OCTOBER DAY MORE THAN HALF A CENTURY AGO...

...when a young Methodist preacher held a church service at Bomarton, then got into his buggy to head for Miller Creek community to perform a wedding ceremony.

The preacher was to marry a young cowboy, Ed Robinson, to a pretty bride-to-be, Miss Minnie Alexander, at the home of her parents. The morning quiet was shattered by a hardriding cowpoke, who hailed the preacher's buggy – waving his hat and yelling – "Wait, wait!"

The excited cowhand blurted out a fact that the large creek coming up, was on a big "rise" – "enough to float a steamboat." Sure enough, it was. The Rev. Mr. McReynolds could not cross it. The good parson was sitting there pondering the situation when the prospective bridegroom rode up – on the preacher's side of the swollen stream, a tributary of the Salt Fork of the Brazos.

"Brother Mc, what are we gonna do?" asked a very anxious and very disappointed young cowboy.

...[T]he preacher said, "Let's try to swim that stream on horseback, maybe we can make it."

"It's my party. I'll go first," exclaimed the cowpoke, who had shucked off his brand new suit and was holding his outer clothing aloft as he guided his horse into the current. (He kept on his long-handled underwear and hat.)

The preacher watched from the creek bank. The 'poke had gone upstream a good ways so he could come out on the other side about the point where they wanted to cross... He tried and failed. The getting-married cowpoke almost drowned, but he held onto his blue serge suit [and returned to his side].

"I'm afraid I can't make it over," the preacher yelled to Ed. Ed just stood there blinking and shaking. "Tell you what, though, go get the girl and bring her to the bank beside you on your side."

Ed struck out to the home of the bride, got her, her parents, and a group of friends and relatives, who had gathered for the big event. The entourage came to the creek bank – the bride radiant in her new white dress, read an account in the *Baylor County News*.

The couple stood on a grassy knoll (a fitting carpet) beside the raging stream. The preacher stood up on a point directly across from them. A crowd of wellwishers had gathered on his side, too. The ceremony was performed here and there.

The creek, a tumbling, sloshing ribbon, furnished wedding music. Greenery beside the creek – wild flowers and bushes, provided the color, plus a sky of blue above their heads.

"I do!" boomed Ed across the stream, cupping his hands to his mouth to be sure he was heard by the preacher across the stream.

"I do," piped a shy Minnie, nodding her head up and down to emphasize her acceptance to the satisfaction of the minister.

"I now pronounce you man and wife," intoned the Rev. Mr. McReynolds. Congratulations were shouted back and forth across the swollen stream.

[Editor's Note: The Robinsons' Golden anniversary was celebrated in Abilene half a century later.]

Tanner Laine, *Cow Country*, 1969

*T*exas is on the *whole a flat country.* More prairie lands than wooded areas are to be found there. The prairies are magnificent, the most delightful sight an eye can hope to behold. For nine months of the year Texas is a green carpet decorated with wild flowers. It is a garden, where the hand of man has nothing to do but gather. Nature alone is sufficient to reproduce the treasures of this vast, fertile park in which every adornment and every fruit of the earth grow without cultivation. The Americans call Texas their Italy, their Andalusia. This praise is no exaggeration.

Although mountains are rare in Texas, hills abound. In most places the terrain offers to the eye irregular and picturesque undulations, which extend like solid waves on a troubled sea…

The forests which Texas possesses are usually located on river banks. More than in any other part of America one finds there those secular giants precious for ship building when their timber has been hardened by the elements. Forests of future masts rise up to the sky as they await the axe of the Americans, who have so far left them untouched. The products of Texas will, as time goes on, become infinitely more varied. The fertility of the soil, which, in all of North America, is perhaps unequaled except in the states of Indiana and Illinois; the mildness of the climate, Texas's heat being tempered by a steady cool breeze; these factors make it suitable for all types of agriculture, whether colonial or European.

From an article in *Journal des Debats*, by Theodore-Frederic Gaillardet, October 26, 1839

---

*T*his is a big country and it produces big men. Now I've seen what Texas is supposed to be.

Richard Nixon, at John Connally's Floresville ranch, 1972

*L*ast night I left Houston on a steamboat to visit San Jacinto Battleground, located between Houston and Galveston and therefore on the route which Admiral Baudin is expected to follow. It was midnight when the steamboat reached the plain known to the Texians as the Battleground. It is immediately below the point where the small stream called Buffalo Bayou joins the larger San Jacinto River. No sooner had we arrived at this scene of recent glory and importance for Texians than the passengers, who filled the steamer to capacity, broke forth into frenzied shouting, mingled with artillery fire and military band music. It was a curious spectacle to witness, this really terrifying explosion of patriotic enthusiasm! The weather was superb. The inhabitants of the plain, aroused by the unexpected cannonade from the river, hastened to light up their windows and to run half-naked to the little row of cannon on the bank, which they proceeded to shoot off. Soon we went ashore, and the patriotic throng, armed with resin torches, formed a fiery frame around the field. There the famous patriotic song "Yankee Doodle" was sung, and the ceremony concluded with three cheers, shouted in not inharmonious chorus by the exultant crowd, who, with this triple adieu, honored the memory of their heroes who had died for their country.

Article by Theodore-Frederic Gaillardet
April 23, 1839, in *Journal des Debats*

I *miss the damned place.* Texas is my mind's country, that place I most want to understand and record and preserve. Four generations of my people sleep in its soil; I have children there, and a grandson; the dead past and the living future tie me to it. Not that I always approve it, or love it. It vexes and outrages and disappoints me – especially when I am there. It is now the third most urbanized state (behind New York and California) with all the tangles, stench, random violence, architectural rape, historical pillage, neon blight, pollution, and ecological imbalance the term implies. Money and mindless growth remain high on the list of official priorities, breeding a crass boosterism not entirely papered over by an infectious energy. The State Legislature – though improving as slowly as an old man's mending bones – still harbors excessive, coon-ass, rural Tory Democrats who fail to understand that 79.7 percent of Texans have flocked to urban areas and may need fewer farm-to-market roads, hide-and-tick inspectors, or outraged orations almost comically declaiming against welfare loafers, creeping socialism, the meddling of ol' feds, and sin in the aggregate.

Larry L. King, *The Atlantic*, March 1975

NEXT STOP, WACO!

"Six-Shooter Junction!" the Katy brakeman would yell into the day-coach. "Thutty minutes for lunch and see a killin'!"

The Land of Beginning Again, Julien Hye, 1952
Because of frontier violence, early Waco was nicknamed "Six-Shooter Junction."

OTHER NAMES FOR THE TEXAS LONGHORN

Spanish cow
Coaster (because they first were found near the Texas coast)
Sea lion (for the same reason; especially a pet nickname used by legendary rancher Shanghai Pierce)
Cactus boomer
Mossy horn (an old, usually emaciated steer)

OTHER NAMES FOR TEXAS HORSES

Cow-horse
Fuzzie (because when wild on the range their manes and tails grew shaggy)
Broom-tail (usually range mares)
Broomie
Broncho
Bronc
Cayuse (a rare variation was "kiuse")
Mustang

82

A HAPPY ENDING FOR THE TEXAS LEGISLATURE

The 63rd session [of the Texas Legislature; 1972] cleaned up the House rules and passed a campaign-reporting law with teeth in it and some species of ethics legislation, and that exhausted reform for the year. Reform expired totally about halfway through the session on Apache Belle Day. The Apache Belles are a female drill and baton-twirling team that performs during half time at college football games. They are real famous in their field, so the House set aside a special day to honor them for their contributions to the cultural life of Texas. Representative Billy Williamson, a political troglodyte from Tyler, hometown of the Apache Belles, served as master of ceremonies.

The Belles, all encased in tight gold lame pants with matching vests and wearing white cowboy boots and hats, strutted up the center aisle of the House with their tails twitching in close-order drill. They presented the speaker's wife with a bouquet of Tyler roses, and made the speaker [Price Daniel Jr.] an honorary Apache Belle for the day. Then Williamson commenced his address by noting that not all Apache Belles were on the floor of the House.

Upon Williamson's instruction, everyone craned his neck to look up at the House gallery, and sure enough, six extra Belles were standing. On a signal from Williamson, the six turned and perched their gold-lamed derrieres over the rail of the gallery. Upon each posterior was a letter and they spelled out R*E*F*O*R*M.

Molly Ivins, *The Atlantic*, March 1975

★ ★ ★ ★ ★ ★ ★ ★ ★ ★ ★ ★ ★ ★ ★

Dave Rudio...described a Texas ranger's killing of a renegade: "The ranger came up and said quietly: 'You're wanted. You'd better come along peaceable-like' The outlaw he began to throw talk. The ranger he said: 'Don't act up. Be sensible and come along with me.' The outlaw, still jawing, started to reach. He hadn't a tenderfoot's chance at that game, for the ranger he just whirled out his own gun, and that outlaw stopped plumb short talking to the ranger and began a conversation with Saint Peter."

The Cowboy, Phillip Ashton Rollins, 1936

IT WAS ONLY A TRIFLING KILLING, ACCORDING TO MRS. HOUSTOUN, A BRITISH VISITOR TO GALVESTON IN LATE SUMMER, 1843....

...The Texas people go on remarkably well with their primitive system of administering justice. During the months we remained in Galveston Harbor, there was no single instance of malicious crime – no street fights, no apparent drunkenness or tumult. It is true that on New Year's day one man was shot; and doubtless this fact would to those ignorant of the details furnish a strong argument in favor of the popular opinion of the prevalence of crime in Texas. The circumstances were as follows. Some children were quarreling in the street; from words they came to blows; when their respective parents who had been drinking together thought proper to interfere. "I say, sir, you call your children away, sir!" This gentle remonstrance not being duly attended to, the speaker went forthwith for his rifle and was in the act of presenting it at the head of his foe (probably as a means of intimidation) when he received his death wound from the other's pistol. No notice whatever was taken of this misdemeanor.

Littell's Living Age, II, August-October 1844

When we were upon the high table-land, a view presented itself as boundless as the ocean. Not a tree, shrub, or any other object, either animate or inanimate, relieved the dreary monotony of the prospect...it is a region almost as vast and trackless as the ocean — a land where no man, either savage or civilized, permanently abides; it spreads forth into a treeless, desolate waste of uninhabited solitude, which always has been, and must continue, uninhabited forever.

Captain Randolph Marcy, recording his first view of the Texas Panhandle, diary, 1849

When we hear a man say 'Texan,' we involuntarily look to see if he has the lock-jaw, or if he has ice in his mouth. There is no excuse for a man to use such a word in a mild climate. The genius of our language requires generally the termination 'ian,' when it is necessary to give a name to the inhabitants of that country. 'Texian' is the name for which we fought, and which shows ourselves independent of all foreign dictation. Let us stand up for the rights of the 'old Texian' against the ruthless Goths and Vandals who are endeavoring to deprive him of that which has blazed to brilliantly from the folds of his banner over all his battle-fields.

From a debate over the etymological correctness of the use of 'Texan' vs 'Texian,' *The Texas Monument,* February 5, 1851

★ ★ ★ ★ ★ ★ ★ ★ ★ ★ ★ ★

Texas is...a hard, hot, uncompromising landscape, interesting mainly for the bizarre fact that its bushes, instead of standing still as they do in Europe, blew about in the wind; and for its population, which was made up of two mutually hostile races, the Randolphscotts and the Nonrandolphscotts.

Alan Coren, *Punch*, May 1982

★ ★ ★ ★ ★ ★ ★ ★ ★ ★ ★ ★

In Texas you call a friend 'old' if you are really fond of him, and you never give offense by addressing him or introducing him by his nickname. The use of nicknames is so common that one gets the impression that all Texas millionaires, are called Jim, Joe, Billy, Ted, Ed, Mike, Kip, Dutch, Slats or something equally breezy, and the value attached to them is so generally recognized that some millionaires have incorporated theirs into their given names.

The Super-Americans, John Bainbridge, 1961

Pioneer Texans *did not speak well of the Comanches.* Was this because they robbed them of everything they [the Comanches] held dear?

The Comanches never "went" to war. (It was at their door, brought to them). They always fought to hold their homes – in defense of their lives and property – against an invading foreign foe. Finally, they were fighting against total extermination. (Not only was it a right, it was a patriotic duty, and there were no slackers.)

It is true that they took a few white people's scalps, but not more than the whites took from them. Perhaps they killed a few hundred whites, but lost at least 35,000 of their own people in a period of 200 years. But they never bombed a city, killing thousands of men and women. Nor did they ever poison a pool of drinking water, as was charged to one Texan. His defense was: "The Comanches may not be doing any devilment now but they might – so I killed them." That attitude drenched Comanche Land with blood.

J. Emmor Harston, *Comanche Land*, 1963

The mesquite *loves life and will grow almost anywhere.* In fact, most West Texans think it prefers the dry red clay or the worst soil God has to offer. It has about its annual bloom a mysterious sense of danger in springing forth prematurely and it is traditional in West Texas that spring isn't safely abroad in the land until the mesquite acknowledges it. The late Frank Grimes, editor of the *Abilene Reporter-News*, made an annual affair of running his poem warning those who would disregard this prophet:

We see signs of returning spring –
The redbird's back and the fie' larks
*   sing,*
The ground's plowed up and the
*   creeks run clean,*
The onions sprout and the rosebud's
*   near;*
And yet they's a point worth thinkin'
*   about –*
We note
*   that the old*
*   mesquites*
*   ain't out!*

A Personal Country, A.C. Greene, 1969

The longer I lived in the east, the more completely I realized that, for better or worse, I was going to be, to everybody's mind, wherever I lived, a Texan.

Cowboys and Cadillacs, Don Graham, 1983

The Alamo is a nice place *to visit but you wouldn't want to live there.*

The Mexican American Devil's Dictionary, P. Galindo, 1973

85

A SUNDRY ASSORTMENT OF HOUSTON WEATHER REPORTS

1. Heat is so severe during the middle of the day, that most of us lie in the shade and pant.

Ashbel Smith, in a letter dated May 1, 1838

2. Everything is so new, clean, fresh looking, as compared with the cluttered, gray life in England. But it's rather warm outside, isn't it?

A.D. George of the Manchester Guardian, quoted in the Houston Post, June 17, 1964

3. When [General Sam] Houston came to Houston

> He beat a quick retreat,
> He loved its wicked people,
> But he couldn't stand the heat.

Letter from reader C.J. Haynes, quoted in the Houston Post, June 2, 1969

4. Rain! Why, it falls in torrents! And muddy! Whoopee!! If there is a town in Texas more muddy than this pleas [sic], tell the Bishop not to send me to it.

Rev. C.H. Brooks, in a letter dated March 10, 1856

We went to the hotel[at Matagorda]...our hostess making herself very agreeable. Mrs. L was a widow, one of the early day settlers, was anxious for emigration to the country, and was very polite to strangers, kept a good table, and had a great deal of customers.

The country was full of bachelors, but very few ladies. When bed[time] came we were ushered into a room where there were several beds.

We did not like this much, as we expected a room to ourselves, but on being told that the gentlemen slept on one side and the ladies on the other side of the room, I opened both my eyes and ears and looked again at my hostess, who did not seem to be jesting. Presently several more ladies came in to go to bed. They went through the undressing operation quickly and were all in bed long before we had got over our surprise at this new fashion in sleeping. We soon undressed but did not divest ourselves of all our garments, keeping on outside garments which were calico wrappers. We had been in bed about an hour when the gentlemen came in one by one until all had retired. I watched with breathless suspense the coming of the last one. This was something we were not accustomed to, and it was several nights before I could sleep – not until nature was completely exhausted and overcome with watching.

The ladies all laughed at us and said, "By the time you have been in Texas a few months, if you travel in the country, you will have to sleep with the man and his wife at the house you visit," as houses were only log cabins with two rooms, one for the house servants, the other for the family. I found this statement correct, visiting some friends in the country two weeks after this who had a small log cabin with two rooms in it, the servants and cooking one, the other to sleep in. I had to sleep with the man and his wife. I slept at the back of the bed, the wife in the middle and the man in front.

Victorian Lady on the Texas Frontier
ed. by C. Richard King, 1971

A BRIEF HISTORICAL SURVEY OF TEXAS COSTS, PRICES AND SALARIES

1838: $5.00 – One year's subscription to the *Telegraph & Texas Register*, a newspaper

1840: $1.00 – One pound of coffee in Austin

1841: $15.00 – One-way fare on the Tarbox & Brown stagecoach between Houston and Austin; travel time, three days

1852: $15.00 – Monthly salary, driver of ox-drawn freight wagon

1860: $2.50 – One-way ticket via railroad between Galveston & Houston; travel time, 2 1/2 hours

1861: $200 – One-way ticket via Butterfield Overland stage, 2,795 miles from St. Louis, through Texas, to San Francisco; travel time, 25 days

1880: $4.00 weekday, $6.00 Sunday – Daily buggy rental at Fort Worth livery

1883: $1.18 – Daily salary for working cowboy on ranches around Tascosa before March 24, beginning of the cowboy strike for higher wages

1883: $1.68 – Daily salary for working Tascosa cowboys after April 3, end of the strike for higher wages

1890: $1.82, $1.05 and 98 cents – Average daily wages for, respectively, men, women and children industrial workers

1891: $360.00 – County judge's annual salary in Borden County

1900: $1.50 – Price per acre of land in Lamb County; financed at 3 percent interest for 50 years

1903: 3 cents – Price per barrel of Texas crude oil

1903: $121.00 – Annual salary, Methodist circuit-riding preacher, Texas Panhandle

1917: $100,000 – Construction price of massive rock headquarters house of 6666 Ranch in Guthrie

1928: $2.50 – Price of live horned frogs at Democratic National Convention in Houston

*T*he first court trial [in Taylor County] was unique. Two men went into the back end of a saloon together. A pistol was discharged. One of the men came out. The other one was found dead. The living man declared that he didn't know what had caused the other's death. A trial was held under the mesquite trees, after which a jury wandered off into the bushes to meditate. Soon a verdict was rendered: "No man is guilty until he's proved guilty. This man denies that he killed the other fellow and nobody swears that he did. We find the gentleman, accepting his own testimony, not guilty."

Attributed to J.B. Masters, *Dallas News*, January 17, 1926

*T*he genuine old-time cowboy – not the occasional one who has done most of the talking – was, it is true, somewhat bow-legged. But his legs were strong; if he held on to a pitching horse he held with his legs and not his hands. It is also true that he did not like to work on foot, but even fifty years ago [1876] he was beginning to build fences and to work with mules and scrapers in making tanks. Then when it came to "mugging" yearlings and throwing down bulls and cows he had on foot to outwrestle the world. Moreover, he often prided himself on his running ability. Lee Russell of Fort Worth is one of the best-known cowmen of Texas. If any doubting reader will sometime get one of Lee Russell's friends to tell of the time out on the Texas-New Mexico line when Russell ran afoot 100 yards against a race horse and won the bet, he will have at least one concrete illustration.

J. Frank Dobie, *Dallas News*, July 11, 1926

*W*hen the Indians robbed houses they invariably took all the books they could find, using the paper to pack their shields. They knew, as well as we did, the resistance paper has against bullets. Paper offered more resistance to a bullet than anything to be had upon the frontier, unless it was cotton. The Indians knew this and stole all the books and paper they could find...

Their shield was made by forming a circular bow of wood two or three feet across, over each side of which was drawn untanned buffalo hide from the neck of the buffalo, the toughest and thickest they could get. They filled between the hide with paper. In times of action, the Indian had this on his elbow and always aimed to keep it at an angle between you and him. Very few of the old-fashioned rifles would penetrate these shields. The rifle I carried then [1861], and still have, would knock a hole right through them at any angle. I once shot an Indian down on the Quitaque. I did not kill him, but he dropped his shield. Between the folds of hide was a complete history of Rome, and the boys had considerable fun passing the sheets around and reading them.

Legendary West Texas rancher Charles Goodnight recalling his days as an Indian fighter
Panhandle-Plains Historical Review, 1928

Executive Department
Columbia 11th Nov. 1836

To the Chiefs of the
Wacos, Towacconnies,
Towassies, Keechies, Ionies,
Comaanchees [sic] and all other
Indians wishing to be friendly.

Brothers,

I have heard that you wish to talk with your
white brothers and to smoke the Pipe of Peace!
Bad men have stolen horses and made war and
brought trouble upon the white and red people.
It is now time to be at peace with each other
and bury the Tomahawk forever. The great chief
of Mexico, Santa Anna, is our prisoner, and he
cannot help you to make war any more upon us.
The Mexicans have told you many things and
you find that they have spoken to you with two
tongues. Hear my words and walk in the white
path, and you shall be happy. You shall have
such things as you wish to swap for. We will pay
you for what you have to sell. If you come to see
me, I will give you presents that you may
remember my talk. I once gave to the chief of
the Comanchee [sic] Nation a silver medal while
I was at San Antonio. I now wish to see him,
with his other chiefs, that we may smoke
together and be friends. I send my friends to
talk with all the chiefs of the Wacos,
Towacconnies, Towassies, Keechies, Ionies and
Comanchees, and to make a writing with them,
and to bring it to a Great Council of Peace.

Sam Houston

From a letter by Sam Houston, attempting to settle Texas'
Indian problems peaceably. The attempt failed.

The first fictional
Texas movie appeared in 1908. It was
made in Denmark, of all places, and it had the
ultimate Texas title: *Texas Tex*. The Great
Northern, a film company located in
Copenhagen, used "genuine" American Indians,
members of a Wild West show on tour, to add
authentic color to *Texas Tex*. Since Great
Northern had offices in New York as well, *Texas
Tex* was distributed in the United States and
billed as an "American story for Americans."
Texas Tex mixed scenes of Western life such as
capturing and taming wild horses with routine
melodrama. A bad cowboy and his sidekick, a
Sioux Indian, steal Tex's horses and abduct his
sweetheart. In the woods the cowboy tries to
kiss her, and she resists. Then the Indian kills his
partner, hoping to have the girl to himself. He
ties her to a tree, but Tex arrives just in time to
coldcock the Indian and reclaim his sweetheart.

Cowboys and Cadillacs, Don Graham, 1983

★ ★ ★ ★ ★ ★ ★ ★ ★ ★ ★ ★

Chivalry, according to the dictionary, means a
mounted society, a world of horseback men. All
the jessamine and guitars and sweet talk...can't
change that definition.

Hell on Horses and Women, Alice Marriott, 1953

★ ★ ★ ★ ★ ★ ★ ★ ★ ★ ★ ★

One of the boys working for me that year
[1879] never changed his clothes from the time
we left Texas till we reached our destination, a
three month's [cattle] drive. But every two
weeks or so, he would remove his underwear,
shake off the gray backs [lice], and put it on
again.

A. Collatt Sanders,
Adventures on the Old Cattle Trail
written in the early 1920s

PANHANDLE LIFE IN 1890

For two and one-half years I never went to the post-office – Colorado City, 115 miles away – nor looked upon the face of a woman. I allowed my beard to grow and, never giving the matter a thought, must have become as tough looking a character as ever bestrode a horse in Texas. It is not strange that, when I did finally go to town and attend a *baile*, Eliza Hudgins would not see fit to favor me, when I sought a dance. Late in the evening, the party broke up in a fight and it was several months before I saw the fair young lady again. But the memory of her drew me back to town and on to Plainview, where her family resided. This time I was shaved and slicked up like a city dude, or as nearly so as a sunburned, calloused cow-hand could be. She smiled upon me and I rushed the case as rapidly as her crumbs of encouragement would justify. We were married in her father's home and I took her back to the Elwood ranch as a new top-hand. As she accustomed herself to the rigors of the open range, she gradually became as good a hand with cattle as many of the men we had. At the time, she was the only woman in four counties and very rarely did she see another of her sex, except on occasions when we could tear ourselves away from ranch duties to ride a hundred miles or so to a dance.

Later our savings enabled us to buy sixteen sections, which we fenced, the two of us, almost entirely by our own labor... Then we got a windmill. I'll never forget how happy we were, standing at the door of the little dugout, watching the flow of the first water the new windmill pumped for us. Then came the cattle, slowly. We'd buy a cow here and a cow there; then we got a good bull and a few young steers for fattening... Our first baby, Mary, was born... She died at seven years...Then came little Bob Lee, who drowned when he was three years old.

Later, after we had proudly built a new house with several rooms, Ruth was born and we were blissfully happy with our two living children.

From this time on, it seemed that everything to which we placed our hands prospered and multiplied.

Frank Norfleet, *Norfleet*, 1924

OTHER NAMES FOR TEXAS

Amiechel (used by ALonzo Alvarez de Pineda, first white man to explore the region in 1519)

Apacheria

Nueva Felipinas

Gran Quivira

Tejas
(first used in 1690)

The Land of Beginning Again

I believe I could *walk along the streets* of any town or city and pick out the real cowboy, not by his clothes especially, but because one can always notice that he has open countenance and almost innocent eyes and mouth. He is not innocent, of course, but living in the open, next to nature, the cleaner life is stamped on his face. His vices leave no scars, or few, because Nature has him with her most of the time.

Unidentified woman, writing in
Frontier Times Monthly, August 1926

As I contemplate becoming a resident of Texas, I feel great solicitude about the nature of the population which will inhabit the country... The planters here have a most desperate opinion of the population there, originating I presume from such villains as have been driven from among them and who have taken shelter in that province.

Letter of January 31, 1829, from Thomas White of
Louisiana to Texas colonizer Stephen F. Austin

History as Texas Saw It

Texas has never lost but one war, the Civil War. And the way it happened was that a Texan who was delirious from fever and was color-blind besides, wandered into the Union lines, thought he was among his own comrades and turned and charged, single-handed, on the Confederates and he wrought such destruction that General Lee had to surrender.

Texas Laughs, Boyce House, 1951

*T*here used to be – and is still yet in places – a good deal of malaria in southeast Texas.

A man moving to this promised land from Missouri drove two spans of powerful, spirited Thoroughbred horses to two brand new wagons. He drove mighty proud, and when anybody would ask him where he was going, he'd boom out in the heartiest voice you can imagine, "Goin' to Texas to get rich."

After a couple of years in the alligator-swamp country, this man and his family had been shaken by so many chills and burned up by so much fever that they were as yellow as pumpkins, and just about as spirited.

He'd had to dispose of his fine horses and painted wagons to buy medicine. Finally he started back to Missouri in an old shackly wagon, each of its four wheels trying to go in a different direction, pulled by a pair of ewe-necked, rabbit-hipped prairie ponies.

When anyone would ask him where he was going, he would squeak out in a weak, whiney voice, "Goin'-back-to-Missouri. Mister-please-gimme-a-chaw-of-terbaccer."

My Rambles, Solomon Alexander Wright, 1942

Die-Ups

Cattle that died naturally on the range. Cowboys were expected to take hides from those dead animals, a chore most ranch hands detested. The name possibly came into use because rigor mortis caused the cattle's legs to stiffen and stick into the air.

Montgomery Ward Woman

This is not a flattering term for women. In Texas of the last century, rural families and communities depended on mail order catalogs, specifically those of Sears & Roebuck and Montgomery Ward, for many needs. And there were few women, so some men found their wives through mail order agencies; too often these were women who, for varying reasons, among them lack of acceptable looks, could not find a husband at home. Thus, any unattractive woman became, in the cowboy's sometimes cruel slang, a Montgomery Ward Woman.

Heehee House

A frontier place of entertainment. Probably the term first was applied to bordellos but it went on to encompass all forms of leisure amusement, from saloons to rough tents in which gambling games like faro and poker were played.

Stove Up

Cowboys used this term to explain their aches and pains and injuries caused by cattle and horse work. "I'm a little stove up..." a cowboy might say, indicating a broken leg. "Stove in" was a way of describing, perhaps, a crushed fender, "Aw, I got over in the bar ditch, run over them fence posts, and stove in my pickup."

WE CROSSED THE TEXAS BORDER AT NIGHT...

...[S]topped at a Howard Johnson, and went down to breakfast the next morning not suspecting where we were. Trained as we are to avoid cliches like the plague, we forgot they often have a basis in reality. That morning we were surrounded by faces from the westerns that had made my youth; there sat John Wayne, Gregory Peck, Gene Autry. I had seen them too many times to be mistaken. And although I can only suppose that most if not all of them were truck drivers, they dressed in the same hats, vests and boots as their cowboy antecedents.

The waitress brought us juice, eggs, two stacks of bacon, toast, griddle cakes, butter, syrup, and jam. "I was wondering, folks," she drawled as she unloaded her tray, "what language that is you're talking."

"What do you think?" I asked.

"Sounds mighty like German."

"No. Russian."

"Just what I thought," she said. "Russian or German."

"They're actually quite different; they don't sound at all alike."

"Really?" She was sincerely surprised. "You mean you're Russians from Germany?"

"No, we're from Russia."

"Germans from Russia?"

In the mind of this middle-aged Texas woman, Russians and Germans were inextricably intertwined.... Shaking her head in confusion, she went over to a group of "cowboys" and, pretending to clear the table, told them about the weirdoes at table four; they say they come from Russia, but they're not Germans. The men turned to have a look at us, but the moment our eyes met they averted theirs, pretending to study the weather outside.

When the waitress came up to us again, she looked worried. "The fellows, they say the papers print a lot about Russia. A lot of nasty stuff. Are the papers lying?"

"Afraid not."

"The fellows say that Russia has the type of government that doesn't permit you to write the books you want. Is that so?"

I was astounded. What a question to be asked in Sweetwater, Texas!

"Yes, ma'am, that unfortunately is also true. You see, I'm a writer and the government kicked me out for writing books it didn't like. That's why we're here."

Suddenly the waitress threw open her arms and said with a warmth I count among the greatest of American charms, "Welcome to America!"

The cowboys smiled reservedly.

Vasilii Aksenov, *In Search of Melancholy Baby*, 1987

I WAS WALKING LEISURELY ALONG MAIN STREET...

...when I heard the reports of two or three pistols in rapid succession, and shortly afterwards I noticed a small crowd collected in front of a shanty, over the door of which was a board with the following legend inscribed on one side: "The First Chance" and on the other "The Last Chance," thus appropriately soliciting the custom of thirsty wayfarers, coming into or going out of [Houston].

I stepped up to one of the crowd collected around this "juicery" and inquired if anything unusual had happened. "No," said he, "nothing more'n common. Bob Sprowls and Arkansaw Jake had a little misunderstanding 'bout a game of poker just now, and Jake 'upped him' with a derringer, that's all." "And where is Sprowls now?" said I. "Well, some of his friends carried him off to the drugstore to see if the doctor could do anything for him, but I reckon he can't do much for a fellow that's got a half ounce bullet through his light." "And where is Arkansaw Jake now?" I asked. "Have they arrested him?" "Arrested thunderation!" replied my informant, "you must be green from the States – he's in there," pointing to the door of the "juicery." "Seth Blake has taken Sprowls' hand, and they are finishing the game – and by the by, my young man," he continued, "you'd better get out of the range of that door, for I heard Arkansaw Jake jes' now tell Seth he was renigging, and I reckon 'twont be long afore another derringer goes off."

John C. Duval, *The Young Explorers*, 1892

Men talked hopefully of the future; children reveled in the novelty of the present; but the women — ah, there was where the situation bore the heaviest. As one old lady remarked, Texas was a 'heaven for men and dogs, but a hell for women and oxen.' They — the women — talked sadly of the old homes and friends left behind...of the hardships and bitter privations they were undergoing and the dangers that surrounded them. They had not even the solace of constant employment. The spinning wheel and loom had been left behind. There was, as yet, no use for them — there was nothing to spin. There was no house to keep in order; the meager fare was so simple as to require little time for its preparation. There was no poultry, no dairy, no garden, no books...no schools, no churches — nothing to break the monotony of their lives, save an occasional wrangle among the children and dogs. The men at least had the excitement of killing game and cutting bee trees.

Life in frontier Texas as described in *Evolution of a State*, Noah Smithwick, 1900

TEXAS EATS

Squirrel & Dumplings

2 squirrels

1 cup buttermilk

1/4 teaspoon baking powder

2 tablespoons shortening, melted

1 teaspoon salt

1 2/3 cups flour

butter

pepper

Boil squirrels in salted water until the meat falls off the bone. Discard bones. Set meat aside and reserve broth. Mix buttermilk, baking powder, melted shortening, salt, and enough flour to make a stiff dough. Roll paper thin and cut in small strips. Put meat back in pot of broth and bring to a rolling boil. Drop dumplings in, one at a time, adding dots of butter and pepper. Lower temperature, cover pot, and simmer for 15 to 20 minutes.

From menu of The Springs Hotel Resort of Sour Lake, circa 1880s, quoted in *Boardin' in the Thicket*, by Wanda A. Landrey, 1990

TEXANESE

Peaked

First, it is not pronounced as it looks. Say it as: peek'-id. It was an early, rural health assessment, as "You shore look peek'-id today." The term likely was as Southern as Tex-Western and perhaps even was coined first in England. It meant that someone looked pale, with sallow skin, the diagnosis of which, in early Texas, probably caused a dose of home medicine, such as a few drops of coal oil (kerosene) on a spoonful of sugar.

THE SUBJECT OF SCALPING IS GRUESOME

…but a few observations made by experienced frontiersmen will not be amiss here. We all understood that the practice of taking a portion of the skin from the head of an enemy, with hair thereon, was to secure a trophy. Usually the Indian took a small piece of skin just back of the crown of the victim's head. But when there was plenty of time and hair was desired for purposes of decoration, perhaps for ornamentation of leggings or saddle, or to pad the inside of the war shield, the entire scalp was removed. In haste at the scene of battle, the victor generally rolled the victim over on his face, knelt with his knee on the fallen one's neck, passed the knife quickly around the portion desired, and with a quick tug, slipped it off. Of course, the victim was sometimes alive. If this were the case, then more honor to the scalper, it was believed.

Early Texas settlers could name more than one man who had been scalped by Indians and left to die but who recovered. Perhaps this last was intentional as the redskins knew better than most that the operation was not necessarily fatal. Nor was the warrior who downed an enemy necessarily the one who scalped him; another brave might be permitted to do this. However, there was sometimes a race, mounted or afoot, on the part of the warriors to see who could be the first to count coup on the victim. It was counting coup that was the greatest honor, according to the better informed frontiersmen

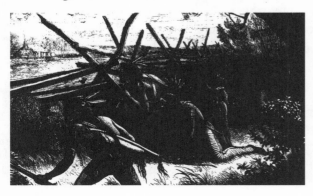

and from the information furnished by the friendly Indians. In fact, the scalp might not be retained long after the return home of a war party. It might be dedicated to some such god as dwelt in the water. If so, it would be thrown into the water after an offering of prayer. Frequently, the trophy was used in the scalp dance and then might be used as decoration for the warrior's favorite horse or even thrown away.

Bois d'Arc to Barb'd Wire, Ken Cary, 1936

★ ★ ★ ★ ★ ★ ★ ★ ★ ★ ★ ★ ★

I am going down the Western slope of life – cannot carry the weights, run the races, nor pack the loads I once could. [But] With Texas air, Texas exercise and Texas habits generally – active, out-door and bracing – I can go on for years barring accidents and ordinary ills.

Sheep rancher George Wilkins Kendall, in a letter to a friend, January 1867

★ ★ ★ ★ ★ ★ ★ ★ ★ ★ ★ ★ ★

A lone Kentucky rifleman raced across the country [in 1835]. Asked where he was going in such a big hurry, he answered:
"Going to Texas to fight for my freedom!"

Traditional, told in many forms about men who came from other places to fight in the Texas Revolution

★ ★ ★ ★ ★ ★ ★ ★ ★ ★ ★ ★ ★

Come what may, I am convinced Texas must prosper. We pay no taxes, work no public roads, get our land at cost, and perform no public duties of any kind.

George W. Smith, land commissioner at Nacogdoches, 1835

★ ★ ★ ★ ★ ★ ★ ★ ★ ★ ★ ★ ★

[San Antonio] is prosperity just in the edge of a lonesome, untilled belt of land 150 miles wide, like Mardi Gras on the edge of Lent.

Poet Sidney Lanier, circa 1870

The decimation took place by the drawing of black and white beans from a small earthen mug. The white ones signified exemption, and the black death. One hundred and fifty-nine white beans were placed in the bottom of the mug, and seventeen black ones placed upon the top of them. The beans were not stirred, and had so slight a shake that it was perfectly clear that they had not mixed them together. Such was their anxiety to execute Captain [Ewen] Cameron that [he] was made to draw a bean from the mug in this condition.

He said, with his usual coolness, "Well, boys, we have to draw, so let's be at it." So saying, he thrust his hand into the mug, and drew out a white bean.

Some of lighter temper jested over the bloody tragedy. One would say, "Boys, this beats raffling all to pieces," another would say that "this is the tallest gambling scrape I ever was in," and such like remarks.

Poor Major Cocke, when he first drew the fatal bean, held it up between his forefinger, and thumb, and...said, "Boys, I told you so; I never failed in my life to draw a prize."

[L.L.] Cash [of Victoria] said, "Well, they murdered my brother with Colonel Fannin, and they are about to murder me."

Several of the Mexican officers who officiated in this...expressed great dissatisfaction thereat, and some wept.

Captain Cameron, in taking his leave of these brave men...wept bitterly, and implored the officers to execute him and spare his men.

Just previous to the firing they were bound together with cords, and their eyes being bandaged, they were set upon a log near the wall, with their backs to their executioners. They all begged the officer to shoot them in front, and at a short distance. This he refused; and, to make his cruelty as refined as possible, fired at several paces, and continued the firing from ten to fifteen minutes, lacerating and mangling...in a manner too horrible for description.

Journal of the Texian Expedition Against Mier,
Thomas Jefferson Green, 1845; Santa Anna ordered Cameron
killed anyway and in front of the execution squad the captain said,
"For the liberty of Texas, Ewen Cameron can look death in the
face," opened his shirt and commanded, "Fire!"

OTHER NAMES FOR COWBOYS

Cowpuncher

Puncher

Hand

Banquero (a variation of "vaquero")

Buckaroo (rare spellings were "buckaru" and "buckayro")

Bucker

Rider

Broncho peeler

Broncho twister

Broncho buster

Goodbye, God. This will be the
last chance I get to talk to you.
We're moving to Texas.

Child's prayer in Arkansas; traditionally
said of several western states

THE HANGING OF JOHN SLIMP

In Coryell and adjoining counties of Texas just after the Civil War there was no law. The best citizens were forbidden to hold office and the few carpet-baggers and freedmen were either too ignorant to render such service or too corrupt to enforce the laws... Many horse thieves and cattle rustlers had so depleted the farmers' and stockmen's herds that patience ceased to be a virtue [and] in order to protect their own stock and families, the best citizens organized a Vigilante Committee...

A man was living there whom every one called "Old Slimp," but his name was John Slimp, at least that was the name he called himself, though no one knew his real name. This man lived on a leased place alone up the river from Moffatt, Bell County, across the river north of the Lower Belton and Gatesville road... He raised corn and feed stuff in the bottom and was supposed to buy and sell cattle for a livelihood. After he was suspected of stealing cattle, one of his neighbors finding the hide of his missing yearling on a pole in Slip's back yard, the Vigilant Committee ordered him to leave the country. He left, but in a few weeks he returned and thereafter he rarely left his hut without being heavily armed. The calves and neighborhood yearlings kept coming up missing, while Old Slimp...kept driving off bunches of cattle to market, though no man could be found who had ever sold Slimp any cattle...

The sentiment of the country was unanimous that Old Slimp was at the head of the thieving and must be put out of the way. The Vigilant Committee, one night, took Slimp from his house and marched him to an oak tree where... The captain asked Slimp if he had anything to say. At first he flatly denied any knowledge of wrong-doing... The captain then ordered the rope to be put around Slimp's neck, his hands tied behind him and his feet hobbled. Then the captain said, "Slimp, you have one minute to live." Then he realized that death was near, and began to beg... Then the captain told him he would be given a few minutes to pray if he so desired. He fell on his knees and out-prayed any man this scribe ever heard before or since. He confessed to God all his crimes and wrongs and begged for mercy like a little child begging its parents. Many of the Committee were in tears. Then he paused. The captain said: "Slimp, are you ready?" and he answered: "Captain Bill, I am ready and willing to go; goodbye. I do not hate you men." Then the captain said, in a low husky voice: "Men, pull the rope."

Slimp's body shot up six feet above the earth. There were two groans, some writhings, then the body swung limp in mid air. With not a word, with just a few whisperings, the fifty Committee men dispersed in all directions and an early passer-by the next morning reported to the Justice of the Peace at Moffatt that a man was hanging from a live oak limb across the river near the Slimp hut.

D.B. Smith of Bonham,
writing in *Frontier Times*, August 1926

Two Texas remarks attributed to Uncle Warren Klein, a Hill Country rancher:

1. *"What do you mean buying groceries, when there's not a drop of whiskey in the house?"*

2. *"It was so dry once, the fish would crawl up out of the creek and hang around the back door, waiting for us to throw out some dishwater. Some years it got so bad out here we had to gather 'em all up and douse 'em with tick powder."*

Quoted in *Long Days and Short Nights*,
by Neal Barrett Jr., 1980

WE HAD OFTEN HEARD OF THE ASTONISHING EQUESTRIAN FEATS PERFORMED BY THE TEXAS RANGERS, RANCHEROS, AND COMANCHES...

and we were anxious to see the riding match between them... We followed the crowd until we came to the San Pedro, a little stream flowing through the western suburbs of the city [San Antonio]. Drawn up in line on one side of the arena and sitting like statues upon their horses were the Comanche warriors, decked out in their savage finery of paints, feathers, and beads, and looking with Indian stoicism upon all that was going on around them. Opposite to them, drawn up in single file also, were their old enemies upon many a blood field, the Texas Rangers, and a few Mexican rancheros, dressed in their steeple-crown, broad-brim sombreros, showy scarfs, and slashed trowsers [sic], holding gracefully in check the fiery mustangs on which they were mounted. A Mexican lad mounted on a paint (piebald) pony, with a spear in his hand, cantered off a couple of hundred yards and laid a spear flat on the ground. Immediately a Comanche brave started forth from their line, and plunging his spurs into his horse's flanks dashed off in a direction opposite to that where the spear was lying for a hundred yards or so; then wheeling suddenly he came rushing back at full speed, and as he passed the spot where the spear had been placed, without checking his horse for an instant, he swerved from his saddle, seized the spear, and rising gracefully in his seat, continued his headlong course for some distance beyond, wheeled again and galloped back (dropping the spear as he returned at the same spot from which he had taken it) and resumed his place in the ranks. The same feat was then performed by a dozen or so each of the Rangers, rancheros, and Indians. A glove was then substituted in place of the spear, and in like manner it was picked up from the ground by the riders, whilst going at full speed... A board with a bull's eye marked upon it was then set up at the point where the spear and glove had been placed. A warrior with his bow in his hand and three or four arrows from his quiver charged full speed towards the mark and in the little time he was passing it planted two arrows in the board. The Rangers and rancheros then took their turn, using their pistols instead of bows, and all of them struck the board as they passed it and several the bull's eye... No feats of horsemanship we had ever seen exhibited by the most famous "knights of the ring" could compare with them.

John C. Duval, The Young Explorers, 1892

A man has got to be at least seventy-five years old to be a real old cowhand. I started young and I am seventy-eight. Only a few of us are left now, and they are scattered from Texas to Canada. The rest have left the wagon and gone ahead across the big divide, looking for a new range. I hope they find good water and plenty of grass. But wherever they are is where I want to go.

Teddy Blue, We Pointed Them North, 1939

100

Hog killin' Day

Years ago...when the first norther blew into East Texas, the jig was up for many a backyard [hog]. Since pork was the main source of meat for most country residents during the winter months, it was important that the hog's last rites be properly executed. The ritual, long and tedious, started early in the morning and lasted well into the day.

First, someone filled the cast iron wash pot with water and heated it while someone else cornered the rooter, tied him, and went for the jugular. Then, when the water reached the scalding point, it was poured into a vat or barrel in preparation for the animal's final bath.

The saying, "You got the right scald," a saying I've heard all my life meaning the food has been seasoned properly, must have originated on hog killin' day because it was necessary that the water be scalding but not boiling. If the water was too cold, it would not loosen the hair; if it was too hot, it would set it. At any rate, when everyone agreed on the water conditions, the hog was immersed head first into the water and twirled around by his feet until his hair began to slip. When this happened, he was pulled, turned over, and dipped into the water in reverse. Generally, more hot water had to be added at this point. Next, the carcass was removed from the water, placed on boards, and the scraping process was begun. This procedure had to be done very quickly before the hair set. When the hair was scraped, the animal resembled a baby's bottom, pink and soft. But he was not pretty for long because his hind legs were soon attached to a singletree (the wooden crossbar used at the front of a wagon or plow) and he was hoisted up to a tree limb or scaffold where the singletree was attached. Finally, the carcass was disemboweled and dismembered.

Wanda Landrey, *Boardin' in the Thicket*, 1990

In 1880, [Englishman] Alfred Rowe arranged to purchase some 8,000 acres along Whitefish Creek from Lewis Carhart… The story relates that on the day the sale was negotiated Rowe and Carhart, after a long tiresome buggy ride under a hot, sizzling sun, arrived at the crest of the hill overlooking Whitefish Creek… The landscape at first seemed unfavorable to the observant Englishman, who reportedly remarked, "This appears to be a very hard country." The diligent Carhart quickly replied "True, my friend, true, but just think of the scope." Rowe then caught the vision of the vast, broad range country, and the deal was completed.

H. Allen Anderson, *The Catch-Pen*, 1991

It was the season of the roundups for the road north across the far plains, when the great steers on their wild spring steel legs came clattering their horns through the thickets, when scores of shouting centaurs rode in dust to the bellowing music of the great herds.

Tom Lea, *The King Ranch*, 1957

"**G**entlemen," answered [William] Travis, "I go with [Davy] Crockett and [James] Bowie. If we hold the Alamo, it is a deed well done. If we fall with it, it is still a deed well done…"

"We have none of us lived very well," said Bowie, "but we can die well. I say as an American, that Texas is ours by right of natural locality, and by right of treaty; and as I live, I will do my best to make it American by right of conquest! Comrades, I do not want a prettier quarrel to die in" – and looking with a brave, unflinching gaze around the grim fortress … "I do not want a better monument than the Alamo."

Texian heroes talking before the final battle, in *Remember The Alamo* a highly romanticized novel by Amelia E. Barr, 1927

While Gen. [Sam] Houston's army was retreating from Gonzales, some of his men camped near a widow's home and made fire of her fence rails. The brave woman gave the culprits a piece of her mind, and just then Gen. Houston rode up and tried to pacify her by saying that as soon as he whipped Santa Anna, he would return and compel his men to make rails for her until she was satisfied. "You'll never come back," she screamed. "You cowardly old rascal. You'll keep a-runnin' as long as your lazy legs will carry you. You look like whuppin' Santa Anna, you a-runnin' like hell an' a-goin' so fast your men can't keep up with you, jest stoppin' long enough to burn a poor woman's rails!" Gen. Houston rode away smiling, and when he became president of Texas he sent her a fine clock as a gift, and saw that she was paid for her rails.

Familiar retelling of a legendary Sam Houston tale, *Frontier Times,* March 1926

★ ★ ★ ★ ★ ★ ★ ★ ★ ★ ★ ★ ★ ★ ★ ★ ★ ★

Some one said that we ought to continue the war and whip them [the Mexicans] until they consented to take back all Texas.

Unidentified soldier, in a letter home during the U.S.-Mexican War, 1847 quoted in Paul Horgan's *Great River, Vol. II*

★ ★ ★ ★ ★ ★ ★ ★ ★ ★ ★ ★ ★ ★ ★ ★ ★ ★

In February of 1877 [buffalo hunter James Ennis] was camped on Sweetwater Creek in Scurry County, Texas. Going out alone on a foggy morning, he shot two bulls, skinned them, and left the hides staked out beside the carcasses. The same afternoon he wounded a bull, which turned and charged him. Ennis dropped his gun and climbed the nearest mesquite tree with record speed. The bull kept charging the tree until it snapped in two and Ennis landed astraddle the buffalo, which, happily for Jim, was so terrified that it tore off across the prairie letting Ennis slide to the ground unharmed.

Ennis recovered his gun, and as night fell he at last found the two carcasses of his morning hunt. He built a fire, grilled some buffalo hump, and then rolled up inside one of the hides to sleep the cold night out. Warm and weary, he dozed off, only to be awakened by a wild jostling that turned out to be a pack of hungry wolves gnawing at the bits of flesh left on the hide, frozen by this time into a steel-like tube. At dawn the wolves withdrew, but Ennis remained trapped in the frozen hide until at last a warm mid-morning sun had thawed it and he was able to crawl out. Back in camp, his fellow hunters scarcely recognized him because during that wild night of the wolves his hair had turned gray.

Austin and Alta Fife, *Songs of the Cowboys*, 1966

When Rain Fell

A short time since the cow was sad,
She scarce would raise her head, begad
Her hoofs were sore, her tail was limp,
Her mane and bangs had lost their
*   crimp,*
And miles she tugged from grass to
*   drink,*
With scarcely strength enough to wink.
The owner, too, looked blue and glum,
And cursed the cattle business some.

But since the rain, the grass is tall,
The cow can raise her head and bawl,
Her side is slick, no bones protrude,
She prances like a city dude.
Her tail is straight, her eyes are bright,
She snorts and dares the crowd to fight.
Her owner, too, digs up the chink,
And asks the boys to have a drink.
God bless the rain,
It makes a man feel young again.
He feels like tossing up his hat,
And howling like a Democrat.

Attributed to an unknown "Western Texas Editor" of about 1900, printed in an undated clipping from the *Bryan Eagle,* circa 1925

The typical Texan is big and breezy, fond of strong language and strong drink.... Above all, Texans are lusty he-men.

Life, 1939

To feel, enjoy, and appreciate a rabbit race in Texas, it must be seen. A man who has never seen a mule-eared rabbit race knows nothing about the glories of the chase. The mule-eared or mountain rabbit will weigh from six to nine pounds and the ears will measure from fourteen to sixteen inches from tip to tip. We run them on the prairie on horseback and with grey-hounds. They run all the time in a road or cow path, if possible, and scorn the protection of fences, bushes, or timber. They run four and a half or five miles and over a dry road…

About three miles from the city [Austin] we reach the big prairie — high, dry, dotted over with little farms and stretching from the foot of the mountains far away into the country. As we come into the prairie the sun is just rising, the morning is lovely as the blush of modesty, and the air is balmy as a maiden's breath… "There he goes!"

The rabbit is up and all eyes are upon him. The dogs are near him in a moment. At first he bounds about in every direction, ears erect, and so badly frightened as hardly to know which way to run. In an instant, however, [the dogs] crowd him, and he strikes a path, lays his ears back, looks about half as large as he did at first, and he who wants to see the sport mustn't stay long at one place. The rabbit takes the lead, the dogs close behind him, and the horsemen bring up the rear. For half a mile they push him hard, and a "green one" would think they had him. Now they press him to the very heels. Watch him! Lord, what running! A wild pigeon couldn't begin to keep up, as gradually he widens the gap till the dogs lose sight of him, and we wait for the fox-hounds which take the track and put him up again in a mile or a mile and a half from where last seen. He has been "squatted" for a few moments and moves stiffly but makes another gallant effort of two or perhaps three miles, and even then no short stock can see his death.

Spirit of the Times, March 17, 1855

★ ★ ★ ★ ★ ★ ★ ★ ★ ★ ★ ★ ★ ★ ★ ★

In the direction in which we had ridden out, the grass was very abundant and the flowers scarce; whereas the part of the prairie in which I now found myself presented the appearance of a perfect flower garden with scarcely a square foot of green to be seen. The most variegated carpet of flowers I ever beheld lay unrolled before me – red, yellow, violet, blue, every color, every tint was there – millions of the most magnificent prairie roses, tube-roses, dahlias, and fifty other kinds of flowers. The finest artificial garden in the world would sink into insignificance when compared with this parterre of nature's own planting. My horse could scarcely make his way through the wilderness of flowers, and I for a time remained lost in admiration of this scene of extraordinary beauty. The prairie in the distance looked as if clothed with rainbows that waved to and fro over its surface.

Charles Sealsfield, *Spirit of the Times,* December 9, 1843

Will Smith, who lived six miles north of the present town of Leonard, and Dan W. Lee had conflicting rights in regard to the claim of some hay land on the Leonard Prairie. Old Dan Lee got the "drop" on Will Smith in the summer of 1876, forced him to dismount, crawl over the prairie on all-fours, and bark like a dog.

T.U. Taylor, University of Texas
The Lee-Peacock Feud, circa 1920s

THE TRAIL DRIVING PAID OFF...

Seven dollar steers in Texas sometimes brought as much as $42 per head in Abilene. Wagons or pack horses were sometimes required to haul the gold back to Texas. A herd of 1,500 steers costing $8.00 per head including expense of driving, might bring $60,000 – a profit to owners of $48,000. Can you imagine what that amount of gold coins would weigh? And the cowboys? They received about $1.00 per day and "chuck." After reaching Abilene at trail's end they might have wages in the amount of $120 coming to them. Many left that same amount in Abilene after buying new clothes, haircuts, "likker" and other pleasures. But, O'boy! Did they have some stories to tell the "ole boys back home." Truth was not necessarily a required element in the stories.

[In 1871] A total of 600,000 Texas cattle plodded their way to Abilene... as a part of 400 to 500 herds involving 5,000 to 6,000 trail drivers.

C.G. Scruggs, *Up the Trail from Texas*
a monograph, 1990

I am going to hell...! The world is bobbing around me!

Alleged last words of bandit Sam Bass after being shot in failed bank robbery attempt at Round Rock in 1878

Above all else the Big Bend country is a lonesome country – big, silent, aloof. The late Jim P. Wilson swore that for the first two years they ranched in the Big Bend he carried Mrs. Wilson's shoes on his saddle every time he left camp. He said that was the only way he could keep her from leaving him. "But even a woman, pining for gossip, wouldn't take out across the Big Bend barefooted," chuckled the old cowman.

Virginia Madison
The Big Bend Country of Texas, 1955

Tunas are the reddish-purple fruit of the prickly pear cactus. Peel them and eat them, seeds and all. Texians always ask the grocers for a can of "tuna fish" instead of just tuna as to make sure that they get fish instead of tuna from the cactus plant.

William B. Miller III, "Mesquite: The Tree That Created Legends," published in *The Catch Pen*,
Collected by Lee Ainsworth and Kenneth W. Davis, 1991

★ ★ ★ ★ ★ ★ ★ ★ ★ ★ ★ ★ ★ ★ ★ ★

The stillness of [the large Texas] prairie is one of the most painful sensations of loneliness a man ever encountered.

Jonathan A. Kelley
The Humors of Falconbridge, 1856

The Brasada of South Texas covers over twenty million acres. These mesquite thickets and cactus patches created an environment found nowhere else in the United States of America. "Thickets are so dense in Maverick and Well Counties that sometimes the rattlesnakes even have to back out." and "Boys, that's thick brush!" men have said so about every county in South Texas. It seems true of all of them.

The Mesquite is a small tree in height. Seldom does it grow over thirty feet tall. Originally named Mizuitl by the Aztecs, its name has been anglicized. It is not Mesquite. It seems this tree has been here always. It was here before Kawas, the Eagle God, brought the Apaches, Kiowas and Lipans to the Southwest. Maybe the Mesquites were the first trees in Northern Mexico and Texas. Quien Sabe? Some things are shrouded in the mists of antiquity (you do not question legends, you just believe them.) The Mesquite is a product of its environment. The roots go deep into the earth to find water. Its bark is thick and rough. The pale green leaves are small to conserve moisture and prevent its loss from evaporation. The blossoms are small and yellow. The seeds grow in pods resembling domesticated green beans. When green, the beans are sweet, almost like cane. The beans dry on the tree and fall off in the autumn. They are relished by deer, javelinas, rodents, cows, horses and humans.

The native Americans taught the Spaniards about making flour from the beans. The native Indios made tortillas from Mesquite bean flour. The Spaniards soon learned to mix the native corn meal with the Mesquite bean flour to make a form of hot cake. When you cover these hot cakes with honey made from Mesquite blossoms or jelly made from Mesquite beans, you have a delicious dish. Of course, if you stuff your fat sides with meals of Mesquite bean hot cakes, Mesquite jelly or honey, fried carna seca [dried beef] from a four-year-old steer, and black coffee, the inevitable will happen: "You will get as fat as a town dog."

William B. Miller III, from "Mesquite: The Tree That Created Legends," published in *The Catch-Pen*, Collected by Len Ainsworth and Kenneth W. Davis, 1991

A soldier and a cowboy had a run-in with some bandits one day down near the Rio Grande. Bullets were hitting too close for comfort. The cowboy and soldier dropped to the ground behind a big boulder, so flat on their bellies as a couple of hungry horned toads. For some time the only sound to break the sun-baked silence was the whine of bullets ricocheting off rocks. Then bored with a battle which seemed to be getting nowhere, and apparently unmindful of his predicament, the cowboy calmly observed: "Ain't bullets in the Big Bend got a lonesome sound?"

Carlysle Graham Raht, *The Romance of Davis Mountains and Big Bend*, 1919

★ ★ ★ ★ ★ ★ ★ ★ ★ ★ ★ ★ ★ ★ ★ ★ ★

In the summer of 1874 we captured a young man named Waldrop on the river near where the town of Medina is now located. He was accused of finding ropes with horses at one end. There were also others accused of similar crimes, and we took them to San Saba where they were wanted, and turned them over to the officers at that place. A little broke-backed man by the name of Ace Brown, evidently the alcalde [mayor] of the town, ordered the prisoners put in a hole in the ground, about 10x10 feet, which served as a jail. Guards were placed around this sweat hole to keep the inmates from escaping. And there we left them, and as we bade them farewell I could see the beads of perspiration standing out on their faces. I heard afterwards that these fellows left that hole one night and got away. I was glad of it.

Tom M. Stevens, a "former Texas Ranger," *Frontier Times*, January 1926

In the early days, a YO [ranch] hand couldn't get into town as often as he does now. When he did, the sudden release from isolation sometimes proved more a curse than a blessing.

That's the way it was with Hen Baker, a cowboy who'd been up the trail with [YO rancher] Gus Schreiner. On one of Hen's infrequent forays into Kerrville, he wound up getting indicted by the grand jury for killing a man with a pocketknife. At his trial, Baker took the stand in his own defense.

While attending a picnic and barbecue along the Guadalupe River, he explained, he decided to appoint himself parking lot attendant. In the course of carrying out those duties, a stranger from Bandera rode up, got off his horse, and challenged Baker:

"I'm the Bull of the Bandera Woods and I hear you're the King of the Kerrville Cedarbrakes. Let's see who's the best man."

Baker noticed the man seemed drunk. He also noticed there was a gun on his hip. Baker shooed him away, and went back about his business.

After the picnic, Hen strolled into the Mint Julep [saloon] for a drink. Sure enough, here came the Bandera Bull, still drunk and still looking for trouble. Baker bought him a drink. The Bull swallowed it in one gulp, folded his arms, and, according to Hen's testimony "… roosters me in the ribs just like that."

Hen then told the jury:

"I didn't have my six-shooter, so I had to cut his throat."

In effect, what Hen was doing was apologizing for bad manners. A frontiersman didn't use his fist or a knife – but as Baker explained, he didn't have a pistol. What was he to do, under the circumstances?

The case was clear enough to the jury, and they found Hen Baker "not guilty."

Neal Barrett Jr., *Long Days and Short Nights*, 1980

THE END OF BILL LONGLEY, A TEXAS MURDERER

The Search

Giddings,
Lee County, Texas

May 18, 1877

M. Mast Esq.,
Nacogdoches, Texas

Dear Sir:

Your esteemed favor of April 24th was received. Allow me to thank you for your interest in the arrest of criminals. [Bill] Longley is today the worst man in Texas – he has committed many murders in this vicinity – he has even murdered a woman. He is about six feet high; weighs 150 pounds; tolerably spare built; black hair, eyes, and whiskers; slightly stooped in the shoulders. I have been told by those who know him that he can be recognized in a crowd of 100 men by the keenness and blackness of his eyes…You will have to take advantage of him – he will fight and is a good shot…

Very respectfully yours

W.A. Knox

The Capture

On yesterday evening, Captain Milt Mast of Nacogdoches County and W.M. Burroughs of the same county, arrived in Henderson, having under arrest one William Longley, a notorious murderer of Lee County, Texas. Captain Mast was corresponding with friends in Lee County and by this means got on the track of this desperado. A $1,050 reward has been offered for his arrest by different counties. He says he has killed thirty-two men…

Panola Watchman, June 27, 1877

The Hanging

Bill Longley was hanged on October 11, 1878, in the northern part of Giddings. This spot now is marked by the houses of the water and light plant…

The day of the execution opened with a murky morning and with rain threatening, but this did not deter the crowds from coming in along the highways and byways and bridle paths, afoot, in wagons, and on horseback. Toward mid-day, the clouds disappeared and the little town of Giddings was thronged with a crowd of 4,000 people…

About 1:30 p.m…Sheriff Jim Brown and his special guards took Longley out of the jail and the melancholy march began…The gallows was erected of framing timber and was thought to be abundantly strong. Longley ascended the stairs with a cigar in his mouth and with rather a jaunty tread. The stair steps vibrated as he ascended about a quarter past two, and Longley exclaimed:

"Look out, the steps are falling," and laughingly added, *"I don't want to get crippled…"*

Longley spoke from the gallows as follows:

"Well, I haven't got much to say. I have got to die. I see a good many enemies around me, and only a mighty few friends. I hope to God you will forgive me; I will you. I hate to die, of course; any man hates to die, but I have learned this by taking the lives of men who loved life as well as I do. If I have any friends here I hope they will do nothing to avenge my death; if they want to avenge my death, let them pray for me. I deserve this fate. It's a debt I owe for my wild, reckless life. When it is paid, it will all be over. I hope you will forgive me; I will forgive you; whether you do or not, may God forgive me. I have nothing more to say."

Prayer was offered by Father Querat,

after which Longley did a very spectacular and unlooked for thing. He kissed Sheriff Jim Brown and the priest, shook hands with everybody on the scaffold, raised his hand and in a clear, ringing voice, exclaimed, "Goodbye everybody." Several from the crowd responded with a last farewell. The black cap was drawn, the rope adjusted, and the signal given. The drop was almost 12 feet… After hanging slightly over eleven minutes, Doctors…pronounced him dead. Dr. Brown took the head in his hands and turned it completely through 180 degrees… Sheriff Brown placed the body in a covered hack and conveyed it to the cemetery in the western part of the town and buried it outside the fence that enclosed the cemetery.

By "The Frontier Native" for *Frontier Times*
June 1926

Texans have moved across the map of history with a kind of innocence and wonder that there are other people in the world who might see life through different lenses. In another way, they are like a friendly, undisciplined Dalmatian that, as it smothers you with its affection and interest, cannot understand why you do not think it is the greatest dog in the world. In a world that often shows signs of weariness, I personally often wish that Texas would grow up – but only a little bit.

Joe B. Frantz, *The Republic of Texas*, 1968

They [the Texans] were citizens of the free and enlightened republic which boasts itself the smartest nation in all creation, and like most Yankees transplanted from their native localities to the rank soil of Texas were lazy, reckless, and rude beyond the conception of anything European.

Littell's Living Age, January/March 1845

The state of Texas is part of Mexico and is on the frontier between that country and the United States. In the course of the last few years the Anglo-Americans have penetrated into this province, which is still thinly peopled; they purchase land, they produce the commodities of the country, and supplant the original population. It may be foreseen that if Mexico takes no steps to check this change, the province of Texas will very shortly cease to belong to that government.

Alexis de Tocqueville, *Democracy in America*, 1835

★ ★ ★ ★ ★ ★ ★ ★ ★ ★

FOUR TEXAS JOKES

1. I won't say it's hot but yesterday I saw a roadrunner trying to pull a worm out of the ground and he was using pot holders.

2. We were so poor when I was a child that I had a tumbleweed for a pet.

3. We were so poor we weren't even considered to be White Trash. We used to go visit White Trash on Sundays.

4. In West Texas, the sight of rain caused a man to faint. Bystanders revived him by throwing sand in his face.

Traditional, and quoted by
Charles R. Farris in *About Texas*, 1981

The Big Bend is not close to nowhere so people ain't had a chance to ruin it. It's just like it always was. When your lungs are full of Big Bend air you seem to forget that you are gettin' older. But I reckon the best thing about this part of Texas is that it's lonesomer than any place else.

Attributed to an unnamed Big Bend resident by
Virginia Madison in *The Big Bend Country of Texas*, 1955

THE KILLING OF JUDGE ROY BEAN'S PET BEAR

When the smoke of an incoming train was seen, Bean would lead the bear around in front of the [Jersey Lily] saloon and tie it to a post. With the arrival of the crowd of sightseers, the old frontiersman…would hand a bottle of beer to the animal and it would quickly drain it to the last drop down its capacious throat.

"Does the bear ever get drunk?" was usually the natural question of some curious-minded passenger.

"Enough beer would make anybody drunk," Bean would reply.

Beer bought over the bar cost a dollar a bottle, but there were always enough interested passengers to make the experiment. The bear was a big source of revenue to Bean, and the bruin seemed to thrive on the beverage. One day a traveling salesman overstepped the bounds of Bean's severe restrictions and was heavily fined. He vowed he would get vengeance. A few weeks later the traveling salesman found himself again in Langtry and at a time when Bean was in San Antonio on one of his periodical visits. The bear was in its accustomed place. A bright thought occurred to the seeker for revenge. He went to the telegraph station, wrote a telegram and signed the name of the Mexican who was in temporary charge of the saloon to the message. It was addressed to "Judge" Bean at his stopping place in San Antonio, and read:

"Bear died last night. What shall I do?"

The telegram was a severe blow to Bean. He wired back:

"Skin bear and ship skin to me here."

The Mexican knew what would happen to him if he disobeyed orders. He went out and looked at the bear. The animal was dosing peacefully in the shade. The Mexican went inside, picked up a rifle and shot the bear squarely between the eyes. He skinned the carcass, and the pelt went to San Antonio by the next train. Bean received it and sent it to a furrier to have it dressed. He came back to Langtry depressed and suffering more or less from a "hang-over."

"What in hell was the matter with the bear?" was the first question he asked.

The explanations which followed were accompanied by a stirring scene in which the Mexican narrowly escaped with his life.

New York Herald-Tribune, October 18, 1925

When I was sixteen years old, I went to Stephenville, Erath County, and entered a school taught by a Mr. Allard. I had been in school only two weeks, when a runner brought word that the Indians were in the country and had murdered the Woods family and that of Mr. Brumley and had burned their houses. Two of the Brumley girls and the two Woods girls had been carried off by the savages.

At the time of this occurrence all the available men were out in pursuit of another gang of Indians that had raided another settlement, leaving no man to take the trail but the teacher, Mr. Allard. In his school there were sixteen boys from 12 to 17 years of age. He explained the situation to us and said: "Boys, I'm going after those Indians; who'll go with me?" Every boy in school, even the small boys, lined up and told him to lead out, we'd follow him to the jumping off place…

About 10 a.m. we started, all armed with double-barreled shot-guns and six shooters and after striking the Indians' trail we came upon the dead bodies of the Woods girls. We wrapped these bodies in blankets and laid them side by side and stretched between two bushes and over the bodies a white shirt as a fright to keep the buzzards away until they could be removed…

Having cared for the bodies of these poor murdered girls to the best of our limited ability, we pushed on with a firm resolve to avenge their brutal murder if we ever came up with the in-

human butchers. When we reached Leon Creek about twenty miles from Stephenville, the water in the creek was still muddy and we knew by that we were close on their trail. We hurried forward until we reached a slope that led off down to Copperas Creek. Here we came up with the Indians and charged them…In the fight that ensued Mr. Allard's horse was shot through the neck with an arrow and fell. Mr. Allard was thrown with great force against the ground, and an Indian rushed upon him to finish him with a lance. Recovering himself almost instantly and seeing his peril, Mr. Allard seized a stone with which he knocked the Indian down and before he could rise the teacher was on him and gave the finishing touch. The action became a running fight for about four miles and only two of the [Indians] got away. Six of us were wounded, myself of the number, having stopped two arrows in my thigh.

On our return we came by where we had found the murdered girls and strapped their bodies on horses and reached Stephenville some time after midnight, very well pleased with our day's work.

Attributed to W.N. Nicholas in *Frontier Times*
February 1926

The sun was fiery hot and the atmosphere like a blast from a hot air furnace, the water salt…Every branch and leaf in this country, nearly, are armed with a point and some seem to poison the flesh. What a blessing the children are not here; they would be ruined.

Excerpt from letters of Robert E. Lee, while stationed at Ringgold Barracks, near present Rio Grande City, August 25, 1856

"YES, SIREE, I SEEN IT WITH MY OWN EYES," SAID CIGARET CHARLIE. "I SEEN A KANGAROO RAT RIDE AN OLD WHITE STEER IN ONE OF THE SKEERIEST STAMPEDES I EVER RODE...

"Oh, them little fellers," and he shook his head. "There are thousands of them in the Pecos Valley. They scratch out holes in the ground for nests and then cover 'em with dome-like mounds of dirt, with several openings for doors. The mounds are hollow and if a horse steps on one he goes down up to his belly. You may see a thousand of them nests in a day and nary a rat. They are wilder than jackrabbits and harder to see than baby antelopes. They have tails longer than most rats, with a little bunch of hair on the end. Their hind legs are extra long and the fore ones extra short. They don't have bags on their buzums to tote the babies in but they have a pair of saddle pockets, one in each jaw, to pack food to their young'uns.

"The boss sold his ranch and was moving out of the Big Bend. We gathered all his cattle, about a thousand head, and they was all kinds, cows, calves, yearlin's and heifers, bulls and steers, all fat an' lazy... On this drive the herd leader was an old white steer, bigger than a saddle horse and almost as gentle. He was a born leader; had a lot of cow-sense.

"One night, riding Setfast...I took a place pretty close to him ... Soon after the moon came up, I be danged if one of them long legged rats didn't prowl out of his hole. When he saw the slick white sides of that old steer he sat back on his hunkers, then he run and jumped on his back. Well, Old Whitey struck

out like a bat outer hell a-flappin' both wings, every crazy cow in that herd tryin' to outrun him.

"It was some race, me and Setfast doing our best to get up to Old Whitey's side so as to swing the cattle around into a mill, and that damn kangaroo rat settin' on Whitey's back holding on like a monkey a-ridin' a circus horse.

"We was about set to turn them when Setfast struck both forelegs up to his belly in a rat nest and turned a complete wildcat. I spread out in front of him on my stumick, like a horned toad. Knowing Setfast was coming over to pancake me, I scratched sand and gravel to get out of his way and got up running...

"After that, we sent a man ahead every evening before sundown to pick out a bed-ground that was free of rat nests and we had no more stampedes."

Virginia Madison, The Big Bend Country, 1955

In one Texas town there is more color of legend and history than can be found in the whole state of Iowa.

J. Frank Dobie, Austin American-Statesman
April 24, 1926

The Three Basic Texas Food Groups

1. *Brown*
2. *Fried*
3. *Well-done*

How to Cattle Drive

On the morning of April 1, 1882, our Circle Dot herd started its long tramp [from South Texas] to the Blackfoot Agency in Montana. With six men on each side, and the herd strung out for three quarters of a mile, it could only be compared to some mythical serpent or Chinese dragon, as it moved forward on its sinuous, snail-like course…

[Trail boss Jim] Flood seldom gave orders; but, as a number of us had never worked on the trail before, at breakfast on the morning of our start he gave in substance these general directions:

"Boys, the secret of trailing cattle is never to let your herd know that they are under restraint. Let everything that is done be done voluntarily by the cattle. From the moment you let them off the bed ground in the morning until they are bedded at night, never let a cow take a step, except in the direction of its destination. In this manner you can loaf away the day, and cover from fifteen to twenty miles, and the herd in the mean time will enjoy all the freedom of an open range. Of course, it's long, tiresome hours to the men; but the conditions of the herd and saddle stock demands sacrifices on our part, if any have to be made. And I want to caution you younger boys about your horses; there is such a thing as having ten horses in your string, and at the same time being afoot. You are all well mounted, and on the condition of the remuda depends the success and safety of the herd. Accidents will happen to horses, but don't let it be your fault; keep your saddle blankets dry and clean, for no better word can be spoken of a man than that he is careful of his horses."

Andy Adams, *The Log of a Cowboy,* 1903

The Fleas Were as Thick as the Sands of the Sea…

Our clothes were actually bloody, and our bodies freckled after a night of warfare with the Vermine [sic]. And the Rats, I cannot convey an idea of the multitude of Rats in Houston at that time [1839]. They were almost as large as Prairie Dogs and when night came on, the streets and Houses were litterly [sic] alive with these animals. Such running and squealing throughout the night, to say nothing of the fear of losing a toe or your nose, if you chanced to fall asleep, created such an apprehension that together with the attention that had to be given our other Companions made sleep well nigh impossible.

C. C. Cox, quoted in
Southwestern Historical Quarterly
October 1902

★ ★ ★ ★ ★ ★ ★ ★ ★ ★ ★

Some twenty years ago William Kelso, who now lives at the mouth of Nueces Canyon, was attacked by an Indian and was shot in the side. He succeeded, however, in killing the Indian. He has suffered at different times ever since from a pain in the spot where the Indian's arrow penetrated him. Recently he has suffered considerably, and a large rising came on his side. Finally it broke and an Indian arrowhead was taken out, covered with gristle.

Galveston News, April 13, 1876

THE BATTLE OF ADOBE WALLS AS SEEN BY THE COMANCHES

In the fight at Adobe Walls, in present Hutchinson County, Texas, June 27, 1874, [Comanche chief] Horse Back was wounded twice and had three horses shot from under him.

He was in full charge although Sata Tejas, Tabbe Nanica, White Horse, White Antelope, Yellow Bear, He Bear and several other chiefs were in charge of their respective groups. Quanah [Parker], then 16 years old, was there but did not lead the raid.

What was the cause of the battle? The furious Comanches – and no other Indians took part – wanted to put a stop to the slaughter of the buffalo for their hides, leaving the meat to rot. The attack was on a band of buffalo hunters, who were outnumbered about four to one. Except for numbers, all other conditions were in favor of the white men.

The name of Adobe Walls conveys a story. It consisted of a group of shacks originally known as Bent's No. 1 Trading Post. It was built about 1823 and abandoned the following year. Fifty years later old man Crego of Henrietta, Texas, used the place as a buffalo hunters' headquarters camp. Located on Bent's Creek, near the South Canadian River, there were three small shacks, made of sunbaked mud bricks. Over the years it had been battered by the elements. Crego used the sod blocks of one shack to raise the walls of another. He then put on a buffalo hide roof and used the buildings in that manner. A little later some hunters from Kansas joined the group and built other shacks alongside the old ones. A picket fence surrounded the shacks and a well, thus forming a stockade. The only entry was by gates. It was built for defense against Indian attacks.

Horse Back had planned the attack for Sunday morning at daybreak, thinking the buffalo hunters would be asleep. But the cracking of a ridgepole, from the weight of a sod roof, awoke the men. Billy Hogue went to the well for water, and…saw Indians approaching. He gave the alarm, the gates immediately were closed and locked, and the doors to the shacks bolted. Two men outside in a wagon were killed and scalped.

The slaughter of the Indians began when the hunters brought their Long Toms [Sharps rifles] and six shooters into action. The Comanches tried to get inside by backing their horses against the gate, while others shot between the pickets. At first the whites fired through windows and partly opened doors. But because of the rain of Indian bullets and arrows, the whites became more cautious. But the Indians had no cover, and the dead and wounded soon were scattered over the surroundings. The Indians were forced to retreat, but returned time after time.

Tom Addington, one of the buffalo hunters…that day, later told [me], "Had those Indians ever gotten inside the stockade they would have made short work of us. I have seen some Indian fighting in my Ranger days, but it was child's play compared to the fight they made at Adobe Walls. They stood their ground and fought like demons… It was the bravest, most foolhardy fighting ever seen…"

Various writers have greatly exaggerated the number of Indians who took part in the Battle of Adobe Walls. Horse Back…declared he had about 100 men. This figure was corroborated by Tom Addington, who said, "There must have been as many as 100 Indians. And many of them were killed…"

Next morning at sunrise all live Comanches were gone… Horse Back said they held a council and decided: "It's no use to fight prairie dogs in a hole." There was mourning in their camps for many moons.

J. Emmor Harston, *Comanche Land*, 1965

THE WHITE MAN'S VERSION OF ADOBE WALLS

The...battle of Adobe Walls occurred on June 27, 1874, when a buffalo hunters' camp, built in the spring of that year in present Hutchinson County, Texas, about one mile from the adobe ruins known as Adobe Walls, was attacked by a party of about seven hundred Plains Indians, mostly Cheyenne, Comanche, and Kiowa, under the leadership of Quanah Parker and Lone Wolf. Most of the hunters at the camp were awake repairing a broken ridgepole when the Indians charged at dawn. The defenders, twenty-eight men and one woman, gathered in (Jim) Harahan's Saloon, (Charlie) Myers and Leonard's Store, and (Charles) Rath and Wright's Store and repelled the initial charge with a loss of only two men. One more man was lost in later charges which continued until about twelve noon, and a fourth man was accidentally killed by the discharge of his own gun.

The Indians, who had been urged into the fight by a medicine man, I Satai, conducted a desultory siege for about four or five days but made no other attacks. On the second day a group of fifteen or twenty of the Cheyenne appeared on a high mesa overlooking the post. The incident formed the setting for William (Billy) Dixon's famous shot. Dixon, inside the stockade, shot an Indian off his horse seven-eighths of a mile away.

Had the Battle of Adobe Walls resulted in a victory for the Indians, it is possible that the settlement of the Southwest would have been delayed for a decade or more.

The Handbook of Texas, Vol. I, 1952

THE MOST FAMOUS RIFLE SHOT IN THE HISTORY OF THE WEST, AS DESCRIBED BY THE SHOOTER HIMSELF

On the third day a party of about fifteen [Comanche] Indians appeared on the edge of the bluff, east of Adobe Walls Creek, and some of the boys suggested that I try the big "50" [Sharps buffalo rifle] on them. The distance was not far from seven-eighths of a mile. A number of exaggerated accounts have been written about this incident. I took careful aim and pulled the trigger. We saw an Indian fall from his horse. The others dashed out of sight behind a clump of timber. A few moments later two Indians ran quickly on foot to where the dead Indian lay, seized his body and scurried to cover. They had risked their lives, as we had frequently observed, to rescue a comrade who might be not only wounded but dead. I was admittedly a good marksman, yet this was what might be called a "scratch" [lucky] shot.

Billy Dixon, explaining his rifle shot during the latter days of the second Battle of Adobe Walls in mid-summer, 1874; written by Olive Dixon in *Life and Adventures of "Billy" Dixon*, 1914

Hen Butter

The wagon cook at the Pitchfork Ranch made this dessert around the turn of the century and gave it its name. Here is a modernized recipe.

1 qt. syrup, preferably cane flavored

1 qt. sugar

1 stick margarine

1 c. Duncan Hines white cake mix

Pinch of salt

8 eggs

1 c. Coca Cola

Mix syrup, sugar, margarine, cake mix and salt in a large Dutch oven. With a heavy spatula stir constantly until the mixture boils for 3 or 4 minutes. After it has boiled for 3 or 4 minutes, set it off the fire and let the ingredients cool thoroughly. Beat up eggs. Put Dutch oven back on the fire. Start stirring and pouring in eggs. Mix eggs well before the contents start to boil. Then let the mixture boil until big bubbles come to the top. Let boil for 3 or 4 minutes. Then add 1 cup of Coca Cola. It is now ready to eat. Hen butter makes a good dessert with hot biscuits. It will keep in the refrigerator a long time.

From the Goen Ranch, Dickens County, Texas, printed in *Trail Boss's Cowboy Cookbook*, 1988

Wherever "Texas" is heard, steers are thought of, and the head of the Longhorn is as emblematic of Texas as is the lone star. Texas and cows are almost synonymous.

J. Evetts Haley, *The XIT Ranch of Texas*, 1929

THE DIARY OF SAM NEWCOMB

A School Teacher at Fort Davis, Texas ★ 1865–66

January 1 [1865] — For the past year Indians have been troublesome, coming into the section in such large bodies that a great many families have left the frontier.... and those who remain are "forted up." There are now 125 persons in the fort and others are preparing to move in.

Jan. 23 — This day was made memorable by the marriage of J. H. Browning and Miss Angelina McCarty. It was a grand occasion, being attended by a number of people from the lower fort, and all the visitors coming prepared to fight the Indians along the way, if necessary.

March 13 —Commenced school here today for a term of fourteen weeks. I have only nineteen scholars at present and most of them are rude, wild and wholly unacquainted with school discipline.

July 8 — A couple of the fort's leading ladies indulged in a fist fight this morning, the result of differences among the children.

November 29 — A large buffalo was driven into the fort this morning, causing a great deal of commotion and excitement. The animal was immediately attacked by forty dogs and killed in a very few minutes.

December 5 — Cold and sleeting and several herds of buffalo drifted by during the day. I have stood in the school house and watched a herd not more than one hundred yards away. I have made some home-made ink, but find it difficult to get it of the proper color and consistency, but it is a case of the best you can do or do without.

December 24 — The first sermon ever preached in Fort Davis was preached here today by Parson Slaughter, and it was the first sermon many of our people ever heard.

January 29 [1866] — My school is continually getting smaller. This is the second time a couple have quit school to get married.

Quoted in *The Graham Leader*, January 29, 1922

★ ★

A TRADITIONAL TEXAS JOKE

When Noah built that ark and it rained for forty days and nights, West Texas got half an inch.

THE COWBOY: 3 VIEWS

The good...

Very few people don't grow up wantin' to be cowboys. It was a good life. It was hard, but you were happy. It was a lot of work and a lot of fun. We spent a lot of time hopin' daylight would hurry up and break so we could run cattle. Many a night we went to bed thinkin' about the good times ahead. Ridin' horses and ropin' calves – that's what it was all about.

The way we worked in the old days made it fun, too. The main thing you appreciated was your horse. We felt like brothers. We helped one another and it made it easier to work. We would depend on each other like family. We were close. We were for one another. We teased each other, but we really respected each other's abilities. That feelin' stays forever. It don't never change. Even today when we meet on the street, we're glad to see each other.

You could call it a hard life, but we made so much pleasure out of it that we had a good clean life. Everybody had respect for a good cowhand. Guess we kinda made history with our lives.

Anonymous

The bad...

It wasn't romantic. It was hard, hard work. At the time, we didn't think much about it, but now you realize – when we were workin' – it was a little bit rough. Up at three in the mornin' for fifty cents a day.

We'd all be millionaires if we had got overtime.

When it rained, it rained on the cowboy. When it got cold, you got cold. You slept on the ground and it felt like a feather bed, while you was praying to the good Lord that a rattlesnake didn't bite. We had to ride rain or shine, heat or mosquitoes. Uncle Tom Ball could tell tales about sleepin' out when it was so cold his slicker would stand up.

We never went to the hospital or quit when we got hurt – not then. We thought it was part of life.

Anonymous

And the sublime...

When I was a young man cookin' in cow camp, I read the Bible a lot, and I used to wonder at the goodness of God as I watched the boys workin' cattle with their horses.

Cattle and horses are mentioned many times in the Bible because they are important for man. God knew that we would need these animals for meat, milk, and work, so He made them right along with man to help him.

Man, cows, and horses have always been together, because God showed man how to work horses, and he was wise enough to make horses faster and smarter than cattle to help man as he began to herd and care for these animals. The men who worked these animals were called herdsmen in the Bible.

As man began to own more and more cattle, it was necessary for him to get help carin' for them. As the rich man in the Bible entrusted his many goods to his steward, the bosses on these ranches had to have help with their big herds of cattle, and so they turned them over to us. But we were faithful stewards, unlike the one in the Bible, and this is our story – the story of the cowboy.

Attributed to Milam Thompson, "Itinerant Camp Cook," by Louise O'Conner in *Cryin' for Daylight*, 1989

WAKEFUL NIGHTS ON STARLIT PLAINS OF THE TEXAS OF 1846

…when the hoot of an owl or the bay of the wolf alone pierced the black void. Days of roving, countless herds of buffalo and Indian hands where no white man had ventured….a tete-a-tete with death before a phalanx of stampeding buffalo – these, to George Andrew Gordon, were adventure. Now they are romance.

★ ★ ★ ★ ★ ★ ★

Gordon went to Texas from Kansas with hunters and became lost from his companions one night. He rode to a hill "where he might see from afar."

★ ★ ★ ★ ★ ★ ★

In about an hour, a faint murmuring came, as of wind sighing in pine trees – but there were none. Could it be a buzz of insects? He could see none near. The buzz became a drone, a roar that shook the earth. And then he saw a monstrous herd of buffalo charging down upon him, a surging black mass that would engulf him.

There was a cluster of trees not far away, and he dashed over to it, tied his horse and clambered into the branches. The center of that mass of animals struck the little grove.

"The width of that sea of buffalo as shown by their trail was more than half a mile," Gordon related. ``My terror was indescribable. Alone, as I feared, far from civilization, without a horse, in a hostile country, with my last bullet in my gun, a braver man than I might have despaired.

"[It was] a spectacle which I fancied neither the white man nor Indian had ever seen… I could have whipped the buffalo on each side of me with a buggy whip, and the heap itself was approaching me, with the buffalo on top of it higher than the fork of the tree where I was perched. It was a great relief when I observed that the roar was lessening, and after 55 minutes of alternate terror and pleasure for me, the mighty host had passed."

It had been a great migration of buffalo from their winter pastures in Texas to their northern haunts of the summer.

Kansas City Star, December 30, 1925

WHY 'ARBUCKLE'S' WAS THE COWBOYS' COFFEE OF CHOICE

The cook's coffee kept the cowboys going day and night. A favorite brand of brew, "Arbuckle Brothers," originated the idea of shipping coffee beans already roasted. Most of the coffee at that time was green and had to be roasted in the cook's skillet. The gaily colored manila bag of that brand was a familiar sight at the chuck wagon. The word "Arbuckle's," printed in bold letters across the front, had a picture of a flying angel in a long flowing skirt with a streaming red scarf around her neck. As a bonus, a stick of striped peppermint candy was in every one pound sack. When the cook hollered out, asking who wanted the candy that night, it was a comical sight to see those tough, rugged cowhands scuffle for the privilege of grinding the coffee beans in order to get the candy stick.

Roze McCoy Porter, *Thistle Hill*, 1980

I recall the first school in this section [Taylor County, about 1879]. A shack of logs was stacked up around a dirt floor. The school term extended over three months. Twelve children were enrolled the first year. Prof. Hale was the first teacher and his salary was $20 per month, paid by private subscription. He had no regular boarding place, but took free lodging at the different children's homes. Each Saturday Prof. Hale went to Buffalo Gap and got drunk, returning on Monday to continue his responsible position as instructor.

Attributed to C.W. Hunt
Dallas News, January 17, 1926

LOST TEXAS

Tee Pee City

Early on, this was a Comanche camp near the South Pease River in Cottle County, and the first settlers in 1879, who were buffalo hunters without spelling competency, found tepee circles on the ground. Tee Pee City became a supply center for passing wagon trains and other transients. When the railroad arrived in southern Cottle County about 1900, Tee Pee City was abandoned.

...**O**n the morning the Missouri-Kansas-Texas (Katy) train I was riding was due to reach Texas, I awoke early, pulled up the blinds, and looked out on the dismal landscape of southern Oklahoma. It was a foggy, chilly January morning; in the half light, the shanties, red-clay gullies, and the run-down farms looked their worst, which can be depressing indeed.

...I dressed quickly, and then went to the next car to awaken the lady I was going to marry. She looked out the window and shuddered. "Will it be like this in Texas?" she asked.

..."No," I said. "I am happy to tell you that the minute we cross the Red River and get into Texas the fog will lift, the sun will shine, people will smile, birds will sing, and the sky will turn a wonderful sapphire."

Stanley Walker, *Home to Texas*, 1956

A soldier and a cowboy had a run-in with some bandits one day down near the Rio Grande. Bullets were hitting too close for comfort. The cowboy and soldier dropped to the ground behind a big boulder, as flat on their bellies as a couple of hungry horned toads. For some time the only sound to break the sunbaked silence was the whine of bullets ricocheting off rocks. Then bored with a battle which seemed to be getting nowhere, and apparently unmindful of his predicament, the cowboy calmly observed: "Ain't bullets in the Big Bend got a lonesome sound?"

Carlysle Graham Raht
The Romance of Davis Mountains and Big Bend, 1919

...FIDDLIN' BY EAR

Uncle Worthy was past eighty in 1905, but he was still a "fiddlin' fool" and when he received compliments on his rendition of *Over the Waves*, which was the hit tune of that decade, he acknowledged the compliments with a gleam in his eye and gave most of the credit to his violin, which he held up for inspection. He said he had had it for "nigh onto fifty years." As he turned the instrument for all to see, there came a faint thump, thump, as if a small piece of leather or a little chip was loose inside...

"Got something in it you can't get out?" asked one of the young fellows.

"Nope. Got something in it I don't want out," came laconically from Uncle Worthy. "...I'll tell you how it all come about.

"I was company cook in G Company when we was sent from San Antonio to help the Rangers run those damn Indians out of the Big Bend and the Devil's River country. We spent fourteen months on duty amongst that many million prickly pear and enough Indians to keep the Cap'n and the boys busy. But fixin' three meals wasn't enough to occupy my time, so I rode a pack mule over to a settlement, and bought, from a down-and-out sheep herder, this ole fiddle, which was shiny bright then, havin' just been bought at old Indianola, the year before.

"Long toward night of about the last day we spent in that thorn-incubatin' region, I was roastin' some venison and musin' over the reasons the good Lord must 'a had for inventin' Injuns when, all of a sudden, somethin' zipped by my head and I felt a stingin' feelin' along the right side of my face... I reached up and felt a round hole in my right ear, which ain't been none too good since. In less than another minute I heard another shot and the Cap'n come ridin' down the side of the arroyo with his Springfield a-smokin'.

"'One shot got the old chief,' snapped the Cap'n. 'He's lyin' where he fell. Don't touch him...

"Next mornin' we pulled out for San Antone and the trail led right by the body of that old Indian chief. The Cap'n permitted us to stop and look at the old cuss's carcass. I reached down and made like I was straightenin' his head out, which had sort of got crooked as he fell... But what I really done was to let my desires get the most of my soldier trainin' and cause me to whack off that old gent's right ear, which I deemed rightly due me in place of mine, which he injured fer what I feel to be the rest of my days. When I collected the compensation fer my ruined ear, I had no place to hide it: so I just slipped it into my fiddle."

The thump, thump, of Uncle Worthy's bit of retribution could be heard again as the fiddle, with a swinging flourish, was adjusted under the shaggy chin, and he settled back in his chair with an air of perfect harmony with the situation.

Virginia Madison, *The Big Bend Country*, 1955

There is the story of what may have been the first Texas pardon. A woman was convicted of murdering her husband and was sentenced to be "erected [?] by the neck until dead, dead, dead." Sam Houston was President of the Republic and pardoned the woman with the chivalrous statement that "when all the men in Texas that needed hanging were hanged, then it would be time enough to start inflicting that punishment on the women."

Walter Prescott Webb, Department of History, University of Texas, written about 1919, reported in *Frontier Times*, April 1926

THE MEANING OF MESQUITE

The Brasada of South Texas covers over twenty million acres. These mesquite thickets and cactus patches created an environment found nowhere else in the United States of America. "Thickets are so dense in Maverick and Well Counties that sometimes the rattlesnakes even have to back out," and "Boys, that's thick brush!" men have said so about every county in South Texas. It seems true of all of them.

The Mesquite is a small tree in height. Seldom does it grow over thirty feet tall. Originally named Mizuitl by the Aztecs, its name has been anglicized. It is now Mesquite. It seems this tree has been here always. It was here before Kawas, the Eagle God, brought the Apaches, Kiowas and Lipans to the Southwest. Maybe the Mesquites were the first trees in Northern Mexico and Texas. Quien Sabe? Some things are shrouded in the mists of antiquity (you do not question legends, you just believe them.) The Mesquite is a product of its environment. The roots go deep into the earth to find water. Its bark is thick and rough. The pale green leaves are small to conserve moisture and prevent its loss from evaporation. The blossoms are small and yellow. The seeds grow in pods resembling domesticated green beans. When green, the beans are sweet, almost like cane. The beans dry on the tree and fall off in the autumn. They are relished by deer, javelinas, rodents, cows, horses and humans.

The native Americans taught the Spaniards about making flour from the beans. The native Indios made tortillas from Mesquite bean flour. The Spaniards soon learned to mix the native corn meal with the Mesquite bean flour to make a form of hot cake. When you cover these hot cakes with honey made from Mesquite blossoms or jelly made from Mesquite beans, you have a delicious dish. Of course, if you stuff your fat sides with meals of Mesquite bean hot cakes, Mesquite jelly or honey, fried carna seca [dried beef] from a four-year-old steer, and black coffee, the inevitable will happen: "You will get as fat as a town dog."

William B. Miller III, from
"Mesquite: The Tree That Created Legends,"
published in *The Catch-Pen*, collected by
Len Ainsworth and Kenneth W. Davis, 1991

★ ★ ★ ★ ★ ★ ★ ★ ★ ★ ★ ★ ★

NO CLOSE RELATIVE OF MINE EVER WAS MIXED UP IN ANY DOWNRIGHT CRIMINALITY....

[T]hough some of the more distant kin were not so lucky. Indeed, almost all of our so-called better families had their black sheep; this was to be deplored, but it was not regarded as a disgrace. I knew one ex-convict who would offhandedly refer to the long years he had passed behind the prison bars as "that time I was working for the government." One day, while helping out on a sheep deal which my father had made, I got into conversation with a friendly, gabby old man who lived a few miles south of us. He said he had had an unusually happy life, and that much of his happiness had been because of the fine bunch of sons he had reared.

"Eight of them," he said. "Wonderful boys. They have been a great comfort to me. You know, only four of them ever were sent to Huntsville Penitentiary."

Stanley Walker, *Home to Texas*, 1956

WE HAD A LITTLE EXCITEMENT, CHASING SOME MEXICAN THIEVES…

[w]ho robbed Mr. Pitcher of everything he had in his little Jim Crow store. John [Robinson] and I were absent from our camp, six days on this trip. There were nine of us in the pursuing party, headed by Mr. Moore, our boss. We caught the outfit, which consisted of five men, all well armed, and three women, two of them being pretty maidens, on the staked plains, headed for Mexico. It was on this trip that I swore off getting drunk, and I have stuck to it – with the exception of once and that was over the election of President Cleveland – it happened thus:

We rode into Tascosa about an hour after dark, having been in the saddle and on a hot trail all day without food or water. Supper being ordered we passed off the time waiting, by sampling Howard and Reinheart's [saloon] bug juice.

Supper was called and the boys all rushed to the table – a few sheepskins spread on the dirt floor. When about through they missed one of their crowd – a fellow about my size. On searching far and near he was found lying helplessly drunk under his horse, Whisky-peet – who was tied to a rack in front of the store. A few glasses of salty water administered by Mr. Moore brought me to my right mind. Moore then, after advising me to remain until morning, not being able to endure an all night ride as he thought, called, "Come on, fellers!" And mounting their tired horses they dashed off at almost full speed.

There I stood leaning against the rack not feeling able to move. Whisky-peet was rearing and prancing in his great anxiety to follow the crowd. I finally climbed into the saddle, the pony still tied to the rack. I had sense enough left to know that I couldn't get on him if loose, in the fix I was in. Then pulling out my Bowie knife I cut the rope and hugged the saddle-horn with both hands. I overtook and stayed with the crowd all night, but if ever a mortal suffered it was me. My stomach felt as though it was filled with scorpions, wild cats and lizards. I swore if God would forgive me for getting on that drunk I would never do so again. But the promise was broken, as I stated before, when I received the glorious news of Cleveland's election.

Chas. A Siringo, *A Texas Cow Boy,* 1885

122

POOR MEALS, {AND} POOR HORSES WERE CONSTANT COMPANIONS OF NEGRO TROOPERS

The post surgeon {in 1870} at Fort Concho put it bluntly. The food was inferior to that provided at other posts. The bread was sour, beef of poor quality, and the canned peas not fit to eat. There were none of the staples common at other posts – molasses, canned tomatoes, dried apples, dried peaches, sauerkraut, potatoes, or onions. The butter was made of suet, and there was only enough flour for the officers...

Off-post recreation, of a sort, was available in the sordid little towns that blossomed around the posts, but a good soldier had no cause to seek trouble – it was awaiting him. If a trooper was unfortunate enough to lose his life in a clash with a white citizen, his comrades could hardly expect that justice would be served. One such citizen, John Jackson, a settler near Fort McKavett, murdered a Negro infantryman, Private Boston Henry, in cold blood, long eluded the law, and in the process shot and killed Corporal Albert Marshall and Private Charles Murray of F Company stationed at Fort McKavett. When finally apprehended and brought to trial, a jury quickly set him free.

★ ★ ★ ★ ★ ★ ★ ★ ★ ★

The year [1877] had been a difficult one...at Fort Concho, and particularly for Captain [Nicholas] Nolan, whose wife had died earlier in the year. Young Lieutenant Hans J. Gasman had returned from a scout to find his infant child, whom he had never seen, dead at the age of six days. One of the telegraph operators had gone insane from loneliness, and Surgeon [J.H.] King's maid had begun "eating dirt." Neither [Colonel Robert] Grierson nor his troopers were popular in the nearby village of Saint Angela [now San Angelo], the sole source of night life in the immediate area. Grierson described the place as a "resort for desperate characters and is mainly made up of gambling and drinking saloons and other disreputable places."

Dreary and dangerous though Saint Angela's "resorts" were for a Negro trooper, there had been only minor clashes until the fall...when, oddly enough, the arrival of a few Texas Rangers brought serious trouble. Several Rangers visited Nasworthy's saloon to drink and dance, and discovered that a number of troopers were doing likewise, whereupon they pulled their six-shooters and pistol-whipped the soldiers. When the incident was reported at the post, Grierson asked the Ranger captain, John S. Sparks, for an apology and instead got the braggart answer that the little Ranger company would whip the entire Fort Concho garrison...

The affair did not end here, however, for the angry troopers armed themselves, went back to Nasworthy's, and shot up the place, killing an innocent bystander. Responsibility for this unfortunate turn of events pointed squarely at Captain Sparks, and he left the Ranger service.

William H. Leckie, *The Buffalo Soldiers, A Narrative of the Negro Cavalry in the West*, 1967

"[Texas] is a beautiful land," said the doctor.
"It is worthy of freedom," answered [Sam] Houston

Dialogue in *Remember the Alamo*, a novel by Amelia E. Barr, 1927

THE LAST INDIAN KILLED IN SOUTHWEST TEXAS

…was a Kiowa who was shot by Captain Arrington's rangers west of Quanah in 1879, and his death brought about a raid by the Kiowas into that section in the way of reprisal. The last white man killed was named Earl and he was slain east of Quanah by the band of Kiowas which came down from the reservation [in Oklahoma Territory] to avenge the death of one of their number, a short time before in the same locality by the rangers. Earl had just arrived in the country and I met and talked to him at the headquarters of the R2 Ranch the night he was killed. He was traveling with Fred and Joe Estes and knew little about the habits and the disposition of Indians. I warned the little party not to leave the ranch that night, as I had been informed that about thirty-five Kiowas were out on a raiding expedition bent on vengence, and that traveling might be dangerous. They did not listen to me, however, but continued their journey toward Quanah, and Earl lost his life.

Attributed to E.A. (Pat) Paffrath of Fort Worth, "a veteran pioneer plainsman," and reported in *Frontier Times,* December 1925

JOHN WESLEY HARDIN IN ABILENE, KANSAS

I had been drinking pretty freely that day and towards night went into a restaurant to get something to eat. A man named Pain [sic] was with me, a Texan who had just come up the trail. While we were in the restaurant several drunken men came in the restaurant and began to curse Texans. I said to the nearest one:

"I'm a Texan."

He began to curse me and threatened to slap me over. To his surprise I pulled my pistol and he promptly pulled his. At the first fire he jumped behind my friend Pain, who received a ball in his…arm. He fired one shot and ran, but I shot at him as he started, the ball hitting him in the mouth, knocking out several teeth and coming out behind his left ear. I rushed outside, pistol in hand and jumped over my late antagonist, who was lying in the doorway. I met a policeman on the sidewalk, but I threw my pistol in his face and told him to "hands up." He did it.

I made my way to my horse and went north to Cottonwood about thirty-five miles, to await results.

John Wesley Hardin,
The Life of John Wesley Hardin
(*Written By Himself*), 1896

★ ★ ★ ★ ★ ★ ★ ★ ★ ★ ★ ★ ★

A Short Pithy Poem

While other good people
*   are lyin' in bed*
The Devil keeps a-workin' in a
*   Texian's head.*
Whiskey is whiskey any way
*   you fix it,*
Texas is Texas any way
*   you mix it.*

Traditional

QUEEN VICTORIA AND THE TEXAS RANCHER

An old, old man got to remembering down in Texas the other day, and when somebody questioned a statement he made, he hauled forth from the tray of an ancient horsehair trunk yellowed letters that bore the haughtiest crest of British royalty and two very famous signatures.

When he showed them around, he not only convinced his hearers that his story was true, but he made public for the first time a tale of both homely and historic value – a tale that casts a very human sidelight upon the most famous of modern monarchs, the late Queen Victoria.

The venerable Texan's name is Shannon … last survivor of that famous family that, headed by Colonel Thomas Jefferson Shannon, prairie-schoonered its way into that vast and howling wilderness in the days of head-rights and the buffalo. The old Colonel, a bluff, hard riding, sharp-shooting old plainsman, is…remembered as the man who introduced the Red Durham strain into the cattle business of the West.

[I]t now appears that that start – probably the parent herd of all the Durham cattle in America today, was a male and two females sent to Colonel Shannon by none other than Victoria, herself, and sent to him merely because he wrote her a letter saying he'd like a sample of the cattle she liked best.

He was only a plainsman living in an uncharted wilderness, but…he sat down and wrote the queen…simply asked her to sell him some of her livestock. He told her who he was, where he lived and what he wanted with it. The order was for a male and two females, and he generously offered to let her set any price she thought was fair.

Two months later the Queen herself wrote. It was a friendly but business-like letter. She said she'd be glad to let the colonel have the stock as he requested, and if he'd pay the freight on them from New Orleans to his North Texas home, she'd be glad to make him a present of them…and in 1848 the bull and two cows landed from a British ship at New Orleans.

The colonel conveyed them carefully from there to North Texas. There were no railroads, but he placed them in wagons. At frequent intervals he unloaded them, fed them, and let them graze for a day or two. He at last got them home in perfect condition and they founded the herd that was the sensation of the old Southwest.

The old colonel never forgot the graciousness of England's queen. He sent her reports from time to time as to how her transplanted stock was flourishing in the New World. He named his first daughter Victoria in her honor, and one of his sons was christened Albert in honor of her consort.

Norfolk (Virginia) *News*, March 20, 1926

Prior to 1885 the idea was generally prevalent that West Texas, especially west of the Cap Rock, could never be developed into an agricultural country. In 1865, Sam Newcomb, a school teacher at Fort Davis, recorded in his diary, "Agriculture is not, and doubtless never will be followed here, owing to the long and dreadful droughts."

Eugene C. Barker, *The History of Texas*, 1929

OLD SAN ANTONIO

This was a very primitive town when we first came here [1838]. The houses were one-story and built of adobe, one room deep with dirt floors and no connecting doors leading from room to room. A person went outside to enter another room from the back. The sills were more than a foot high, the window sills were three feet wide and the walls were three feet thick. The windows were iron barred and one could sit in the window seat and chat with a passerby or flirt with an admirer. The dirt floors were kept hard by sprinkling after each sweeping, which was done with brooms made of wood tops, the kind that are bushy and covered with yellow flowers…

The houses of the very poor were merely poles, driven into the earth close together and the cracks filled with mud. Dried beef hides were spread on the floor and the family sat on these to eat, breaking off small pieces of tortilla and folding these to form a spoon to dip up their chili con carne and frijoles. The coffee was black, or, if diluted, goat milk was used. Frequently, you saw a baby in a hammock hanging from the rafters. The hammock was made of hide…

There were no timid, frightened women there…nor were there any women with frazzled nerves. Vicissitudes were their daily atmosphere and God's fresh air was their lipstick…

I remember the dreadful epidemic of cholera which followed the end of the war in 1865. People died on the streets, many from fear. So fast did they die and so many that there were no men to make their coffins. People were forced to nail pine boxes together as quickly as possible, haul them to the cemeteries and bury them in trenches side by side. But tragedy often has its comic side. There was a man in town who had never heard of prohibition, and his task of burying the dead was a grewsome [sic] one. He must have something to give him courage, so he took his courage in hand and started up to the cemetery on Dignowity Hill with a pine coffin on his dray.

His eyesight was uncertain [and] the wheel struck a stump and when the driver looked back to ascertain what was the matter he saw his dead man sitting in the road with the broken coffin shattered about him. The corpse had been [only] dead drunk.

Attributed to a Mrs. H. Lucas, *San Antonio Express*, November 22, 1925

DINNER WITH QUANAH PARKER

I made a lot of drives, but never made a drive like the first big drive I made. My Uncle Henry decided to drive five thousand head over into the [Indian] Territory (now Oklahoma) one spring, on account of the grass shortage. The grass was good over there, and we started out. Well, I'd never seen any Indians to speak of, and just after we got over the line there, somewhere north of where Vernon is now, our herd ran right through an Indian village, and it was Quanah Parker's to boot. Well, the first thing I knowed about it was when I rode right up to an Indian tepee (you know, they all lived in tepees in them days), and I saw about fifteen Indians in a bunch. I didn't know whether to run, shoot, or just go straight up. They didn't say anything, either, but just stared. I can't make you feel the way I felt then, and I just know that you couldn't have bent my hair anyway because it must have been straight up and stiff as a board. One of the Muleshoe old-timers, old Bill Porter…, he rode up behind me and said something to them in Indian. They never smiled, but grunted, and everything seemed to be all right. I never did get over my scare, though, and was ready to ride at the drop of a hat. Not toward them redskins, either.

Then, to top it all off, about thirty Indians, Quanah Parker in the bunch, came over to the chuck wagon and had dinner with us. The menfolks joked around, and after quite a bit of talk, we went on our way.

W.L. (Bill) Dobbs, quoted in *Texas Cowboys*, edited by Jim and Judy Lanning, 1984

Most ranchers did not allow drinking among the cowhands, would not even permit the presence of liquor. So cowboys had to find the nearest settlement saloon – usually on Saturday night – to quench their thirst. These remote and indispensable saloons were given the nickname "Whiskey Ranch,"and often, by extension, the entire community would carry the nickname.

TEXAS TRIUMPHANT

A geological fact: Texas has twice as many Pike's Peaks as Colorado's Pike's Peak, which the latter state insists is a squatty 14,110 feet high. Texas' Pike's Peaks are located in:

1. Edwards County – rising to 1,905 towering feet.
2. Pecos County – the elevation, modestly, is not given on present maps, but this promethean mountain can be seen from passing Santa Fe Railroad cars about 22 miles southwest of Fort Stockton (on your left, headed west).

THE LONE EAGLE CRASHES IN TEXAS

At the post office in Pensacola, Florida, [Charles] Lindbergh got the long-hoped-for acceptance into the Army flying school. He was told to report to Brooks Field, San Antonio, Texas, on March 15, 1924.

That was still a month away, enough time for him and [flying companion, Leon] Klink to get to California, [where] Lindbergh could enlist on the Coast and take a train back to Texas.

Lindbergh and Klink were ready to take off by February 20. This would make the trip to California and back to Texas by March 15 a rather near thing. But by carrying extra fuel to increase the plane's range, they thought they would make it. Two five-gallon cans of gasoline were lashed to the wing next to the fuselage. "It was quite a job leaning out of my cockpit, into the slipstream, and unlashing one of those cans; and then, empty, lashing it back again. But with the aid of a steamhose slipped over the nozzle, I hardly spilled a drop," Lindbergh wrote. They made San Antonio in five flights.

At their next stop, in Camp Wood, Texas, they found no decent landing field, so they blithely put down in the town square.

Of course, the town went wild with curiosity and excitement. There was nothing extraordinary to Lindbergh about landing in a large square. But the wind shifted, and the planned takeoff the next morning had to be redirected, down one of the town streets. It was a possible runway, but had one dangerous point between two telegraph poles. They were only two or three feet farther apart than the wingspan of the Canuck [airplane]. Lindbergh thought about it. "After all, one drove a car regularly between objects with only a few inches clearance. Why shouldn't one do it with an airplane?"

He would mark the exact center of the street and keep the plane headed perfectly straight; this would give him at least a foot clearance on each side. But something went wrong. Three inches of the right wing failed to clear the pole; the plane spun around and crashed into a hardware store.

There was a splintered propeller and a damaged wing tip... The store owner refused payment for the damage done to his shop by the Canuck; it had been an interesting experience and good advertising, he said.

Walter S. Ross, *The Last Hero*, 1964 (time ran out and Lindbergh never got to California; he repaired the plane and flew back to San Antonio to enlist March 19)

"Next time two hours hangs heavy on your heads, spend it on our porch. Along in the cool of the evenin', we present 'Sunset on the Chisos' in natural color and on the widest screen on earth. It's pure beauty gone plumb loco in thin blue air. A million pairs of 20-20 eyes can't take in all its beauty. All props ten times older than the pyramids. All sunsets painted personally by the Lord."

Sign posted on wall of general store near Terlingua in the Big Bend National Park of Texas

WHY DICE PLAYERS PRAY TO TEXAS

If you judge notoriety by the number of times the name of a place is spoken, the likelihood is that the most famous towns in Texas are Tenaha, Timpson, Bobo, and Blair. The reason for this is that there are so many dice players in the world. When trying to make ten with dice, crap shooters everywhere are apt to holler Tenaha, Timpson, Bobo, and Blair, even though they may not know what the words mean. These four towns are strung out along U.S. 59 in the East Texas county of Shelby.

Now how in creation did four little places in East Texas ever get to be so common on the tongues of dice players? I once set out to solve that mystery. At Tenaha, Bobo, and Blair I found no one who could shed any light on the matter.

At Timpson, I located R.R. Morrison, Colonel, U.S. Army (ret.), who said the old dice shooter's cry had its beginning right there in town just before World War I. Morrison was then captain of a local company of infantry organized as Fory's Fusileers, named in honor of a Timpson railroad agent, H.R. Fory. The Fusileers later became Company B, 3rd Texas Infantry, of the National Guard, and Colonel Morrison led the company to France in World War I.

Just before leaving home the infantrymen in that company had a few dice games, as soldiers anywhere are apt to do before going overseas, or even when they're coming home, for that matter. Anyway, while talking to the dice as crapshooters do and calling on them to make ten, one of the boys happened to yell, "Tenny-haw!" Which inspired another, who was apparently betting his friend would make the point, to answer with "Timpson!" and somebody else threw in Bobo and Blair. This was a natural thing, for the four towns lay within a few miles

of each other along the railroad and passengers were accustomed to hearing the stations called in that order. And it made a nice alliterative phrase, pleasing as it rolled off the tongue.

The names of the soldiers who applied this cry to crap shooting will remain forever a mystery, but the fact is clear that the phrase sailed to Europe with Fory's Fusileers. There it fell on fertile ground and spread to dice games the world over. During World War II in Europe I heard dice players from New York and Pennsylvania, Ohio, Nevada, and California and various other states invoking the dice to make ten in the names of Tenaha, Timpson, Bobo and Blair, but I never found one who'd believe me when I explained that those are the names of four small towns in Shelby County, Texas.

Leon Hale, *Turn South at the Second Bridge*, 1964

[**A**bout 1900] When Scottish inspector John McNabb visited the Spur [Ranch], he insisted on always carrying an umbrella and walking everywhere he went in a business suit with starched collar and cuffs, a bowler hat, and expensive shoes. This apparition created chaos among the wild and skittish cattle and derision among the cowboys. When McNabb and his wife came upon a group of cowboys castrating calves, she chided them for treating the "cowlets" in such a fashion. The cowboys' retort was they were not cowlets but "bullets."

Marisue Potts, *Home on the Range, Scottish Style*, a monograph, 1990

"As Another Christmas Is Just Fading From Memory."

"I am reminded of the first marriage that ever occurred in this section [Taylor County] among the white settlers. It was in 1879. Sawdie, an old bachelor, and Frony Hinard, an old maid, had sparked long enough — they wanted to be tied. The cowpunchers had been watching this courting quite awhile and were betting on the day when the parson would stop these old kids' bashful behavior and squirrel-squinting smiles. At length the night arrived and the dust in every cow trail in these quarters was stirred."

Here the speaker was interrupted: "What was the full name of the groom? Sawdie who, or what Sawdie?"

"Young man," his eyes flickered with fun and his mind ripp'ed over a period of forty years, "we didn't question settlers who came West about their private lives. We called a man by the sound that he gave to himself. Nobody especially cared to rake up kinfolks on the frontier. And not many people bothered us with their biography. The groom was Sawdie — just Sawdie. I guess that if his and Frony's family ever multiplied the young ones were called Little Sawdies unless they had occasion to drift further West.

"Sawdie and Frony were at the two-room log cabin that Christmas night, when John Creager, Sawdie's best man, arrived. Creager's coat wasn't a stylish cutaway garment, but his trousers were short of cloth. He was an exceptionally tall cowpuncher and extra sized breeches couldn't be bought this side of Fort Worth. In fact, he didn't have any Sunday pants, and he borrowed any pair of trousers that the others were not using at the camp, which stopped halfway between the knees and the shoe-tops. He wore white summer socks, from necessity, you might surmise.

"After all the cowpunchers had arrived they were so tightly crammed between the log walls that, when Sawdie and Frony were asked to join hands for the ceremony, Sawdie was too bashful and scared to ask the boys to widen out so that he might loosen his right arm that was wedged in the jam, and, if I remember right, he was tied to Frony with the left hand clasped.

"A big beef supper awaited the crowd, spiced, of course, with Kentucky sour mash.

"After the ceremony and feast the fiddlers began to tune up the catgut, which was a signal for the gents to arm the ladies to the center of the floor.

"The dance started with the old quadrille and as many as could crowd upon the floor turned about to the tune of the fiddles. And then the old square dance was carried out while the ladies and the gents promenaded and paraded. As the dance continued the sour mash jugs gurgled oftener. At 2 o'clock the next morning John Creager fell, a drunk. But that caused no interruption. Bert Brewer was selected for the new best man in John's stead, and the dancers romped on until daylight peeped in at us across the hills."

Attributed to J.B. Masters, Dallas News, January 17, 1926

Translation of the Laws, Orders and Contracts of Colonization From January, 1821, Up to This Time, In Virtue of Which Col. Stephen F. Austin Has Introduced and Settled Foreign Emigrants in Texas

---

Title of first English-language book printed in Texas, November 1829, by Godwin Brown Cotten at the now-disappeared town of San Felipe de Austin

THE PLAN

You know where to find the Indians; you know what atrocities they have committed; you know how to punish them. The means and men are placed at your disposal to do it, and now all the rest is left with you.

I need not repeat to you the orders given to all commanders whom I have sent out to fight Indians, that women and children will not be killed – only men who bear arms. Of course, I know that in attacking a village, women and children are liable to be killed, and this cannot, in the rush and confusion of a fight, particularly at night, be avoided; but let none be killed willfully and wantonly. We make war upon men who have murdered and robbed our people.

Letter from U.S. Army General James H. Carleton to Colonel Kit Carson, upon the latter's departure to fight Indians in West Texas, October 22, 1864

THE ATTACK

Winter of 1864-65 – Tsenho Sai, "Muddy-traveling winter," so called because the mud caused by the melting of heavy snows made travelling difficult. The Kiowa and Apache, with a part of the Comanche, made their winter camp on the South Canadian at Duahal Doha, "Red Bluff," on the north side between Adobe Walls and Mustang Creek, in the Texas Panhandle. While here early in the winter they were attacked by the famous scout Kit Carson, with a detachment of troops assisted by a number of the Utes and Jicarilla Apache. According to the Indian account, five persons of the allied tribes, including two women, were killed. The others, after a brave resistance, finally abandoned their camp, which was burned by the enemy [Carson's troops]. One of those killed was a young Apache warrior, who was left behind in his tipi in the hurry of flight.

James Mooney, *Calendar History of the Kiowa*, Seventeenth Annual Report of the Bureau of American Ethnology, undated

On last Thursday afternoon, a terrible gale of cold wind swooped down upon this devoted section while in its shirt-sleeves, that cleared the thoroughfares in a few brief and hurried good-bye moments, killed business dead, stopped all out-door work, sent men tumbling into their overcoats, and in a few hours froze all creation stiff and hard.

The gale blew great guns all of Thursday night, and on Friday morning the thermometer actually went down to 1 degree above the point of zero!

The Colorado was frozen entirely over at Bluffton, Marble Falls and other crossings where the water was comparatively shallow and still. The ice ranged from half to over an inch in thickness, which is unprecedented. At Marble Falls, it took over two hours to cut a passage for the ferry boat on Friday. The Llano River was also a mass of ice in places. Mr. J.J. M. Smith saw a horse pass over it at Llano town. Hamilton Creek was frozen all over as far as the eye could reach with ice two and three inches thick and the boys had a lively time sliding.

Burnet Bulletin, January 1866

ONE RATHER DISPARAGING CHARACTER DESCRIPTION OF THE TEXAS BANDIT, SAM BASS

It was well-known by the acquaintances of Sam after his arrival in Texas that he was intensely ignorant and wholly illiterate. He could not read a word; nor could he write his name until taught by a school boy named Charles Brim, in the town of Denton, about the year 1874, and it was with much difficulty that he learned to do this.

When he arrived in Texas, Sam was about 19 years old and he was quite as poor a prospect for a hero as ever blossomed into notoriety. He was about five feet eight inches in height, dark sallow complexion, dark hair, and brown or hazel eyes. He had a thinly scattered black beard, which habitually appeared about a week old. He was stooped in his shoulders, and wore a downcast look, more a look of embarrassment than of villainy. He rarely spoke, except when under the influence of whiskey, and when he did, his words were drawled out with a shrill, nasal twang that was devoid of melody, and exhibited a total absence of refinement. He was dull in all but trickery.

Authentic History of Sam Bass and His Gang,
Author unknown, printed in the Monitor Book and Job Printing Establishment, Denton, Texas, 1878

Henry Mims, though 60 years ago as near death as a man may come, missed it to live to the age of 109 years and nine months and came to an end at Globe [Arizona] on Christmas Day.

Mr. Mims was born in Alabama in 1816. At an early age he moved to Texas where he resided until four years ago when he came to Arizona.

The elder Mr. Mims was for some time a Texas ranger and after that was a cattleman in that state. He enjoyed the distinction of being one of the few men that ever survived a scalping, and no man living or dead was ever scalped more thoroughly than he was 60 years ago near Duncan Prairie, Texas.

One night he and two other men stole out to watch stock against the incursions of Indians but they were seen by a band of hostiles which stole upon them and Mr. Mims was stricken down and scalped. The other two men fled and were pursued by the Indians. The white men made their escape and the Indians, doubtless believing Mims to be dead, did not return to him.

He had been struck down near a log and he rolled into the shadow of it after the Indians left. Later he crawled to the little settlement near by where he received attention and quickly recovered.

He remained in good health and his faculties remained unimpaired up to the time of his illness which resulted in his death.

Phoenix Republican, December 27, 1923

People make a mistake to rate the so-called Texas character too highly. There have been some wonderful Texans, but in general Texans have little to brag about. The state was settled mostly by second-rate folks on the lam from Tennessee. What can you expect from such people?

Stanley Walker, *Home to Texas*, 1956

cowboy has muscular arms and shoulders; he obviously does manual labor at times, he doesn't really drink enough beer to justify the stomach; but it is there, and he has a tendency to pat it. When his wife is particularly pleased with him, she may pat it. By some feat of engineering, the shirt reaches around the stomach and stays tucked into the Levis, which by a similar miracle, stay up.

Next the watcher will notice the Levis. He will wish to give his "501s" away: the cowboy will have on neither "501s" nor bell bottoms. He will have on boot or cowboy cut Levis, well washed and ironed (presumably by the same accommodating woman who irons the shirts). The crease will be ironed in according to the way the pants legs fall, not according to the seams. If the [cowboy] aspirer tries to match the side seams and iron a crease straight down, he will find, when he puts his pants on, that the crease seems to wind about his legs, giving a peculiar appearance to this stance. The Levis are not "flood or highwater" pants: they are the length which cause the hem to break across the front of the boot and to just drag the ground in the back. After several wearings, the hem in the back of the Levis will be worn off and raveled. The watcher should not attempt the short cut of cutting the hem off in the back; it must wear off and ravel. These Levis will usually have a button fly instead of a zipper, but it is important either way that they be tight and that they do not bag. These Levis are worn with a belt that has a large buckle...

The back right hand pocket will have a peculiar circle worn on it from the inside. This has been worn by the ubiquitous can of "Skoal" – snuff – which is carried there. In the left pocket in back will be the billfold, or wallet, with varying amounts of paper money, a driver's license, a gas credit card, and little else. This billfold will not have a plastic picture album in it.

Mildred Boren, *The Real Thing: How to Look, or Avoid Looking, Like a Real Cowboy,* a monograph, 1990

The cowboy seems to wear long sleeved western shirts even in the summer. They are likely to be gray or blue chambray, and starched and ironed by the cowboy's wife or mother. The younger cowboys may have on cotton knit shirts with a pocket. These knit shirts do not say things on the back, nor do they express obscenities. This form of self assertion is saved for bumper stickers. Whether knit or chambray, the shirt has a long tail, which is tucked in the Levis, those being positioned under a usually prominent stomach, "beer belly," or paunch. The

A *Texan ain't nothing but a human being way out on a limb.*

John Wayne, *The Searchers* (the movie), 1956

SAM HOUSTON LAYS DOWN THE INDIAN LAW

Republic of Texas
Executive Department
March 28, 1843

To Maj. Benj. Bryant, Indian Agent.

Sir: your letters were handed to me by the Lipans and Toncahuas. I will send you some forms of returns as soon as they can be prepared. It will be of some importance to have a complete census of those tribes.

I hope the commissioners will succeed in making a desirable treaty at the Waco Village. If they do, I am anxious that you should cultivate sentiments of friendship on the part of these Indians towards the other tribes. I am desirous of removing every cause of excitement to the Indians on our frontier. The future prosperity of Texas only requires peace to ensure its protection. I send you a copy of a letter which I had forwarded to you by Yonsey, a Toncahuas. I am afraid he did not deliver the original. Until the country has more ability to bestow favors than at present, I am anxious that the Indians should not resort here. To those who have come contrary to my wishes, I have made small presents. I have written by them a letter to Gen. Flaco. I hope it will be interpreted to him with care. I send him four plugs of tobacco. To his wife I send eleven shawls, the mother of young Flaco that was slain. Of his murder I know nothing, only it is said that Mexicans from the Rio Grande killed him. Maj. [Jack] Hays has written to me on the subject. When I get new particulars of his death I will write you and you can inform his father of the facts. If the Lipans and Toncahuas will go out to take satisfaction for his death, tell them by no means to harm women and children. The warrior scorns to hurt a woman or child and only fights with men. I will never shake hands with a red brother that has stained his hands with the blood of women and children. He is a "squaw" and a coward himself.

I will direct the Indians that are here to communicate with their tribes not to come to this place except on important business that cannot be done by the agent, and I will tell them so to speak to their people. And that they are to listen to your talks and walk in the path which you point out to them. When I wish to see them here I will write to you and you can communicate to them my desires.

You will permit no persons to trade with the Indians, nor go amongst them, without leave from you; and should you give leave to any, you will report the same to the government by the first opportunity. I have the honor to be

Your obt. servt.,
SAM HOUSTON

137

A *glorious revival* was carried on for two or three months [in Sabine County, about 1838], resulting in the immersion of twenty people. We all went into the water at the same time, and Brother [J.T.] Bryant baptized us in twenty-two minutes. There were men there thirty years old who had never seen any one baptized. Some came twenty-five miles to witness it.

From that time churches began to be organized and revivals were held. We would take our wives and children on Spanish ponies to preaching six or eight miles from our homes. We did not know but we should be attacked by the Indians on the way, or at the house where the services were held, so we always took our guns with us. We would stack our guns in one corner of the house, and put a guard on the outside, to prevent a rush on the house before we were aware of it.

We went to church in our shirtsleeves, and wore our moccasins when the weather was warm, and no one ever fainted or became insulted in those days. They did not have an instrument to grind the music out, but everybody sang. There was not so much formality then as now, but there was a great deal more spirit.

We used to pay the preacher then, too, but we did it by dividing our meat and bread with him, and the sisters would spin and weave him a nice suit of jeans to wear to his appointments. The men would take their deer skins to town and barter them for a hat and shoes for the preacher to wear, while we wore our homespun pants and shirts and moccasins to church.

Letter from S.F. Sparks to Reverend J.L. Walker of Bruceville, March 16, 1895

God made Texas when he was a small boy wanting a sandbox.

Traditional, quoted in *Folklore on the American Land*, 1972

★ ★ ★ ★ ★ ★ ★ ★ ★ ★ ★

Throughout the more than four-century span of her history Texas has been the meeting point of alien peoples and diverse heritages, so that today she represents the focal point of many conflicting cultures. The Spanish influence lays a heavy hand upon her past; the Rio Grande, her southern border, is the international boundary line with Mexico; at her western extremities lie Isleta and El Paso, among the oldest European outposts on this continent; and against her western boundary impinges the bilingual culture of New Mexico. In the east remain strong traces of two Anglo-American traditions, that of the Kentucky and Tennessee frontiersmen, and that of the Old South. Upon her northern sections the practicality of the Middle West presses down. Within her borders the German of early colonists is still spoken, and the dialects of Indians. In the upper Panhandle men yet young remember the days of free land; there are dugouts still inhabited by the original homesteaders.

These are the cultures which fringe Texas. She stands at the center, self-sufficient, receiving them all, dominated by none – absorbing them all: those of the Mexican, the Kentucky Colonel, the Kansas wheat farmer, the Cajun; and by some mysterious alchemy converting them into the Texas way of life.

Donald Day, *Big Country: Texas*, 1947

A FRONTIER HOME

The home described was located in the forks of the Bear creeks, Parker County, Texas, about three miles west of the Tarrant County line. It was on the real frontier, on the borders of the Indian country, and during the time described herein [1860s] Parker County was the "hot bed" of Indian raids and Indian attacks.

The frontier house consisted generally of a main room, 16 x16, with a big fireplace, a front porch the full length of the house and a shed in the rear, containing kitchen and dining room combined in one room. Cooking was done on a fireplace because cooking stoves had not yet made their appearance on the frontiers of Texas. Bread was baked in an old-fashioned "baker" or oven, which consisted of a cast iron oven about 10 inches in diameter, six inches deep with three legs protruding from the bottom. It had a lid or cover with a rim around the outer edge from one-fourth to one-half inch high. The "baker" was placed on the live coals of fire; and when hot the biscuits were placed therein; the lid was placed on top and coals of fire placed on top of the lid.

The coffee pot was of generous proportions, of the same general outline and size of the camping pot today. It had its handle and its spout; but it was placed on live coals of fire and was liable to take a tumble without warning.

In the kitchen in addition to the "baker," the skillet, the coffee pot and the boiling pot, there was the "piggin," the "noggin," and the old dasher churn. The "piggin" was a small cedar bucket six to eight inches in diameter with one of the staves extended above for the handle. This was the universal milking vessel. The "noggin" was a small sized "piggin" with the handle absent. The buckets were all of the red cedar variety.

Our beds consisted of four-posters. Often the posts were extended from the floor to the bed and not above. Springs and mattresses were unknown. A bed tick was filled with straw and placed on rope cords that gridironed from side to side rail and from head rail to foot rail. The straw bed was placed on this rope of gridirons and the luxurious old feather bed on top of this. Underneath this main bed was the ever-present trundle bed that shoved under the main during the day, and was brought forth at night out in the middle of the floor. It was the bed for the children while the grownups occupied the main bed. If company came some of the homefolks had to take quilts and make a pallet on the floor of the kitchen.

T.U. Taylor, University of Texas, 1925

OLD TEXAS JOKE

"Yes, siree," the Amarillo rancher said to the visitor, "We got them high winds blowing on us almost ever' day. You jes' learn to kinda lean into 'em. One day last November, I think it was, the wind jes' stopped, and all the chickens in the Panhandle fell over."

Texans, in the 19th century, were victims of many diseases which no longer are general health problems. Malaria is a good example. From coastal Texas north, generally in the eastern half of the state, malaria was a scourge for anyone living near water, which, of course, bred mosquitoes that spread the disease. All along the Brazos River – even into far north Texas – malaria went by the name "Brazos Bottoms." Quinine, when available, was the usual treatment for the fevers and sweating symptoms.

Papa's Barbecue Goat or *Barbado*, Texas Style

This was originated by Malcolm Jernigan, Sr., a rancher from the "Hill Country" of central Texas, which is a major sheep and goat producing area, famous for barbecue goat, *barbado* and lamb.

20 lbs. goat or *barbado*

1 c. salt

1 dry jalapeño (ground)

1 tbsp. black pepper

1 tsp. cumin (approx.)

Barbecue Sauce

2 c. sugar (to taste)

1 c. prepared mustard

1/2 c. apple cider vinegar

1 tsp. salt

1 tsp. black pepper

Mix salt, jalapeño, black pepper and cumin. Sprinkle meat generously. Cook slowly on grill 2 hours (or less, depending on cut of meat). Be sure meat is well above fire (at least 20 to 24 inches). Meat may be brushed with cooking oil occasionally to prevent dryness. While meat cooks, prepare sauce.

At least 30 minutes before removing from fire, brush meat with sauce so it will "set." Continue cooking and turn the meat often, brushing on sauce at every turn.

From the Seven Jay Ranch, Mullin, Texas, printed in *Trail Boss's Cowboy Cookbook*, 1988

I *was a young fellow when I first started out* to be a 'cowman' and the height of my ambition then was to see my brand on every 'cow brute' that I came across. I'll never forget my first visit to Fort Worth, or to the 'Fort' as it was then called. We came through it one cold, rainy day. There were a few log cabins set 'round in a square, with one larger one, the commissary, at the back side of them. All of them had port holes to shoot through. Outside of the Fort proper, there was a box room store or two, six or seven saloons, some of which had poles set up for rafters with buffalo or cowhides for the roof. The postoffice was there, which made the place unusually interesting, for getting mail was an important thing then. You see that has been a long time ago. We were driving a one-horse team and a yoke of oxen that 'geed and hawed' to the names of 'Rock' and 'Tony.' It got colder and colder all the way and the week before Christmas we landed in Wise County in a two-foot snow, and camped in a little log school house till the cold spell broke up. Then we set out to find a place to live in for the balance of the winter. Houses were scarce as hen's teeth then, and we were lucky to chance on Ira Long, then captain of the Texas Rangers, and a better man never lived than he. He let us move in his log smokehouse, and I've often thought since no house has seemed finer nor better than did that little old log cabin that cold winter of '77.

William Simpson, quoted in *Dallas Semi-Weekly News*, 1925

Mexico
March 25, 1843

Dear Mother:

I write to you under the most awful feelings that a son ever addressed a mother, for in a half hour my doom will be finished on earth, for I am doomed to die by the hands of the Mexicans for our attempt to escape the [illegible] Santa Anna that every tenth man should be shot. We drew lots, I was one of the unfortunates. I cannot say anything more. I die, I hope, with firmness. Farewell. May God bless you and may He in this, my last hour, forgive and pardon all my sins. Farewell.

Your affectionate son,
R.H. Dunham

Letter written in Mexico City's Perote prison by one unfortunate member of the Mier Expedition, a band of 250 Texans. The famous black bean drawing occurred there. The 17 Texans who drew black beans were executed. Major Dunham was one. The mother could not be located, and the letter was never delivered, but was lost and, years later, found in an early Waco post office building. The original now is in the Alamo museum.

A PLAGUE OF GRASSHOPPERS

In the fall of 1848 the grasshoppers made their first appearance in Travis and other neighboring counties. They came with the early fall winds in October, in swarms from the north, lighting and depositing their eggs everywhere; always when it was convenient selecting sand soil to make their deposits in. After remaining a short time, and eating the fall gardens, they suddenly disappeared, no one knows where. The warm sun of the following March again brought the little hoppers out, and after eating the crops up, in May they suddenly rose and took flight towards the north. The crops were again planted, and the season being favorable, there was an abundant harvest. We saw nothing more of them until in October, 1856 when they again came in swarms with the early north winds. After eating the blades off the wheat, and depositing their eggs, they disappeared. In the spring of 1857, myriads of little grasshoppers, about the size of fleas, hatched out and crawled out on the ground. Until they were about three weeks old they did not travel, or eat much. At that time they were about half grown, and after shedding they started on foot toward the north, preserving as much regularity and order in the march as an army of well-drilled soldiers. Exercise seemed to have a wonderful effect on their appetites, for as soon as they commenced traveling they became perfectly ravenous, devouring almost every kind of tender vegetation, being extremely fond of young corn, but preferring young cotton to anything else. They had no respect for place or persons, marching through the houses with impunity; and what was worse than all, they were cannibals, for if you would cripple one and thrown him down, his companions would eat him up instantly. When about six weeks old they again shed their outer garments, and came forth full grown grasshoppers with wings well developed, but nicely folded up, only waiting a few days sunshine to dry and unfold and fit them for use. A few days afterwards, they all rose at once as if by common consent, and took their flight towards the north. In the fall of 1857, they paid us a third visit, acting precisely as they had formerly done, with one exception. On former visits, when once they bid us farewell and started on their flight, we saw no more of them, but in the spring of 1858, after having our crops in a part of the country destroyed by our own native grasshoppers, raised on the soil, a swarm of foreigners, hatched and bred in the south, between the Colorado and Gulf of Mexico, were met in their journey north by adverse winds and driven down upon us, the poor, hungry, half-starved things staying with us ten days – just long enough to eat the most of the remainder of our crops. In the fall of 1858 we saw them again, high up in the clouds, passing towards the South; none, however, stopped here, and we saw nothing of them returning in the spring. It is to be hoped that the last one of them found a grave in the Gulf of Mexico. In flying their wings glitter in the sun, and the whole sky has the appearance of being filled with moving flakes of snow. They come with the north wind in the fall, and return with the south wind in the spring.

Samuel J. Wood, *Texas Almanac*, 1860

✪ ✪ ✪ ✪ ✪ ✪ ✪ ✪ ✪ ✪ ✪ ✪ ✪ ✪ ✪

By Hercules! – The man was greater than Caesar or Cromwell – nay, nearly equal to Odin or Thor! The Texans ought to build him an altar.

High praise for Jim Bowie, attributed to English author Thomas Carlyle, quoted by J. Frank Dobie, *Tales of Old-Time Texas*, 1928

ON MARCH 18, 1937, THE SUN ROSE, AS PREDICTED, AT EXACTLY 6:24. A.M., AND SET, AS PREDICTED, AT 6:27 P.M., AS IF NOTHING HAD HAPPENED

…It was a sparkling spring day, although unusually warm. The trees were hazed in green, the redbuds were in full bloom. So were the dogwoods.

The day routinely wore on. At Gaston [High School], as well as the other schools in the area, the last class period was nearly over. Then at approximately 3:10, the school at New London blew up, killing at least 194 children and teachers. The exact number has never been determined. It was the worst school disaster in our history.

We jumped in a car and drove to London, not comprehending the magnitude of what we might see. Thousands of people had begun to converge, and we had to park nearly a mile away and then stumble across fields to get there.

What we saw has been described by Walter Cronkite, then a young reporter, as "…one of the most ghastly scenes I ever saw. Those oil field workers whose children were buried there were sobbing as they tore away at the rubble with their bloodied hands, uncovering body after body."

It was later determined that teacher Lemmie Butler, working in a basement level shop class, had reached for the electrical switch on a sander. He flipped the switch. It sparked.

Boom!

The force of the explosion pushed the eight-inch concrete foundation and the 30,000 square foot building completely off the ground and then it collapsed in ruins. The roof rose twelve to fifteen feet in the air. It is estimated that six hundred people were in the building at the time.

A military board established to determine exactly what happened concluded that a leaking two-inch line had allowed gas to accumulate in the crawl space under the building. The crawl space ran the length of the 254-foot long, 58-foot wide structure and varied in depth from two to six feet.

Soon an inchoate mass of desperate men began clawing through the ruins… The better half of man's divided nature was made manifest, confirming, perhaps, that there exists a universal bond of human sympathy… On the other hand, it wasn't long before some sonofabitch was hawking souvenir picture postcards.

The oil companies released all of their men. They mobilized and came by the thousands…. For hours, the only tools the men had were their bare hands, covered with blood, some of it their own. Two thousand men cleared the debris. The work did not stop when the night came… When one man dropped from exhaustion, another quickly took his place. It is estimated that these men removed five million pounds of brick, concrete, and steel in less than twenty-four hours, some of it in peach baskets passed from hand to hand…

The bodies were temporarily laid out on the football field (nearly all of the football team was killed), and the dying and wounded were rushed to hospitals… The funeral homes were pathetically inadequate. Cronkite remembers rows of "good-looking boys and pretty girls looking as if they were asleep" lying under sheds… Agonized parents sped from place to place, frantically searching for their children, trying to make identification. Sometimes the only thing they recognized was a shoe or a scrap of cloth.

The scene at the cemetery was the macabre compounded – the nightmare of a madman.

Dad was among another small army of men who came in their heavy work shoes, their khaki pants and shirts – the unmistakable uniform of the East Texas roughneck – bringing their shovels and pickaxes [to dig graves]. A tent was thrown up, and Mother took charge of the food. Somehow, from somewhere, sandwiches, bottled drinks and tubs of ice were brought in... Aunt Ladd and Lillian McGee.... went into the woods, gathered twigs and broken limbs, built a fire, and made hundreds of gallons of coffee in a No. 3 tub.

The funerals began... Services were held simultaneously. The sound of the gospel hymns, of prayers of supplication, of preaching, and of terrible, unbearable grief intermingled in the bright, rainwashed air.

The explosion occurred on Thursday. On Saturday afternoon the men at the site, shattered and bone-tired, went home to their families. It is said that several of these nameless, unsung heroes, had nervous breakdowns and never recovered. By Sunday night the funerals were over.

A generation was lost.

William T. Jack, Gaston High School,
Joinerville, Texas, 1989

THE HARSH REALITY OF WESTERN TEXAS IN THE 1850S

We crossed the Brazos and came to a very rough country, difficult to pass through on account of briars and scrub oaks...[and] one opinion prevailed with us, viz; that the dangers we encountered and the privations we suffered had not been in vain, establishing as they did the fact that for all purposes of human habitation – except it might be for a penal colony – those wilds are totally unfit. Destitute of soil, timber, water, game, and everything else that can sustain or make life tolerable, they must remain as they are, uninhabited and uninhabitable. Perhaps some use can be made of the mineral resources, but that will have to be done under a load of peril to life that few will be willing to encounter.

W.B. Parker, Expedition Through Unexplored Texas, 1856

FERRY TOLLS ACROSS THE NUECES RIVER IN 1847

For each and every wheel to a wagon, buggy, or carriage: 25 cents.

For each and every pair of oxen and horses: 25 cents.

For each man and horse: 25 cents.

For each man: 12 1/2 cents.

For each loose horse: 10 cents.

For each head of sheep, goats, or hogs: 3 cents.

Paul S. Taylor,
An American-Mexican Frontier, 1934

XIT RANCH ORDER NO. 11

No employee of the [XIT] Company, or of any contractor doing work for the Company, is permitted to carry on or about his person or in his saddle bags, any pistol, dirk, dagger, sling shot, knuckles, Bowie knife or any other similar instruments for the purpose of offense or defense. Guests of the Company, and persons not employees of the ranch temporarily staying at any of its camps, are expected to comply with this rule.

General Rules of the XIT, 1929

I WELL REMEMBER THE FIRST MAN I EVER SAW KILLED

…The killing occurred on the corner of Goliad Street and Main Plaza in San Antonio one moonlight night in 1857. The boys of the old town were wont to congregate on the plaza, especially on moonlight nights, where they played ball and other games until bedtime.

In 1857 there lived in San Antonio a man named Jonathan Hackett, who conducted a small business on Commerce Street. Hackett was a bachelor and lived alone in the rear of his place of business. He was a man who was well thought of by the citizens of the old town generally and was regarded as a quiet, peaceable man and good citizen. There was also living there at the time a man named Bob Wilcox, who was a handsome, dashing man. The population of San Antonio at that time numbered many sporting characters, for at that time the old town was a paradise for gamblers.

Wilcox and Hackett met one day in the latter's place of business and had an altercation over some business matter, the nature of which I do not recall. On the evening of the killing a crowd of boys who had been playing on the plaza were sitting on the curbstone of the sidewalk when Hackett and Wilcox chanced to meet on the corner of the street above mentioned. Within a few feet of where the boys were sitting the quarrel between the two men was renewed and suddenly Bob Wilcox drew a Bowie knife and stabbed Hackett twice in the stomach and the latter sank to the sidewalk. I well remember seeing the flash of the knife in the moonlight and shall never forget the thrill of horror which ran through me when I saw the victim fall and the blood from his wounds flowing over the sidewalk. Hackett was dead within a few minutes.

Wilcox fled and was never apprehended, though I have always heard that when the Civil War came on he enlisted in the Confederate army and was killed in one of the battles in Virginia.

Taylor Thompson, *Frontier Times*, April 1924

✦ ✦

[In Montague County] is a mountainous hill or arm reaching out into the [Red River] valley. Here a young man by the name of Giles Gordon was overtaken by a group of Indians and badly spiked [wounded with arrows]. He escaped, but one Indian youth raced him to the gate of the white man's home. In recent years, Mr. Gordon heard that this Indian was still living on an Indian reservation in Oklahoma and went over and looked him up and had a nice visit with him.

Interview with Vera V. Thomas, *Dallas News*, October 20, 1929

In 1837, after the Mexican war, our land office reopened, having been closed during the war. Congress met and enacted a law granting to every man who was the head of a family, and who had an honorable discharge from the army, a league of land [three square miles]. But this condition was to last for only a short time.

To give a correct idea of courtship at that time, and of marriage also, I must have a beginning corner. In most cases the engagements were made at the cowpen gate. Many of the men lived in camp, and being bashful, did not have the courage to visit the girls at the houses, but went instead to the cowpen where they would find the girls milking.

Of course after the law giving land to married men was passed, every man, young and old, who did not have a wife started out in search of one. Soon all the girls were either married or engaged, some marrying as young as twelve years of age. One young man, whom we will call Sam, came in from the army rather late, and like all the others, started out to hunt a wife, but all his girl friends were either engaged or married except one, a widow, Mrs. Sikes. Later, he found a girl named Lizzie who was, he decided, to be preferred to Mrs. Sikes, so one morning he started out courting and found Lizzie at the cowpen.

He offered her all the inducements he could to marry him, telling her about the land they would get... Sam urged his case and told her that was no one left except the widow and herself.

"Well, why didn't you take the widder, Sam?" asked Lizzie.

"Wa'al, I had some serious objections," said Sam.

"What are they?" inquired Lizzie.

"Wa'al, I found on close examination she had lost an eye; then she's red-headed, roman-nosed, and worse than all, she smokes a gourd-neck pipe that will hold half a plug of tobacco, and I have always had a horror of being burnt."

When Lizzie reached the house she discussed the matter with the old folks and got their consent to the marriage. Then Sam was called in and they set the wedding day, agreeing on the [following] Thursday.

It took ten dollars then to get married, and the question now with Sam was how he could raise that ten dollars. He went to the judge and asked him if he would accept an order on a country store nearby. The judge said, "Yes, that would do," so Sam went to the merchant to make some arrangement with him to pay this order, and the merchant finally agreed to take deer hides, and if he could not kill enough deer a few coon skins to finish out. So all Sam's friends rallied to help him kill his necessary number of deer and coons. When the skins were carried in there was lacking one in number, but one of the crowd had carried an opossum skin, and having on a coonskin cap, he cut the tail off his cap, fastened it to the 'possum skin, and this went in for change.

This seemed to be satisfactory to the merchant, so Sam got his order and carried it to the judge. The marriage took place at the appointed time.

From a speech by Newton C. Duncan of Wheelock, Texas, read to delegates of the Old Settlers' Association of Bell County, November 1904

LIEUTENANT KIRBY WRITES HOME ABOUT HIS FIRST STAGECOACH RIDE IN TEXAS

I left home for my post [Fort McKavett, Texas] December 1st, was joined at Salisbury, N.C. by Glenn, who made the trip to Texas with me.

…I thought [San Antonio] was the last place in the world I would select for beauty or pleasure, but I have changed my mind since. There are worse places. The houses are low and awfully ugly, and the inhabitants are a mixed race of Mexicans, negroes, Frenchmen, Germans and Americans.

Now comes my one hundred and eighty miles stage ride across country from San Antonio to McKavett [near Menard], the most interesting part of my trip. In fact, I would have preferred to have it less entertaining.

Having heard in San Antonio of two recent murders on the road, I purchased a large revolver before leaving. Twelve miles out we met a conveyance containing the corpse of a young man who had been murdered the night before but a few steps from the road. This did not make me feel very comfortable nor tend to lessen my vigilance. I reached Fredericksburg late at night, took a room at the hotel and slept till five in the morning.

I again set out, this time in company with Mr. Blacker, a district judge in western Texas. About 11 p.m. I dropped into a doze from which I was awakened by a man yelling at the driver to turn out of the road or he would blow his d__d head off. I saw a man about ten yards off, pointing a gun directly at the door. I seized my pistols and offered one to the judge, asking him to use it, but he declined, saying, "There is no use; there's a large gang of them and we will all be killed if we resist."

I concluded it would be better to surren-

der. I had time to take all my money except five dollars and put it down my left bootleg, putting my small pistol down my right boot and my watch in the case of a pillow that was lying in the seat. As soon as I was out they took me to the rear and demanded my money. I gave them my purse and they, finding but five dollars, swore that I had more money and that if I did not tell them where it was they would blow my brains out in case they found it.

Now if you have never looked down the barrel of a six-shooter within a few feet of your head, I can assure you that it is not pleasant, especially when it is held by a man whom you have no reason to doubt will pull the trigger under certain conditions, which conditions are pretty certain to be fulfilled in the next minute or two. I pulled off my right boot first, telling them I had a pistol in it. While they were searching that and looking at the pistol, I pulled the other boot off cautiously, pressing my heel against the roll of money and succeeded in throwing it out on the ground, and when they looked in the boot it was empty. They then gave me back the small pistol.

Before we left the boss [bandit] said, "You may tell the Menard people Dick Dublin has come back to stay awhile."

…Those who know say that McKavett is the most pleasant post in Texas. The country is very barren-looking, the vegetation being stunted and the streams few and shallow except during freshets [rains] when they are impassable. There have been five persons shot and killed within less than three-quarters of a mile of the post since I arrived, and it is said to be rather quiet compared to what it was some years ago.

Letter written by Lieutenant Harry Kirby,
February 22, 1877

*January 8, 1865, at Dove Creek, 18 miles
southwest of present day San Angelo, a tribe of
Kickapoo Indians was attacked by a troop of
Confederate soldiers. The soldiers had mistaken
the friendly Kickapoos for Comanches, and the
misunderstanding became a massacre of eighty
Indians – men, women and children. Thirty-five
soldiers were killed. Years later, one of the surviv-
ing Kickapoos told the Indians' side of the battle:*

"We had lived friendly with the white
people many years. They said they were our
friends and we believed them. The great [Civil]
war came on. We did not know why our white
friends wanted to kill each other. They led some
of our young men into war and some never
came back because they were killed. They went
in for twelve months, then they came home and
said they did not want to fight with the white
soldiers any more. Our old men held a council.
They kept the fires burning three days. The
white men had been fighting three years.
Soldiers came and killed our cattle. They took
all our corn. Sometimes they were white soldiers; sometime Pin Indians. Our old men said it
was not our war, and no man could say when
peace would come back. They said as long as
there was no peace, the war trail would lead
through the Kickapoos' country. They told our
people they must go to Mexico where they
could live in peace. When the white men quit

war and made peace, the Kickapoos could come
back to their lands. Five of our chiefs went to
see General Smith. He gave them papers. He
told them they could take their people to
Mexico. When the corn was ripe and all gathered, we started. It was a long journey but we
had strong arms and hearts, and wanted to get
away from the war. We crossed Red River and
kept above the settlements all the way. Six white
men came to us on the Brazos. They were
friendly. They asked many questions. They saw
all our horses. They did not claim any of our
horses. We told them to look at all our horses.
After that we saw few white men until the
morning of the fight. We had a fight with the
Comanches two days before on the Concho.
They shot one of our men in the eye with an
arrow. He died that night.

"When the soldiers came up that morning,
one of our chiefs wanted to talk. He went out of
the thicket with a white cloth. They killed him.
Then a young woman went out with a white
cloth. They shot her down. They killed her baby
also. Her name was Oo-lath-la-hi-na. She had
gone to school at Fort Gibson. She could write,
and read. She spoke good English. She said, 'I
will go and talk with the white captain. He
thinks we are Comanches. The white men won't
shoot a woman.' They killed her. Then we had
to fight or stand still and be killed like rabbits.
Our young men wanted to follow them when
they ran off, and kill all. Our chief and old men
said no. We must go quick. They will bring
more soldiers and surround us. We buried our
chief and Oo-lath-la-hi-na that night. We carried
our wounded with us. Many died on the way.
We traveled day and night till we crossed the
Rio Grande. We were hungry all the way. We
were sad and wanted revenge. We took no scalps
in that fight. The battle ground is one day west
of the Concho River."

John Warren Hunter, *Hunter's Magazine*, 1911

GOD IS ON TEXAS' SIDE

An early settler wrote back to his brother to come to "God's Country." He came and the two brothers saddled up two Texas ponies, mounted them, and rode all day over the range. As far as the newcomer could see, the prairies were covered with cattle, horses and sheep. He raised up in his stirrups, looked and finally exclaimed, "Hooray for God!"

Traditional, this version printed in the
Dallas Semi-Weekly Farm News, 1923

The first cattle outfits that took the trail in 1871 were described as "tough." In fact the men had to be tough as hickory nuts to stand the hardships. There was usually an old Confederate wagon with a negro cook and a span of work bulls. Little bedding was carried and no tents. The food taken along consisted of sorghum molasses, beans, bacon and plenty of salt, but no sugar… A trail outfit was made up of from nine to 11 men, including the wagon boss, cook, horse wrangler and six or eight cowpunchers, usually the latter number. Two of these rode on the lead, or point, two on the flanks, two on the "swing," and two "drag" drivers.

Life on the trail in the early '70s was not exactly a bed of roses. The boys would start north with from 1,500 to 2,000 cattle that were as wild as buffaloes and take them a thousand miles through an unknown country.

[On the trail] the first break of day was breakfast time. Then a short time was allowed for letting the herd graze before they were thrown into the trail. At noon if water was reached, half of the boys would ride into camp to eat and change horses, hurrying out to relieve their comrades. The herd was kept on the trail till the sun began to get low, then it was grazed into the bedground. The first guard would hold until 10 o'clock; the second till midnight; the third till 2 o'clock and the last guard held till day-break. On bad nights half the men stood guard till midnight or later, and if the herd was acting badly and half the punchers could not hold them, the whole outfit would ride all night. Then they would throw the herd into the trail and ride all day. "Catch up your sleep next winter," the trail boss would say. "This herd's got to move if the earth stops running."

Loss of sleep was the worst thing on the trail. I've many a time rubbed tobacco in my eyes to keep them open, but when you rode into camp finally and got a cup of hot coffee you'd forget it and even be ready for another guard without resting.

It was a pretty sight to see a big herd strung out on the trail in the morning, the sun glistening on their horns – half a mile of solid cattle with horse herd and wagon in the lead. The silver conchos on spurs and bridles and the pearl-handled six-shooters of the cowpunchers flashed in the sun and they made a brave showing. Cowpunchers of that time wore the best quality of clothing and took great pride in their outfit. They got to be a distinct type and class. They would go back to Texas after a drive north, work all winter gathering a herd in the brush and then start north again in the spring.

The proudest boast of any of them was "we held the herd." Also few of them ever quit a friend in a tight place. There are not many of them left. Many have gone with the longhorns which are but a memory in the northwest today. A few are living on their ranches mostly up and down the Rocky Mountains. They were a type, and that type has vanished from the west as completely as the buffalo.

Interview with E.C. Abbot (aka "Teddy Blue"), Missoula (Montana) *Missoulan*, August 20, 1922

I am not so old but what I can remember when we got that train in West Texas. And I can remember when dresses were dresses, and the sight of a girl's ankle was as rare as a Democratic victory...

I can remember when there wasn't an ice factory west of Fort Worth, and there wasn't any ice except in winter, I can remember when houses were not screened, and I had to fan the flies away from pa while he took an afternoon nap. Every day at dinner one of us kids had to mind the flies off the table while the grownups ate. We had breakfast before day, and ate supper by a lamp light, in those days.

I remember when the preacher and the Smiths and Jones' were invited to our house for Sunday dinner and supper, and I was lucky to get to eat at the third table. I remember when ma and the girls would bake all day Saturday. Folks would always apologize when they didn't have anything to eat but four cakes, twelve pies, a boiled ham, seven kinds of preserves, and five fried chickens.

I can even remember when boys played baseball Saturday afternoon instead of Sunday and went swimming instead of bathing, and, best of all, there weren't any bathing suits in those days.

I can remember when we had our meal and flour ground at the grist mill and went to the county seat 3 or four times a year to buy a few clothes and a sack of sugar and a can of soda.

I can remember when we used to drive ten miles to church in a wagon, and the young folks did their courting on horseback instead of in automobiles.

But them days is gone forever.

"Lone Star Bachelor," *Farm and Ranch*, January 1930

He was sitting in the shady corner of a little country store on the outskirts of Marfa, wiping the sweat from the wrinkles in a face that had weathered too many summer winds. With a wry grin, he solved one of the great mysteries of life.

"Do you know why cowboys always wear the brims of their hats turned up on the side?" he asked.

"No, sir, I don't," I answered.

"It's so they can sit three abreast in a pick-up truck." It made sense to me, and he was a cowboy. He ought to know.

Caleb Pirtle III, *The Genuine Old Fashioned, Down-Home Home-Grown Official Texas Cookbook*, 1990

How Texas Got Its Lone Star

The sight of the Lone Star flag should always recall to mind a noted Texas patriot and statesman. He belonged to the famous house of Smith, known near and far the world over. This particular member was Henry Smith, a native of Kentucky, who took the trail for Texas in 1821, when about 33 years old. After spending some time on the northern border of Texas in the pioneer settlements along the Red River he became a permanent resident of the municipality of Brazoria, where to anticipate the story somewhat, Henry Smith had the good (or ill) fortune to become the first governor of the then Mexican Province of Texas.

In Smith's day overcoats had large brass buttons. It happened that the buttons on the coat of Governor Smith had the impress of a five-pointed star. A few days after he was inaugurated Governor he was spending the day at the home of his friend, Mr. Polly, on Bailey's Prairie. A messenger arrived with important papers. After reading and signing them the Governor said: "Texas should have a seal" and forthwith he cut one of the big buttons from his overcoat and with sealing wax stamped the impress of the Lone Star upon the documents.

T.B. Baldwin, writing in the *Dallas News*, June 24, 1934

A DAVY CROCKETT STORY

In 1834, [Davy] Crockett presented himself for reelection [to the U.S. Congress from Tennessee], but since the predominant party had no need of men who chose to think for themselves and vote on their own judgement, he was defeated and his political downfall accomplished.

"As my country no longer requires my services," he wrote, "I have made up my mind to leave it. I have a new row to hoe, a long and rough one, but I will go ahead! I told my constituents they might all go to hell, and I would go to Texas!"

John S. Mayfield, writing in *Frontier Times*, October 1934

TEXAS

An Englishman Explains How to Chase Comanches

Indian hunting, in my experience, is not what one would call pleasant sport; there are so many things you must not do. For instance, you mustn't stop to kill any game, however much you want meat, for your shot may alarm an Indian scout; you mustn't make a fire in the daytime, lest the smoke should give warning to the watchful foes; and then you must press on as fast as you can ride on the trail, to have any chance of catching them.

For these Comanches are horse-Indians, and ride active, wiry ponies barebacked. All the provisions they carry is a little jerked beef; their arms are bows and arrows and lances, and being wholly unencumbered with clothing, they get over the ground, whether mounted or dismounted, at a surprising rate. To catch them without plunder would be most difficult; but when they have made a big haul, this is your chance to come up with them – only you mustn't lose any time. I may add that the Comanche doesn't want to fight, and won't if he can avoid it, unless the party following him is a very weak one; he wants to get away with his plunder, but if driven into a corner he will fight like a wildcat.

R.H. Williams,
With the Border Ruffians,
1868

The first strand of barbed wire ever strung in Coleman County was run by Clark Mann around a section of land on Jim Ned Creek, which is now a part of the Morris lower ranch. This was in the year 1880....

The first cost of wire was about 20¢ a pound at the railroad, which at that time was Fort Worth or Round Rock.... The first real barbed wire pasture fence of any consequence erected in Coleman County was built by the late Col. W. H. Day about the year 1881. He fenced what was then and ever afterward known as the Red Wire pasture, being so known because the wire used in fencing was painted red. From 5,000 to 7,000 acres were enclosed in the Red Wire pasture, except when it was opened by wire cutters.

...Col. Day had a man hired to look out for the cutters. One day the wire cutters took charge of him by use of threats or force, made him take a hand and cut for an entire day.

The cowmen were hard put in holding their fences intact and it was many years before the country became pacified to the passing of the free open range. One day during the troublesome days, J. L. Vaughn, who was greatly harassed by the depredations of the wire cutters, was heard to remark at the rock store in the town of Trickham that "he wished the man who invented barbed wire had it all wound around him in a ball and the ball rolled into h___l."

Dallas Semi-Weekly Farm News, February 1924

THE DEATH OF JOHN WESLEY HARDIN

As Reported in the *El Paso Daily Herald*
August 20, 1895

Last night between 11 and 12 o'clock San Antonio Street was thrown into an intense state of excitement by the sound of four pistol shots that occurred at the Acme Saloon. Soon the crowd surged against the door and there, right inside, lay the body of John Wesley Hardin, his blood flowing over the floor and his brains oozing out of a pistol shot wound that had passed through his head. Soon the fact became known that John Selman, constable of Precinct No. 1, had fired the fatal shots that had ended the career of so noted a character as Wes Hardin…

This morning early a *Herald* reporter started after the facts and found John Selman, the man who fired the fatal shots, and his statement was as follows:

"I met Wes Hardin about 7 o'clock last evening close to the Acme Saloon. When we met, Hardin said: 'You've got a son that is a _____, cowardly _____ of a _____.'

"I said: 'Hardin, there is no man on earth that can talk about my children like that without fighting, you cowardly ____ ____ ____ ____.'

"Hardin said: 'I am unarmed.'

"I said: 'Go and get your gun. I am armed.'

"Then he said: 'I'll go and get a gun and when I meet you I'll meet you smoking and make you pull like a wolf around the block.'

"Hardin then went into the saloon and began shaking dice with Henry Brown…

"About 11 o'clock Mr. E.L. Shackleford [and I] were drinking and I noticed that Hardin watched me very closely. When he thought my eye was off him he made a break for his gun in his hip pocket and I immediately pulled my gun and began shooting. I shot him in the head first as I had been informed that he wore a steel breastplate…

"I was not drunk at the time, but was crazy mad at the way he had insulted me."

THE STATEMENT OF WITNESS FRANK PATTERSON:

"My name is Frank Patterson. I am a bar tender at the Acme saloon. This evening about 11 o'clock J. W. Hardin was standing with Henry Brown shaking dice and Mr. Selman walked in at the door and shot him… Mr. Selman said something as he came in at the door. Hardin was standing with his back to Mr. Selman. I did not see him face around before he fell or make any motion…Don't think Hardin ever spoke. The first shot was in the head."

THE STATEMENT OF WITNESS E.L. SHACKLEFORD:

"At the time I met Mr. Selman he was in the saloon drinking with several others… I advised him as a friend not to get under the influence of liquor. We walked out on the sidewalk and came back into the saloon, I being some distance ahead of Selman, walking towards the back of the saloon. There I heard shots fired. I can't say who fired the shots, as I did not see it. I did not turn around, but left immediately. The room was full of powder smoke, and I could not have seen anything anyhow."

THE STATEMENT OF WITNESS HENRY BROWN:

"We…were shaking dice. I heard a shot fired and Mr. Hardin fell at my feet at my left side. I heard three or four shots fired. I then left, went out the back door, and don't know what occurred afterwards. When the shot was fired,

Mr. Hardin was against the bar, facing it, as near as I can say, and his back was towards the direction the shot came from. I did not see him make any effort to get his six-shooter. The last words he spoke before the first shot was fired were, 'Four sixes to beat,' and they were addressed to me…"

Nine months later, John Selman was shot four times while arguing with U.S. Deputy Marshall George Scarborough in an alley behind El Paso's Wigwam Saloon. Selman died of his wounds, April 1896

When the roundup was over we then went back to our routine work, but, before getting down to routine duties, the waddies always took a little spell in Amarillo to shake off the roundup fever.

Amarillo was a pure cow-town those days [pre-1900] and run by stage. There were just a few womenfolks in the town, and they were at a premium. Most of the waddies would make the town after the roundup, and some of the boys would stay until all their money was gone. Some of the boys played the gambling joints, some just soaked themselves in the "pizen," and some went sally-hooting in the sally joints. Any kind of joint that a fellow wanted was in the town to satisfy the waddies' wants.

I was just a kid, but the older waddies took charge of me so I wouldn't get taken in, or get in wrong, and the boys held me down to earth, but I watched and saw the op'ra.

I saw some shootings and many bear fights. Nearly all the saloons in Amarillo, at that time, had bull-pens at the rear of the joints. The purpose for which the bull-pens were built was to have a place to shunt the fellows who became overloaded where they could sleep off the load of "pizen"; also, to prevent interference from the law or meddling gentry who were looking for a chance to swipe a roll of money. The bull-pen was also used for a battle ground. When a couple of fellows got riled at each other they were shunted into the bull-pen to cool off. The saloon bouncers would take the guns away from the riled men and push them into the bull-pen to settle the argument, bear-fight fashion. That method saved a lot of shooting, but could not be worked in all cases, and there was an occasional shooting.

Richard Murphy, quoted in *Texas Cowboy,* edited by Jim and Judy Lanning, 1984

☆ ☆ ☆ ☆ ☆ ☆ ☆ ☆ ☆ ☆ ☆

If you want to obtain distinction in this country, kill somebody.

Statement by a Fort Belknap soldier to journalist/author Albert Richardson, *Beyond the Mississippi,* 1867

☆ ☆ ☆ ☆ ☆ ☆ ☆ ☆ ☆ ☆ ☆

It may be of interest to note…that of some 3,700 new prisoners committed to the various state institutions during 1938, only thirteen were cowboys.

J.H. Plenn, *Saddle in the Sky,* 1940

A FEW WORDS ABOUT THE HABITS OF PLAINS INDIANS

The Camanche and Kioways are the most numerous tribes in the Southwest, have similar habits, but do not speak the same language, nor do the Kioways roam as far south as the Camanches. The Camanches are the "Lords of the Plains." They are the most warlike and powerful and number over twenty thousand. They are separated into three grand divisions, the Northern, Middle and Southern, and these subdivided into bands commanded by separate chiefs. They suppose that their forefathers came from a country towards the setting sun. They acknowledge a supreme ruler and director, whom they call the Great Spirit, but in their devotions appeal directly to the sun and earth, saying that one is the great cause of life and the other the receptacle and producer of all that sustains life; accordingly when they eat or drink they sacrifice a good portion to the Great Spirit, saying that otherwise he would be angry and bring upon them ill fortune. They say that they cannot worship God, he is too far off, but they can worship the sun, who is between them and the Supreme Being. Some of their chiefs have visited Washington and returned with strong impressions of the strength of the whites, but the most of them believe the Camanches to be the most powerful nation in existence, and any opposition to this idea only subjects the relator to ridicule and want of confidence. Captain [R.B.] Marcy relates a conversation he overheard between a Camanche and a Delaware, in which the latter endeavored to prove to the Camanche that the earth was round, and that it revolved round the sun. The Camanche indignantly asked if he took him for an idiot, that any man could see that the earth was perfectly level by only looking off over the prairie, and moreover his grandfather had been to the west end of it where the sun went down behind a wall…

When a Camanche warrior dies he is buried upon the top of the highest hill near camp, with his face to the east. His war horse is killed and his weapons burnt up, his other animals having their manes and tails shaved close as a symbol of mourning. For a long time after the decease the relatives and friends assemble morning and evening to cry and howl and cut themselves with knives… When a young warrior dies they mourn a long time, but when an old person dies they mourn but little, saying that they cannot live forever and it was time they should go. They believe all go up to a place above where they are happy, that they are permitted to visit the earth at night, but must return at daylight.

W.B. Parker, *The Expedition Through Unexplored Texas*, 1856

[In early Texas] There weren't a lot of drunken brawls, however, as people claim. Of course, there were some, but they were in the minority. Liquor was cheap in the old days, but few people used it to excess. Why, in the piney woods stores, there was always a forty gallon barrel of free whiskey for the consumption of customers, and I never saw a drunk man in East Texas the whole time that I was out there. Those who got drunk were usually the people who had been out in a wilderness for months at a time…and many of the old trail drivers. Yes, they usually made things roar when they got to town – as a general rule because they were half mad from the solitude of the plains.

Telvis Clyde Smith, *Brownwood Bulletin*, undated but about mid-1930

At the End of the Day on a Cattle Drive

...The trail boss would wave his hat about his head in a tired circle and then in the direction for the two men riding on each side of the herd to point the lead steers to their bed ground. He directed them to a spot where the grass was succulent, or, if it were a hot night, to a rise where the breeze would be cool. No timber should be close, for Indians or rustlers might lurk in it, and a nearby ravine might prove a cattle trap in case of a stampede.

The first of three or four watches took over. The wrangler roped and dragged dry branches to the chuck wagon or gathered cow chips and sunflower stalks for the cook fire. He helped cooky unload the wagon and after dinner wash the dishes, too. Everyone wanted to be on the good side of the man whose sourdough biscuits were proof of his skill, and whose coffee was called six-shooter coffee because it was deemed so strong that it would float a pistol. The men ate their fill of beans, called Pecos strawberries, potatoes, onions, steak, and often boggytop dessert, which was stewed fruit with a biscuit covering. Whiskey was forbidden in most trail outfits, so a man fortified himself against the night with a second cup of the potent coffee, made by boiling grounds for half an hour...

Some cowboys read in the evening by the light of a hard-twisted string stuck into a cup of tallow. Some read the stars, to which they gave their own trail names – the Diamond, Ellenrods, Job's Coffin, the Seven Stars, Midnight Triangle, and the Big Dipper.

If the camp were a muddy one, cowboys lay down to sleep in a triangle, so that each man's head was on another's ankle. As the night hours slipped by, tired men on watch took chewing tobacco from their pouches, mixed it with saliva, and rubbed it on their eyelids to keep awake... Let a cowpoke complain, and the boss would remark, "You can sleep all next winter."

Richard Dunlop, *Great Trails of the West*, 1971

A SAM HOUSTON STORY

It was out in front [of Salado's Stagecoach Inn] on the eve of the Civil War that Old Sam Houston, piqued at his fellow Texans for trying to take Texas out of the nation into which he had struggled so hard less than two decades before to bring it, stood up before an audience of rednecks and spoke for the Union.

"But General Sam," cried a frontiersman, "we could whip them Yankees with cornstalks."

"But," fired back the old man, "those Yankees won't agree to fight with cornstalks."

Traditional, this version from Richard Dunlop's *Great Trails of the West*, 1971

★ ★ ★ ★ ★ ★ ★ ★ ★ ★ ★ ★ ★ ★ ★

It was the town of Clarendon, a devout community, which furnished the courts of Tascosa, the near-by cattle boom town, with a means of punishment for thorough recalcitrants. When an offender went too far at Tascosa, he was sentenced to ten days in Clarendon. That was the nearest thing to solitary confinement for a cowhand who liked his likker.

[Before the Clarendon rule was established] law violators were tied in Jack Ryan's saloon. One such prisoner was Jack Martin, who was bound tightly on a December evening in 1881. However, Jack's arms were left free and during the night he tore his blanket into shreds and formed a rope. With this improvised "lariat" he lassoed whiskey bottles from the shelf behind the bar and enjoyed his night's imprisonment very well, thank you.

[Tascosa] was some place. The fiddler in Tascosa was named "Snake" Thompson, and he had another claim to fame besides his prowess with the bow. He brewed his own whiskey and got his nickname because he claimed he put snake heads in it to make it strong.

Curtis Bishop, *Lots of Land*, 1949

THE TEXAS RANGER IS NOT SO HANDSOME AS AN EIGHT-DOLLAR-A-WEEK DRY-GOODS CLERK

…but he is more courageous than a Numidian lion and tougher than a Mexican burro. His language might sound a little barbaric in a London drawing-room, but he can successfully ride a broncho pony and kill a…horse thief at five hundred yards with his eyes shut… It is possible that he cannot tell the difference between the hypothesis of atomic evolution and a lunar eclipse, but he knows a "rustler" at sight and can name half the fugitives in Texas. Taken altogether, the ranger is a tough case and most of them have been born on the headwaters of Bitter Creek, where the natives are "wild and woolly and hard to curry." The further you go on this Classic Stream, the tougher the citizen. Underneath this rough exterior the Ranger hides a heart as simple and guileless as a child's and a soul whose tenderest chords are instantly touched by human misery or woe. He cleans his gun, washes his shirt and repairs his saddle on Sunday, but he will share his only dollar with a man in want, and throw his last biscuit to a hungry dog. His salary is meager, and he does not profess to love his country as dearly as he does a candidate for the Legislature, but he will tackle a bunch of rustlers single-handed, and round 'em up, too. He never saw the inside of a college, but he has been the advance courier of civilization, and has made life and property safe in Texas. Half the time he receives no credit for his work. He does his duty all the same. Short-sighted Legislators grumble and growl when they are called upon to pay him his pittance, and every year cut down the appropriation… Penurious tax payers insist that he is a burden upon the State. He returns them their stolen horses and cattle, brings to justice the man who robs them on the highway, and guards their homes day and night…

The Ranger is hardly ever out of the saddle. He is the original and only "solitary horseman" who has been scouring the plains in search of redskins ever since the dawn of the dime novel. He is Young America's beau ideal of border chivalry. The Ranger can ride harder, fight longer, live rougher, and make less talk about it than anything that walks on two feet. He wears a sombrero and spurs, thus accoutred, and with a two dollar government blanket, he will defy alike the rains of summer and the snows of winter. He generally dies with his boots on, and as the State does not furnish rosewood caskets and cemetery lots for her fallen soldiers, his comrades wrap him up in an old blanket and,

> In an unmarked shallow grave,
> They lay him down to rest;
> His saddle for a pillow
> His gun across his breast.

Alexander Edwin Sweet
Texas Siftings, September 1882

☆ ☆ ☆ ☆ ☆ ☆ ☆ ☆ ☆ ☆ ☆ ☆

HOW TO CALL A GIRL WAITER IN 1885

Once when [freight driver Bill Harelson and I] stopped for dinner at a little hotel at Paint Rock [near San Angelo], Bill began his meal by gulping down a cup of coffee, and then, reaching for his sixshooter, shot a hole in the dining-room floor. Whereupon the girl waiter placidly entered from the kitchen. Holding out his cup and saucer at arm's length toward her, Bill smilingly said, "Another cup, please." It appeared that I was the only one to sense anything extraordinary about this mode of calling a waiter.

Attributed to S.J. Houghton of Dallas, circa 1930

A FRENCHMAN DIES IN TEXAS

The last time I was on the buffalo range was in 1875. We went in November and came back the following March. We had to go to the Clear Fork of the Brazos River and camped in the Sand Ruff Cave, said to be twelve miles from the Big Springs. While at Sand Ruff Cave, Ad Holt, of St. Louis, Missouri, came down with a bunch of men to slaughter buffalo for their pelts.

Among them was a Frenchman, whose name I did not know, as he was always known to us as "Frenchy." Frenchy would follow the skinners and get the tongues to pickle. He did this pickling by taking a large buffalo hide, driving the four corners down with stakes, leaving enough slack in the center for it to bag, and make a container for the brine. Then he would fill the container with tongues, later shipping them to St. Louis. He was a great lover of buffalo liver, and one evening Frenchy borrowed my Winchester to kill a buffalo for its liver. About sundown, I heard him fire one shot west of the camp. At supper time Frenchy had not returned. Then it was too dark to look for him, but next morning we organized a searching party and went to where we thought the shot came from the evening before. We found Frenchy dead, also the buffalo, with my Winchester lying near. He had shot the buffalo, without killing it instantly, and it had gored him to death. Evidently he had tried to climb a small tree, about the size of a man's wrist, as it was bent over and the bark peeled from it. We buried him there, and I suppose his remains are still where he was buried.

W. N. Brazzil of Louise, Texas, circa 1924

THE TEXAS HILL COUNTRY IN SPRING: ONE ASSESSMENT

He walked out of the valley, as lean as a mesquite post and just about as gnarled, his eyes harsh and stubborn like the land around him. He paused to kick at a clump of prickly-pear cactus that held on selfishly to a patch of dirt that had washed down among the rocks. He looked out at the bluebonnets, the Indian paintbrush, the clover, the purple, orange, and red haze that ran up and down the gentle hillsides without going anywhere at all, the beauty amid the bristles.

In the rugged valley from whence he came, he saw the face of Texas the way the mythical Texas is supposed to be: big and empty, delicate yet defiant, tough as boot leather and just about as polished.

"This land ain't worth a plugged nickel," he explained, a definite German accent rolling off his tongue. "I've seen cows walk for ten miles just tryin' to find an acre of grass to chew on. 'Bout all you can raise on it is rocks, and a little Cain now and then."

He paused and sighed.

"It's poor, useless, good for nothin' and too dadgummed hard to even leave a footprint.

"But ain't it pretty?"

And so it was. The old man grinned again, bent low into the wind, and slowly shuffled away. I looked close. There were no footprints behind him to even prove he had ever come to or from the valley that separated Kerrville from Medina.

Caleb Pirtle III, *The Genuine Old Fashioned, Down-Home, Home Grown Official Texas Cookbook,* 1990

THE FINAL YEARS OF JOHN WILKES BOOTH

THE DEATHBED CONFESSION:

David E. George, a wealthy resident of the [Indian] Territory, who committed suicide here, on his death bed announced himself to be John Wilkes Booth, the assassin of President Lincoln. He stated that he had successfully eluded the officers after shooting Lincoln and since had remained incognito. His statement caused an investigation. Surgeons examined the body and stated the man to be of the age Booth would be at this time, and that his leg was broken in the same place and in the same manner as that of Booth after jumping from the president's box at Ford's Theatre following the assassination. All the time George has received money regularly from unknown sources. He had previously attempted suicide at El Reno [Oklahoma]. It was at El Reno that Mrs. Harper, who was mentioned in George's dying statement, had befriended him and had listened to a similar supposed death bed confession. No reason for the suicide is known. George maintained to the last to his attendants that he was John Wilkes Booth, and his general appearance closely resembles that of Booth.

Enid (Oklahoma) *Wave*, January 17, 1903

IN TEXAS:

If traditions are to be relied upon, Booth spent a number of his fugitive years in Texas. Many older citizens of Glen Rose and Granbury recall with interest, one John St. Helen (the man later known as David E. George), who lived in and about the two towns for several years…

On the southwest corner of "the square" in Granbury stands an old building, now occupied by Bowden's drug store and confectionery. This is the building, according to the "old timers" of Granbury, in which St. Helen operated a saloon. "The Black Hawk," a title given to the resort by St. Helen, was very popular and was operated in keeping with his fastidious taste.

This strange man's business seemed not to be a matter of necessity with him. It appears that all times he had more money than his stock in trade warranted, and he apparently took little interest in his vocation… His favorite occupation was that of reciting Shakespeare, not from a book, but from memory. *Richard III*, so the story goes, was his special preference… Tennyson's "Locksley Hall" was another of his favorites, and upon an occasion when he gave this as a reading it left an impression upon those who heard it that the years have not effaced…

The man [Booth/St. Helen] is said to have had property holdings in Dallas, Fort Worth and other Texas towns. An incident is told in connection with his having been seen upon an occasion in Fort Worth. Col. M.W. Connolly, a former newspaper man of that city, one-time editor of the old *Gazette* under Walter L. Malone, and a man of integrity, published the following:

"One night I was in the Pickwick Hotel barroom talking to Gen. Albert Pike, who had come down from Washington on legal business…Captain Day of Day & Maas, proprietors, was behind the bar. That was in 1884 or 1885. Tom Powell, mayor of Fort Worth, joined us, and Temple Houston, son of Gen. Sam Houston, was there. I started to bid General Pike goodnight when suddenly he threw up his hands, his face as white as his hair and beard, and exclaimed, "My God! John Wilkes Booth!" He was much excited, trembled like an aspen, and at my suggestion went to his room… I took no further interest in the matter, but later learned that the person [seen by Pike] had moved to the Territory. I have never seen John Wilkes Booth to know him positively, but I am strongly of the opinion that the man who died at Enid as David E. George was Booth.''

Mary Dagget Lake, *Houston Chronicle*, undated; circa 1929

THE END:

The mummified body of David E. George was last reported on exhibition as that of John Wilkes Booth at carnivals and side shows throughout the United States. Thus, it was that he who had known no rest in life knew none in death.

Frontier Times, November 1930

A PARTIAL LIST OF KANSAS LADIES WHO GREETED TEXAS COWBOYS AT THE END OF A TRAIL DRIVE

Poker Alice
Alabama Jane
Cayuse Laura
Cowboy Anna
Poker Nell
The Crying Squaw
Snowplow Bowers
Wild Horse Kate
Madame Bulldog
Dutch Jake
Yellowstone Nell Chinnick

**The Texas Trail was no mere cowpath.
It was the course of Empire.**

A description of the Chisholm Trail by historian Phillip Aston Rollins, 1912

THE LAST SURVIVOR OF SAN JACINTO

To excuse his poor performance in the battle of San Jacinto, on April 21, 1836, Santa Anna charged that Houston's army was composed of soldiers of fortune. That was far from the truth. Of the 877 officers and men on the muster rolls at San Jacinto, 707 definitely lived in Texas before independence was declared. Although it is impossible to determine when the other 170 arrived, no doubt many were Texas settlers before the Revolution…

A typical San Jacinto veteran was Alphonso Steele, a Kentuckian who reached Texas in November of 1835. Steele, age nineteen, joined the army in March, 1836, and was one of the thirty-four Texans wounded at San Jacinto. Steele recalled that:

"I got my gun loaded and rushed on into the timber and fired again when the second volley was poured into them. In that timber they broke and ran. As soon as I got my gun loaded again I ran on a little in front of our men and threw up my gun to shoot when I was shot down. Dave Rusk was standing by me when I was shot. He told some of the men to stay with me but I told him, 'No, take them on.'

"One of our men in passing me asked if he could take my pistol but by this time I was bleeding at the nose and mouth so I couldn't speak, so he just stooped down and got it and went on."

Steele and six other veterans attended the seventieth anniversary celebration of the battle of San Jacinto [1906]. Steele outlived the rest. He died July 7, 1911 at Mexia.

June Rayfield Welch, *Tell Me a Texas Story,* 1991

THE HANGING OF JOE WILLIAMS

On June 13, 1868, just after breakfast a foot-traveler by the name of Thomas Bird passed our home on Bear Creek in Parker County, Texas, and asked me the distance to Weatherford, and I informed him that it was twenty miles. I remember distinctly the way he was dressed. Late that afternoon in the southern part of Weatherford while resting on the side of the road, he was shot by...Joe Williams. Parties heard the shot, and coming along the road they found Joe in the act of robbing the man. Joe escaped in the brush. Later on in the trial, Joe claimed that he first shot at a bird and that the man disputed his word and kicked him, whereupon Joe shot him, as he claimed, in self-defense. Evidence however, showed that Joe fired but one shot and nearby parties heard only one shot.

...South of Spring Creek [Joe] stole a large iron gray mare from Captain Bob Blackwell and went east, taking the old Buchanan road. Officers went in pursuit and captured Joe about twenty-five miles southeast of Weatherford, shooting him in the left elbow. Dr. Millikin dressed Joe's arm and it was almost well when he was hung....

The trial came off in the next term of court. The jury was out thirty minutes and returned a verdict of "guilty." On November 14, 1868, Joe was sentenced to be hung on December 18, 1868. The writer and the rest of Parker County attended the hanging. It occurred about two miles west of town. The gallows was crude but effective. The sheriff, Wes Hedrick, had two green poles, each terminating in a fork, cut and sunk into the ground securely. Between the forks a green pole some ten inches in diameter was laid. The rude gallows was erected in a valley surrounded by nearby hills and the crowd on horseback was like a cloud.

Joe was brought out of jail and made to sit on the box of his own coffin in a two horse wagon. A strong guard formed a hollow square around him, and he was driven to the place of execution.

...The sheriff placed the black cap over his face, adjusted the noose, the driver hit the team a sharp blow that jerked the wagon from under Joe, and he was left dangling in the air. I remember distinctly that the rope stretched to such an extent that his feet came from within two feet of the ground.

T.U. Taylor, University of Texas, April 1924

Last Friday, July 31 [1868], my son Herman, 18 years old, while driving a wagon from one yoke of oxen on his return from Camp Verde, was suddenly attacked by five Indians on horseback about 5 o'clock in the afternoon near Mrs. Denton's farm on the well traveled road between Comfort and Kerrville.

The Indians advanced towards the wagon yelling horribly. My son, however, did not lose his nerve. Having stopped the oxen, he jumped from the wagon and opened fire immediately on the Indians, felling one who was nevertheless able to crawl back and hide in the brush. The others, seemingly scared, retreated for the moment and followed their wounded comrade to his hiding place.

This pause gave my son the time necessary to reload his gun. He had hardly done so when four unwounded Indians trying a different maneuver, charged by at full speed, some 150 paces away. Stopping suddenly, they tied their horses fast and attacked him afoot from both sides, making all kinds of jumps and not standing still for a moment. Three of the Indians fired with six-shooters; one used a bow and arrow. My son could defend himself only with his rifle and a six-shooter, keeping under cover of his wagon as much as possible.

After the Indians had emptied their six-shooters, the wagon box and wheels being hit in several places, they did not cease the attack. Instead, they kept closing in more determinedly

than ever, using their bows and arrows. When my son had only two bullets left, he retreated into the nearest brush, so as to gain sufficient time for re-loading his gun. Meanwhile, the Indians searching the wagon took possession of everything in it – a wagon sheet, two blankets, a pair of shoes and the provision box – and hurrying back to their horses, made off.

My son having reloaded his gun, returned to his wagon fortunate to be still in possession of his scalp.

Herman Stieler, *Freie Press Fuer Texas,* August 3, 1868

★ ★ ★ ★ ★ ★ ★ ★ ★ ★ ★ ★ ★

The first huisache trees in Texas were planted over a hundred years ago [circa 1832] at De Leon's Crossing [of the Nueces River in San Patricio County]…

One of the Mexican commissioners, sent by the Mexican government to the Irish Colony [town of San Patricio], brought them with him and planted them on his hacienda. From these trees huisaches have spread over the state, until now they are as much a part of the native landscape as mesquite. They have other names: papinae, sweet acacia. They have small sensitive leaves and a pair of thorns (almost every native plant has thorns, prominent or concealed) at each node. The leaves close at the touch of the hand. At intermittent periods they are covered with a profusion of fragrant, yellow, fuzzy balls, the size of marbles; and the trees, with several stems arching from the same root, are graceful.

The Mexicans, for centuries, have brewed a tea by boiling the bark. They drink it before breakfast and at bedtime. It is used for internal injuries and bruises. The huisache, because of its early pollen, is also important as a source of honey. In France, it is cultivated for perfume.

Dallas Morning News, June 26, 1932

THE RED BEDOUINS OF WEST TEXAS

In roaming over the plains of the Southwest I was struck with similarity to the steppes of Tartary and the deserts of Arabia, but not more so than with the resemblance of the inhabitants of both. The nomads of the old world and the wild Indians of the prairie have no permanent abiding place, but where their lodges are pitched are their homes. Their respective governments are patriarchal, sanctioned by the masses, and guided by the counsels of the elders. They never cultivate the soil, but subsist upon plunder and the chase. They are alike in their attachment to the horse and expertness in horsemanship. Coinciding in their views of the rights of property, they consider stealing from strangers as perfectly legitimate, are the greatest marauders on earth, and he who is most expert and successful is the greatest among them. In minor and domestic customs they are identical. Polygamy is allowed, they sit cross-legged upon mats, are very fond of tobacco, and saddle, bridle and mount their horses from the right side; they also eat with their fingers. The estimation in which a successful robber is held is illustrated by an anecdote of an old chief, who said he had four sons who were a great comfort to him in his declining years, as they could steal more horses than any young men in the tribe.

W.B. Parker, *Expedition Through Unexplored Texas*, 1856

Chief Ten Bears

AN INTRIGUING PRAIRIE MEETING WITH A COMANCHE CHIEF IN THE WILDS OF WEST TEXAS

August 10 [1854] – about noon Indians were seen approaching, and pretty soon Ke-tum-e-see, a chief of the Southern band of Camanches rode in, accompanied by two of his wives. He told us that he had been riding very hard and far to overtake us…had been six days on our trail, following it through a good portion of the upper Brazos country, where, like ourselves, he came near perishing for want of water…

Ke-tum-e-see was a fine looking man, about fifty years old, full six feet high, with a dark red bronze complexion. His wives (these were two, and the youngest of four whom he commanded) were mere children, the one about eighteen and the other not sixteen years old. Both were pleasing in their appearance, but entirely different, the youngest being chubby and dark, the eldest lean and as fair as a quadroon. Whether it was by accident or from choice that the chief made his selection I know not, perhaps a spice of both, though he gave us to understand he was quite an epicure in such matters.

An odd mixture of wealth and poverty marked this trio. K-tum-e-see was dressed in corduroy leggins and buckskin moccasins, much worn, an old torn, greasy, checkered cotton coat, and a six-penny straw hat, whilst his bridle was ornamented with perhaps fifty dollars worth of silver. His wives were attired in dark calico skirts with leggins and moccasins in one piece like a boot; their clothes thin, dirty and common, and heads bare; the hair short, thick and uncombed, whilst their bridles were similarly ornamented as the chief's; and the youngest, who appeared to be the favorite, wore in addition a girdle studded with silver broaches, very heavy, showy and costly. The wives rode astride, driving the pack horses, who bore their scanty stock of cooking utensils, blankets, skins, etc., and as soon as they arrived, set diligently to work to unsaddle, unbridle and lariat the horses, and make from bushes and blankets a temporary shelter for their lord. The chief threw aside his riding dress and came up to our tent to dine, "in puris naturalibus," except his red blanket. The only ornament or appendage he wore was a long tail of buffalo hair, descending from a bunch of eagle's feathers, fastened on the crown of his head and reaching in a four-fold plait to the ground; a mark of his rank in the tribe…

W.B. Parker, *Expedition Through Unexplored Texas*, 1856

SEVERAL EARLY TEXAS NEWSPAPERS

The Cotton Plant: San Felipe, 1829

The Mexican Nation: San Felipe, 1831

The Redlander: San Augustine, 1837

The People: Brazoria, 1837

The National Banner: Houston, 1838

The Civilian: Houston, 1838

The Intelligencer: Houston, 1838

The Mosquito: Houston, 1838

The Western Texan: San Antonio, 1848

The Flea: Jacksboro (Fort Richardson), 1869

The Plowboy: Lubbock, 1871

The Busy Bee: San Marcos, 1874

The Iron News: Llano, 1884

The Kicker: Ozona, 1891

The Spy: Mason, 1893

The Daily Thomas Cat: San Marcos, 1898

The Pointer: Dripping Springs, 1905

THERE WERE PARTIES IN THOSE DAYS

…They were held at unpainted country houses with clean-swept yards. This was a long time ago when one of my jobs, getting ready for the big event, would be to clean the yard so it would be fit for company to walk on…

Yards in the country at the time I am talking about seldom had grass. More likely a yard would be hard-packed dirt and it could get dirty the way a floor did and so it needed to be swept and picked up. We gathered mesquite thorns and dead leaves and rusty staples that had popped out of the fence. We picked up sticks and clods and pebbles and we swept the yard over and over until it was slick as slate and if a dog threatened to trot across it we would swing a broom at him because we didn't want any tracks showing.

When we got the yard ready we sat on the door of the storm cellar and talked about the smells coming out of the kitchen. Popcorn being popped. Candy being made. Chicken being fried, on Saturday afternoon instead of Sunday. How strange that was, and good.

The best time for one of these parties was a cool calm night, the kind that promised frost before morning. Kerosene lanterns would be hung out on the porch and everybody looked better in the dim light.

Lanterns at country parties always upgraded personal appearances. Girls, for instance. The homely ones looked nice. The plain ones looked pretty. The pretty ones looked beautiful. These were exciting times…

There would be games. Simple games that made the heart pound. Names would be drawn out of a hat, a girl's name and a boy's, and the two would then hold hands and walk all the way around the house in the dark and the boy would have to make clever remarks to entertain the girl

during the trip. I would say, "I swept the yard." And she would say, "You did?" Just as if sweeping yards was a noble calling and nobody without creative calling would sweep one.

We'd have songs, too, and fiddlers would play, and stories would be told, and you'd hear lots of laughter and get wonderful things to eat. There were good parties in those days.

Leon Hale, *Texas Chronicles*, 1989

[South Texas Rancher] Shanghai Pierce once built a church in his vicinity and engaged a preacher to come and dedicate it. But the preacher got his dates mixed and was absent on the Saturday appointed for the ceremony. The crowd assembled around the new church, and old Shang was there dressed in his Sunday best, but nobody knew where the minister was. They waited until the sun began to sink. Many of them had traveled miles on rugged roads to see the building dedicated. To avoid disappointing them, Shang finally got up and said a speech and dedicated the church himself.

The preacher came on the following Saturday, but there was no crowd. After lingering awhile around the empty building, he drove over to the Pierce headquarters and inquired what the matter was, saying he had come to dedicate the church.

"The church?" said Shanghai."Oh, that's already done. I dedicated it last Saturday."

"*You* dedicated the church, Mr. Pierce?" asked the preacher, astonished.

"I dedicated it," said Shanghai.

The clergyman then whispered that softly solicitous question which is so often on the lips of ministers: "Do you belong to the church, Mr. Pierce?"

Shanghai bellowed back: "Hell, no! It belongs to me."

Frank Goodwyn, *Lone Star Land*, 1955

AN EARLY LETTER TO GERMANY

"You ask whether I can advise people to come here. That I cannot do. Although anyone who wants to farm here and cares to work, will do as well here as anywhere. The land is still cheap _ good land with wood, which is a necessity here, where the land on which one raises corn must all be fenced. There are no herders here as in Germany. Here cattle graze where they will. There are not from 1,000 to 1,200 people here. Only 10 or 12 died last year. This shows that the climate is healthy. I write no lie. Whoever does not want to come may stay at home. I advise no one to come, but I write the truth. I shall never leave here. I do not care to have things better than they are here. One lives in peace. When taxes are due, one can always pay them. The taxes are the least of one's cares. As for my health, I am healthier here than I ever was in Germany… In town are a number of pretty homes, good when one considers the age of the community. There are already farmers here who in one year sell from 600 to 800 bushels of corn and keep enough for their own use. The soldiers' fort – Fort Martin Scott – 2 miles from town (*eine halbe Deutsche meile*) brings the town much trade. And now more and more soldiers are being sent to the grant for the safety of the German settlers… I believe Fredericksburg will grow to be a prosperous city. The evidence lies before one's eyes. Immigrants are still arriving, and all are well pleased. Anyone with money can buy cultivated farms with houses as good as anywhere, and as cheap…Please send me several dozen long and short pipes, which I can easily sell here, also a *spiel doose* (music box). When you send these things, please include something for my wife. You will know what will please her."

Letter from Fredericksburg merchant Conrad Wehmeyer to his half brother, Heinrich Kespohl, in Huttenhausen, Westphalia, January 1852

In the Spring of 1888, a trail of covered wagons headed by my father came to a stop at a little place known as "Up-on-the-draw." A town was organized and established. Father named it Plainview on account of the unobstructed view in all directions. Amarillo, which was 85 miles distant, could be seen in the mirage on clear days…

Our first home was a tent…Our second home was a 'dug-out.' It was a nice cozy, warm place and in it we lived until lumber could be hauled from Amarillo. As well as I remember, father built the first frame house in Plainview.

All of our food supplies came from Amarillo and as the journey was long and tedious, we bought in large quantities – sugar, flour and apples by the barrel and raisins by the sacks. Our meat consisted of beef, antelope and bear. We had acres planted in fruit trees. Material for clothes was also bought in Amarillo – not by the yard but by the bolt. I remember all my little aprons were just alike and how glad I was when the bolt gave out so my clothes would change color.

Attributed to Jane Lowe Quillen in the *Fort Worth Star-Telegram*, February 2, 1932

BOOGER RED'S LAST RIDE

Tom (Booger Red) Privett was a legendary rodeo cowboy bronc rider for five decades, never, tradition contends, being thrown in a public performance. For many years Privett operated his own small western touring show and performed with Buffalo Bill and the Hagenbeek and Wallace Circus. His standard offer was $100 to the owner of any wild horse he could not ride. He never had to pay. Among his fabulous exploits was riding 86 wild broncs in one day and winning, at age 58, the best all-round cowboy title at San Francisco.

The number of wild horses that Booger Red rode during his life would be impossible to estimate, but he must have averaged at least two a day for fifty years and that makes 40,000. Booger lost some of them but never one in a show ring. He would travel many miles just to engage a horse of bad reputation. He was some-what like a Texas ranger for the bad horses; it was his job to show them that they were not so bad.

He was not a big man, height 5 feet 5, weight 158, hair was red as the sunrise, voice a gentle baritone…

It was hard for the great rider to quit. He went to the rodeo at Fort Worth the year [1924] before he died and disguising himself by a cap and low quarter shoes, climbed to the top of the grandstand.

He did not want to ride. He had won the top money at the show time and time again, as he had won saddles and other kinds of awards all over the world for his skill with horses. But there was trouble that day. There was difficulty in snubbing a horse and the crowd cried for Booger Red. The Booger sat still. He wasn't afraid, he was tired – he had had about fifty years of wild horse taming and it was beginning to tell. The cry still continued for the Booger.

Then some woman spotted him and out he came. He snubbed the horse and rode him to great applause. It was his last ride. Next year he died at the age of 68.

San Angelo Morning Times, April 25, 1933

The true Texan in his heart is truly a universal nationalist. He thinks not of the waters of the Rio Grande as a boundary line on the west and south, but rather the Pacific Ocean; and on the east the Red River is but a small barrier between him and the Atlantic.

His mind extends over the Canadian border for his northern divide line. Whether he be a native or an adopted son of Texas, he soon begins to expand his vision far and wide, and prides himself on the magnificent dimensions within her confines, wherein states and nations could nestle and be forgotten.

Attributed to 'G.A.L.' in the
Georgetown Sun, Spring 1933

When the time came we started to Dallas. It was a distance of about 300 miles and for over 200 miles of this we did not see a single house.

Attributed to Judge Emanuel Dubbs, recounting a trip from the town of Mobeetie in the Texas Panhandle to Dallas in 1879

COMING TO TEXAS BY OX WAGON IN 1864

We were two months on the road [from Alabama]. Every family brought all the tools it could and one brought an entire blacksmith shop, with bellows, anvil and hammers. Another had a turning lathe to make shears, looms and spinning wheels.

We soon found that everybody was your friend except the Indians. No one had to buy land, just preempt a homestead and live on it three years and get a patent on it. One had a home, plenty of wild game. Coffee, sugar and salt we had only occasionally. The women folks spun and wove the cloth to make our clothes. Our shoes were made of the hides of buffalo and deer.

When we got out of bread, we used the curd from clabber milk. We usually did without sugar until we found a rich bee tree, and then we had all the sweetening we needed. We drank milk out of a gourd…

Our houses were made out of logs. We could go anywhere and cut our timber, then split and notch the logs and when we got them to the right height we gradually drew them in until we got to the center, then we would take our boards we had prepared and cover the house, weighting it down with straight poles. We took mud and rubbed all the cracks. We burned lime rock and got lime, which we mixed with buttermilk to make a mortar and covered the mud with it. We built the chimney the same way. The doorway was always on the south side. The floor was dirt. All the neighbors helped in building each other's home.

We broke our land with bull-tongued plows pulled by oxen. If you got a half acre broken in a day, that was doing well. We plaited rawhide ropes by hand and dropped our corn by hand.

When somebody went to town, which was not often, the lady would never want more than the usual salt, sugar and coffee, if that. I was almost grown when I saw a calico dress. We thought the woman wearing it must be somebody mighty important. When she was asked where she got such a fine dress, she said, "Aleck paid a dollar for it and I made it!"

Remembered by Elias Hardcastle in the *San Antonio Express,*
January 5, 1932

In 1881, the Panhandle was very sparsely settled, houses and families being few and far between. Dugouts were then common and on this particular Christmas the people gathered in the biggest dugout in the neighborhood for their celebration, the place belonging to Joe Browning, a well known citizen of Dickens County. The tree was a Chinaberry full of yellow balls, the balls gleaming like gold amid the white cotton trimming of the tree. In addition, wreaths were made from algerita bushes, the green adding a pretty finishing touch to the festive scene. On the tree were all the gifts that were favorites of years ago. Dolls of all kinds and toys for the little girls and red-topped boots with brass toes and other things equally liked for the boys… There were but six children to enjoy the tree and the treats but the little folks had a good time and so did the older folks. A big dance was also held at the Matador Ranch. As wild game was plentiful in those long ago days, Christmas dinner was bountiful and turkeys were not in demand.

Frontier Times, February 1927

★ ★ ★ ★ ★ ★ ★ ★ ★ ★ ★ ★ ★ ★ ★ ★

REAL COWBOYS DON'T DRINK MILK

Often, in Texas, when we tried to buy milk at a ranch, where there were thousands of cattle, there was not a drop to be had. The owners would not even take trouble to have it even for themselves.

Lydia Spencer Lane, *I Married a Soldier*, 1892

AN 1848 TEXAS CHRISTMAS DINNER MENU

Wild turkey, with cornbread dressing

Ham, boiled, then baked brown

Dried peach pies

Cornbread and biscuits, cooked over an open wood fire

Yams, roasted

Sweet potato pie

Coffee

Egg-nog

Whiskey, straight

Remembered by Melvina "Aunt Viny" Chessher, age 97, in the *Houston Chronicle*, December 14, 1930

In 1850, I attended what I knew later to be an unusual wedding. There lived about a half mile from us a family by the name of McNair… In this family there were three sisters, who formed the novel idea of being married on the same day. After the marriage ceremony the feast was spread… There was a high-light at the feast which I never forgot. At the end of the long table was a large jug of whisky. And this a Presbyterian wedding! I was standing near when a man walked up to the table, picked up a glass, poured it half full of whisky and drank. As he drained the glass, he bit a piece out of it and threw it away. I have no doubt that was not the first drink he had indulged in.

Remembered by Hilton Milam Dodson, age 93, in the *San Antonio Express*, summer 1932

LET HIM WHO IS WITHOUT SIN CAST THE FIRST NOOSE

It was right funny. [About 1871] I knew a fellow by the name of Denny Murphy, who drove off more cattle than anybody else… He was just a better rustler. The cattlemen decided that Denny had better be killed. He had just left a few days before with a big herd of cattle for Denver, Colorado. The boys at Fort Griffin made up a posse, loaded up on whiskey, and started after Denny. They tried to get some of us to go, but we wouldn't go. They overtook Denny's outfit out on the Pecos about 12 o'clock one day. Denny had an idea they were up to something, but had his cook prepare a good dinner for the boys. After dinner, they told Murphy what they had come for. He just sorta grinned, and said: "Now boys, I don't mind you fellows hanging me, but I have one request to make. I want an honest man to do it. If there is a single man in the crowd that is honest, and that hasn't done just what I have, I want him to put the rope around my neck." The boys began to grin and look at each other. After a hearty laugh they all got back on their horses and rode back to Fort Griffin.

Emmett Roberts, from an interview in the *Anson Western Enterprise,* 1933

I had succeeded in transplanting myself from a state [Michigan, about 1875] where the people – good citizens who loved God and nature – had accepted and, as a rule, lived up to the Ten Commandments; where, when trouble arose between men, it seldom was carried to a point beyond a fist-fight.

But in the section of country [Texas] I had now entered, different conditions and codes prevailed. The War of Rebellion [Civil War], then so recent, had caused numerous men who had survived it, and who had committed all sorts of desperate crimes, to seek refuge in the wilds of the land of chaparral and cactus, where the strong arm of the law seldom entered, and where, when it did, the refugee would be apt to have a little the best of it. A majority of the ranchmen in the country preferred aiding a white refugee to helping bring him to justice. The preference sprang from a motive of self-protection, for the enmity of such characters was a most dangerous thing. As there was in that section but little employment other than working with stock, naturally these men took up the life of the cowboy – when their time was not occupied dodging State Rangers or robbing stages and small settlements. Almost every dispute had to be settled with a gun- or knife-fight or else assassination. Such people, added to thieving bands of Mexicans and Indians, wild beasts of many sorts, and other terrors such as centipedes, tarantulas, and rattlesnakes, were a help in making life interesting…

I did not let anyone know where I hailed from. A 'blue-bellied Yankee,' even if he were but a boy, was about the most unpopular thing in Texas at that period. With many people, anyone who came from the country lying to the north of the Red River was a Yankee.

James H. Cook, *50 Years on the Old Frontier*, 1923

[T]exan] Jim Mitchell was noted for his remarkable mastery of horses. His performances in Europe with Buffalo Bill electrified ten thousand people at a time… Mitchell accompanied Buffalo Bill on his first two years' tour of Europe [and] made the greatest record of his life as a bronco buster; …a thrilling account of his work reads as follows:

"An impression prevailed among some of the spectators that these wild, bucking horses are trained after the manner of circus horses. Nothing can be further from the truth… They simply are wild horses spoiled in the breaking. There is one black mare that they call Dynamite that is without exception the wickedest animal I ever saw. You are to understand that when a man attempts to mount her, she jumps into the air, and turning a back somersault, falls upon her back with her heels upward. To escape being crushed to death is to employ the marvelous celerity and dexterity that a cowboy alone exhibits. On Monday, Jim Mitchell undertook to ride this animal. It was necessary for four men to hold her and she had to be blind-folded before he could get on her, and then letting out a scream like a woman in pain, she made a headlong dash and plunged with all her force into a fence, turning completely over head first and apparently falling upon the rider.

"A cry of horror rose from the spectators, but the rest of the exhibition went on. Poor Jim Mitchell was dragged out bleeding and maimed and led away. What was the astonishment of the multitude when the other refractory animals had had their turn, to see Dynamite again led out, and Jim Mitchell, limping and pale, come forward to make another attempt to ride. 'No, no,' cried the spectators, 'take her away.' But the indomitable cowboy only smiled grimly and gave them to understand that in the cowboy's code a man who fails to ride his animal might as well retire from business. It was do or die.

"For fifteen minutes the fight went on between man and beast. Animal strength against pluck and intelligence. I never saw a multitude brought to such intense interest. It was the gladiatorial contest revived. The infuriated beast shook off the men who held her like insects. She leaped into the air and fell on her back. She laid and groveled. But Jim Mitchell got upon her back by some superhuman skill and then he was master. As he punished the animal mercilessly and swung his hat triumphantly, the concourse of people stood up and cheered long and loud."

San Antonio Express, March 8, 1904

A LETTER FROM THE FRONTIER

"Dear Brother and Sister and family:

It is with great pleasure that I now take the privilege of dropping you a few lines in order to let you know that we are all up and about. Lucy has been puny all winter, though is mending now. I sincerely hope when these ill-composed lines reach your absent hands, may find you all enjoying the best of health and doing well also. I haven't much news to write that is worth relating. Your connections are all well with the exception of Mrs. Welch. She is right poorly with the eresipelas [sic]. I guess you have heard that Silas was married. Malaki's wife has a fine son. Toke's wife has a fine son. I have forgot their names. Tom Wright got up here last Tuesday. He brought me a letter from home. They are all well except little Molly; she has the chills.

"I can inform you that the boys had a fight with the Indians day before yesterday. The fight lasted about three hours. Bob [her husband] and Tom Wright were in the fight. The Indians made a raid in the town of Comanche Tuesday night about an hour before day and took the Sheriff's horse out of the stable and took Teverly's buggy horses and one of his mules; cut them loose from the door they were tied to and took one from Dick Kiser and several other horses, and then they came by here and took two stray horses…There was a company of men up by daylight and they caught the Indians about one o'clock on the Colorado, 30 miles away and fought them five or six miles. They got one Indian scalp and wounded three or four others. The Indians didn't do no damage to our men, only killed one horse and wounded 2. Bob found a big knife and a blanket. Several of the boys found blankets. They got one six shooter and one shield. There were 19 Indians and 17 white men. The Indians killed one of Dick Kiser's dogs. He lamented mighty about the dog.

"I will tell you what I have been doing. I have been trying to spin every chance. I have spun – yards of blanket warp, eleven yards of filling and some knitting thread. I am now spinning some harness twine to try to weave. My shoulder pesters me a great deal when I card and spin. I have went to the doctor's here to see if they could cure me but they have not done it."

Letter from Mrs. C.M. Neal, Comanche County, April 19, 1861, to a sister, Mrs. Disa Cox, near Belton in Lavaca County; the letter required a month to be delivered

★ ★ ★ ★ ★ ★ ★ ★ ★ ★

The feet of Big Foot Wallace, famous Texas Indian fighter, were not big, according to Mrs. Annie Grimes of Fort Worth, who knew Wallace.

Popular conception for nearly a century has credited the big fighter, whose battle with an Indian in a West Texas canyon is a gem of Texas history, with wearing shoes size 14. "Big Foot used to visit our home a great deal and his feet really were very small for so tall a man," Mrs. Grimes said.

There are two conflicting stories of how Big Foot got his name.

Mrs. Grimes said that Big Foot once explained to her how he came by it. Down near Austin an Indian with record-breaking feet was killed. In some way Wallace was given credit for the deed. Afterwards he was labeled "Big Foot."

Another oft-told explanation is that Wallace was captured by Mexicans during the War of Texas Independence. He drew a white bean and was spared facing a firing squad. He was sent to Mexico City as a prisoner. There were no shoes in the city large enough for him, so he had to go barefoot until a pair was constructed.

Frontier Times, September 1934; Note: for the record, Big Foot Wallace was 6 feet 2 inches tall, weighed 230 pounds and wore size 11 shoes

Wash day came *once a week*. There were no rubbing boards, or washing machines; and it was a back-breaking process. The rubbing was done with the hands and the only aid they had was an invention of the frontier, the "battling stick" and the "battling bench." The "battling bench" consisted of a cottonwood slab four to six feet long and some twelve to eighteen inches wide and three or four inches thick. It was supported on four legs and was about two and one-half feet from the ground. After being thoroughly soaked the clothes were placed on this "battling bench" and the good wife then plied her "battling stick" which consisted of a long paddle flattened out….

The soap was all home made, either "hard" or "soft." The "ash-hopper" was as common on the frontier as the family churn. A cottonwood log, at least twelve inches in diameter, was cut from two to twelve feet long. A V-shaped trough was cut into the log from end to end. It was placed firmly on blocks in an inclining position with the trough on the upper side. A rectangular framework was constructed about the trough with side and end rails. Boards or planks were placed with their lower ends in the V-shaped trough and the upper ends resting on the side rails, the length of the boards being something like four or five feet. Their ends were closed by other planks. Into this "hopper" ashes from the wood fires were placed until it was filled. Water was then poured over the ashes and allowed to soak and leach through. This formed lye which reached the bottom of the V-shaped trough and flowed out in the lower end into a crock and an earthen vessel. The lye was carefully stored away.

In the meantime all the bacon rinds and all forms of hog fat had been collected and carefully preserved. The lye and the fats were the chief ingredients of the soap. In a huge iron pot the lye and grease were placed with an appropriate amount of water, and the boiling process began. After completion the soap remained on top of the water several inches thick. It was then poured into soap buckets and was there kept "soft" or later was laid out on planks and permitted to harden. At a later time concentrated lye could be bought in small pint cans in the stores and the "ash-hopper" disappeared from the frontier life.

T.U. Taylor, University of Texas, 1925

North of 36

The term used to describe a cattle drive from Texas up the Chisholm Trail beyond the 36th parallel line of latitude, a few miles south of present day Oklahoma City; the expression was used as title for an early novel, which spawned three Hollywood movies.

Soaking wet from top to bottom, your boots plumb full of water and your toes squishing in it, and why us boys liked to be cowboys and could stand it, I can't say. I reckon it were the excitement.

Jesse James Benton, *Cow by the Tail*, 1943

Go get your man. Get him alive if you can; dead if you must, but don't come back until you get him.

Traditional slogan of the Texas Rangers

ON DECEMBER 1, [1866] I HAD A REFRESHING BATH IN THE SAN ANTONIO RIVER

…and the next day came in sight of the city. We felt at once that we were in a strange country, or at least among a strange people. The town is one of the oldest in the union, contemporary with San Augustine and Santa Fe, and its old cathedral church of San Felipe de Bexar dates away back, having been built by the generation immediately succeeding the men who were fellow adventurers with Cortez… There are three plazas, or public squares, the Main Plaza, the Military plaza and the Alamo plaza, on the latter of which stood the ruins of what may be considered, or should be, the Mecca of Texas, the historic building known as the Alamo… To the everlasting disgrace of Texas, no noble monument marks the spot; in fact, when I first saw it, it was part of a livery stable.

The climate of the part of Texas so far seen by me had taken fast hold on my mind approaching the ideal…the following verbatim entry in my diary, written in December, 1866, on the climate, I have never yet seen fit to alter:

"Beyond doubt, the balmy and glorious climate, the gorgeous skies, the glowing sunsets, the pure and bracing atmosphere, and splendid land-scapes, cannot be surpassed on the continent; and in the near future, when the railroad shall have traversed its immense distances, and the six-shooter and bowie [knife] shall have been replaced by the plow and school-house, no portion of our vast heritage will present so many attractions to the emi-grant, the tourist, or the invalid, as the Empire State of the Southwest."

H.H. McConnell, *Five Years a Cavalryman*, 1888

☆ ☆ ☆ ☆ ☆ ☆ ☆ ☆ ☆ ☆ ☆ ☆ ☆ ☆ ☆ ☆ ☆ ☆

THE NEW YORK TIMES THINKS TEXAS IS SOUTHWESTERN POLAND

The name Texas is Celtiberian or Spanish. Some tell us it has the meaning of "Paradise," … the suggestion, no doubt, of a Karankawa buffalo-hunter; and others…seem to think it meant *Friend*, a much feebler sort of guess. But, as in all original cases of the kind, nature herself has vindicated the sense of the nomenclature. Texas meant and means *Plain*, in the Celtic – the great plain near Spanish Seville being named Dehesa. Texas and Poland were named in the same way, and for the same reason, meaning level or plain countries. There was a Texas, or raised platform for the noble family, in the hall of every prince and baron of the medieval ages, and it was spelled Dais – a term curiously mistaken for a canopy.

From a book review, *New York Times*, 1874

We have often heard of Nowhere,
and supposed it somewhere in Texas.

Galveston Texas Times, December 7, 1842

An Old Ranger Remembers

A hundred names of men I knew down there come to me, and most of them, I suppose, now dead. Hard lives, hard men, maybe – but they come back to me like murmurs of far-off voices sometimes, something soft, like a flute's sweet note that has a message to tell. Maybe I didn't see them so soft those days, because it was all too close. Life is something like a gun battle. A man doesn't know what he really thought until the shooting's over. That's the way I went through a lot of things down there. Never saw the danger then.

J.K.P. Lankford, remembering his Texas Ranger life along the Rio Grande in the *San Antonio Express*, May 25, 1930

Tall Tales of Yesteryear

When times in early Texas really got tight, whisky vendors sold pond water and doctors never got any more complicated cases than bellyache. One newspaper reported that corn had got so scarce and pigs so lean they were crawling through cracks in the pens until the farmers stopped them by tying knots in their tails. The next year things improved and it became impractical to build cribs for the tremendous corn crops, so they chinked and daubed the rock fences and built roofs over the fields. Sweet potatoes, that year, had to be taken to the sawmill to be cut up. A father was mournfully quoted: "When I send my two boys for corn and see them staggering under the weight of an ear, one at each end, I can't help but feel sorry for them. (Some of these ears of corn got so large that they snapped off the stalks when half grown, but no loss – the kernels were used for building stone fencees.)

Donald Day, *Big Country: Texas,* 1947

January 21, 1941, W. Lee O'Daniel was inaugurated for his second term as Texas governor. The former flour salesman threw a barbecue on the governor's mansion lawn and invited all Texans. Twenty-five thousand showed up. Here's the menu:

☆ Meat: 17,000 pounds – including one buffalo, many steers, goats, sheep, and calves

☆ Hot dogs: 12,500

☆ Bread: 3,200 loaves

☆ Buns: 6,500 buns

☆ Onions: 1,250 pounds

☆ Potato chips: 1,000 pounds

☆ Lemonade: six 45-gallon barrels, refilled all day from 24,000 lemons and 1,000 pounds of sugar

☆ Coffee: 900 gallons

☆ Pickles: 6,000 pickles, served in four 45-gallon barrels

☆ Cheese: 500 pounds

☆ Paper plates: 20,000

☆ Paper napkins: 50,000

TEXAS RANGERS TAME KILGORE'S OIL FIELDS WITH CHAINS OF STEEL, AND A LITTLE LEAD

Robert (Bob) Goss and M.T. (Lone Wolf) Gonzaullas were sent to Kilgore during the oil boom to "restore order and preserve the peace." Both were Texas Rangers... Goss arrived in Kilgore, February 28, 1931, after being released from hospital where he had spent 20 days recovering from a bullet wound. Gonzaullas preceded him by a few weeks.

Law enforcement officers, overwhelmed by the great mass of people and the necessity to protect them from harm, many times resorted to the swift justice of a lead slug to curb lawlessness of a violent nature. As one of the old-timers put it, "There were too many of them, and too much was going on. We simply didn't have time to arrest, jail and appear in court against each and every thug who came along. We stopped crime by stopping them...a dead hi-jacker don't ever hi-jack again! The word gets around and soon the new ones steer clear of the town, too – it's just that simple."

Within a short time after the boom started, the county jail was chock-full of prisoners, and some method of holding additional prisoners was of utmost importance. The Rangers neatly solved this by putting into operation one of the strangest jails ever known – "The Trotline." It was first situated at the corner of Main and Commerce Streets... [and] consisted of a log-chain strung in a rough square around the trunks of small trees. At intervals along this chain smaller chains were fastened with a "cold-shut [snapping lock]." The prisoners were secured to the other end which was looped around their necks and fastened with a padlock. Care was taken to fasten the lock tightly against the back of the neck so that the prisoner could not pick the lock. This "Trotline" was later moved to an abandoned church, where it remained until the building was sold to a man who converted it into a dance-hall.

Al Eason, *Boom Town: Kilgore, Texas*, undated, but about 1960

"I WILL DESCRIBE [JIM BOWIE'S KNIFE] TO YOU, FOR I HAVE FREQUENTLY SEEN IT AND HANDLED IT."

"It was 17 1/4 inches in the blade, two inches in width until within five inches of the point when it widened a half-inch and then curving backward a little...to a point. It weighed just three pounds. The handle was made of the lower part of the horn of an elk, sawed in two halves and neatly riveted onto the shank of the blade, the handle and blade being 23 inches in length, with a handsome cross-piece where the two joined. The knife was ground down and then put on an oil-stone until it was so sharp that it would shave the hair off one's hand, so admirable was its temper. The sheath was made of two pieces of thin pine wood neatly covered with alligator skin. It could be used for both cut and thrust, and it never failed when Jim Bowie got a fair blow."

James Madison Wells, former Louisiana governor, quoted in the *San Antonio Express*, June 5, 1889

In the Beginning: Old Tascosa

When I came to Tascosa [about 1880] there were only three other American women in the Panhandle country west of Fort Elliott. They were Mrs. Charles Goodnight (he was a big cattle man), Miss Lizzie Rinehart and Mrs. Tom Bugby, wife of another big ranchman…. There was a Mexican girl here in Tascosa, Senorita Piedad Romero, daughter of Don Casimiro Romero, the richest man around. She was called 'The Belle of the Llano Estacado.' She was pretty.

When I came here Tascosa was the only town in the western Panhandle of Texas. Where Amarillo is now was a buffalo ranch then. The nearest town on the north was Dodge City [Kansas], 242 miles away…. Everything we used was freighted in from Dodge. That's why needles cost 10 cents apiece, and it took a small fortune to buy enough material for a new dress. To the south there were only the cattle trails that led down over the wild and unsettled plains to the cattle ranches along the Gulf Coast and to old Mexico. I've seen 10,000 cattle in one herd, all Longhorns, come driving up across the prairie to swim the Canadian [River] here, and go up to the railroad at Dodge City or up to summer in Montana. I've seen one-fourth million cattle swim the Canadian here in one year. Now look at it. The railroad came through; it missed Tascosa; towns sprang up along the line; people moved out from here and Tascosa died.

Attributed to Ms. Frenchy McCormick, faro dealer and last resident of old Tascosa, interviewed in the *Kansas City Star*, December 1930

TEXAS POETICAL

Plentiful Texas

Texas, Texas, what do you think,
Plenty of grapes, but no wine to drink;
Plenty of creeks, but no water at hand;
No corn for your horses, but plenty of land;
Plenty of horses, but none to ride;
Plenty of poverty – plenty of pride;
Plenty of cattle, no butter or milk;
No dress for the dairy, but plenty of silk;
Plenty of hides, no leather that's tanned,
Though the scrubby mesquite encumbers
*   the land.*
The finest of soil, though rarely a peach;
Plenty of all things, though seldom in reach.
Plenty of rain, when it comes down at all;
Enough and to spare would it come at
*   your call;*
Plenty of bacon, year before last;
Plenty again when there comes a good mast;
Plenty of stone the cisterns to wall;
But never the time to do it all;
Plenty of time, but a great lack of leisure;
Plenty of young folks too lazy for pleasure;
Plenty of wind, no drawback on that;
When the old men get to talking, plenty
*   of chat;*
Plenty of stories – the half of them lies;
With idlers and braggarts they need not
*   surprise;*
O, land of great promise never fulfilled
What a country you might be if people
*   so willed;*
All teeming with plenty, with beauty
*   and health;*
Every requisite here for comfort and wealth;
But with jerked beef and coffee men
*   have enough;*
And women get happy on a bottle of snuff.

Author unknown, written before 1870

179

THE TEXAS WOLF BOY

Some twenty months ago a woman living on the banks of the Brazos missed her 3 months [sic] old baby from the pallet where she had left it lying during an absence of a few minutes. Search was made for the infant, but no trace of it could be discovered and the whole affair was wrapped in mystery until a few days ago.

A party of gentlemen riding through a somewhat unfrequented portion of the thick woods that border the river…were startled by seeing a strange object run across the road. Thinking at first sight that it was a wild animal, several of the party were about to fire on it, when the one who had been nearest to it called to them not to shoot but to run it down instead.

This was done with difficulty, for the underbrush was thick, but at last the creature was overtaken in a dense copse. It was half running, half leaping, first on all fours and then nearly upright.

The gentlemen dismounted and attempted to lay hands on it, but chattering frightfully and savagely biting and scratching, it broke away from them. They could see it had a human face, though the brown body was covered with long, tangled hair, and the nails on the feet and hands so long as to be claws. It ran with incredible swiftness, getting over fallen trees and dense masses of creepers at a rate that obliged its pursuers to exert themselves to the utmost to keep it in view. It finally ran into an immense oak tree that lay uprooted on the ground, and the hollow trunk of which formed a yawning cavern. By dint of poking in the tree with sticks, the party succeeded in driving out an old wolf which immediately took to its heels. It was not pursued, as it was not the object sought. This, too, was finally dislodged and lassoed with a lariat made of hides. It bit and scratched so fiercely that it was thought advisable not to approach it, and it was half dragged, half led home with the lariat about its neck howling and yelping like a wolf.

The fact of the woman's child having disappeared was well known to all, and it was decided that this must be the child.

The wolf had evidently stolen it, and for some reason adopted it as its own. The mother declared this conjecture was correct, claiming that her child had had a malformation of one ear, which peculiarity was found in the monster.

It is kept tied up in her cabin, suffering no one to lay hands upon it, and is fed on raw meat, as it refuses to touch any other food. The woman has hopes that she may yet re-awaken the human in it, but in the meantime she is reaping a harvest from the crowds who come daily from all parts of the country to inspect the strange creature.

From a "correspondent at Sandy Point, Brazoria County, Texas," published in the *Pittsburgh* (Pennsylvania) *Dispatch*, 1889; the "strange creature" finally "died in captivity."

Mr. Big Foot Wallace Tells Some Whoppers

A few weeks after my arrival [in Virginia] I went to a "fandango" that was given for my especial benefit. There was a great crowd there, and everybody was anxious to see the "Wild Texan," as they called me. I was the "lion" of the evening, particularly with the young ladies, who never tired of asking me questions about Mexico, Texas, the Indians, prairies, etc. I at first answered truly all the questions they asked me; but when I found they evidently doubted some of the stories I told them which were facts, I branched out and gave them some "whoppers," which they swallowed down "without gagging." For instance, one young woman wanted to know how many wild horses I had ever seen in a drove. I told her perhaps thirty or forty thousand.

"Oh! now! Mr. Wallace," she said, "don't try to make game of me in that way…!"

"Well, then," said I, "maybe you won't believe me when I tell you there is a sort of spider in Texas as big as a peck measure, the bite of which can only be cured by music."

"Oh, yes," she answered, "I believe that's all so, for I have read about them in a book."

Among other "whoppers," I told her there was a "varmint" in Texas called the "Santa Fe," that was still worse than the tarantula, for the best brass band in the country couldn't cure their sting; that the creature had a hundred legs and a sting on every one of them… when they sting and bite you at the same time, you first turn blue, then yellow, and then a beautiful bottle-green, then your hair all fell out and your finger nails dropped off, and you were as dead as a door-nail in five minutes, in spite of all the doctors in America.

"Oh! my! Mr. Wallace," said she, "how have you managed to live so long in that horrible country?"

"Why, you see," said I, "the only way to keep them at a distance is to 'chaw' tobacco and drink whiskey, and that is the reason the Temperance Society never flourished much in Texas."

"Oh!" said she, "what a horrible country that must be, where the people have to be stung to death, or 'chaw' tobacco and drink whiskey! I don't know which is the worst."

"Well," said I, "the people out there don't seem to mind it much; they get used to it after a while; in fact, they seem rather to like it, for they chaw tobacco and drink whiskey even in the winter-time, when the 'cow-killers' and sting-ing-lizards are all frozen up!"

John C. Duval, *The Adventures of Big-Foot Wallace*, 1870

★ ★ ★ ★ ★ ★ ★ ★ ★ ★ ★ ★ ★ ★

I went to Texas and ran wild on her prairies.

William Sydney Porter (O. Henry), in a letter to a friend, about 1905

★ ★ ★ ★ ★ ★ ★ ★ ★ ★ ★ ★ ★ ★

EARLY TEXAS LAND MEASURES

1. *A Caballeria*: 125 acres
2. *A Labor*: 177.1 acres
3. *A league*: 2.63 miles
4. *A sitio*: one square league (4,428 acres)

CHARLIE GOODNIGHT EXPLAINS HOW TO CATCH FIRE AND EAT PRAIRIE DOGS:

Charles Goodnight and Texas were born in the same year – 1836 – and Goodnight grew up to survive several adventurous lives: cowboy, military scout, Texas Ranger, trail driver, first Panhandle rancher. Goodnight knew how to endure in a harsh West Texas environment, and shared those skills in interviews shortly before he died in 1929. In some instances, I have condensed and paraphrased the interview.

Making Fire

"The 'catching of fire' by a pioneer plainsman became almost a science within itself.... As matches were unknown, other means of obtaining fire were necessary, the most common of which was the use of punk [decayed wood, used as tender] and steel. But in the prairie country, where there was no punk, the frontiersman had to turn to other ways of obtaining fire. A substitute for punk was frequently prepared as follows: Red corn cobs were burned to ashes, then the ashes were put in a tin plate and made into a very thin mush with water. Into this mush colored calico was put; when dried, this would catch fire readily from flint and steel.

"In spells of rain the rangers were soaked and a fire became a matter of serious concern. Perhaps their powder alone was dry. As a last resort, the scout rubbed a damp rag through powder held in the palm of his hand, until it was saturated with half-melted explosive. Then he slipped off one of his Spanish spurs, placed a percussion cap upon the end of a rowel, and wrapped the powder-laden rag round the rowel below the cap. He hit the cap sharply with the back of his Bowie knife. The rag caught the sparks and flashed into a blaze as the powder burned; and from this blaze the kindling was set."

Curing Thirst

"Water was very hard to find; and near the Plains the water was not only scarce but extremely bad. Most of it was undrinkable. In case of dire thirst, placing a small pebble in the mouth would help; a bullet was better, a piece of copper, if obtainable, was better still, and the prickly pear [cactus] was best of all. A piece of prickly pear which had the stickers cut off and had been peeled, when placed in one's mouth, would keep it moist indefinitely. And if the drinking water happened to be muddy, a thin slice of pear was peeled and placed in it. All the sediment adhered to the prickly pear and sank to the bottom, leaving the water clear and drinkable.

"On the Plains, a scout was always glad to see a mesquite bush. In a dry climate – the climate natural to the mesquite – its seed seems to spring up only from the droppings of an animal. The only animal on the Plains that ate mesquite beans was the mustang. Mustangs rarely grazed out from water more than three miles… Therefore, when a scout saw a mesquite bush, he knew that water was within three miles."

More Prickly Pear Lore

"Prickly pears, peeled and pounded to a pulp, make an excellent poultice for wounds. There is nothing better, unless it is cold mud. Either will relieve the pain and remove the fever and poison. A prickly-pear poultice is especially good for rattlesnake bites. Further, when the stickers have been singed off by fire, the pears are splendid food for cattle. The pears are good food for man, too….

Alternative Dining

"When the Rangers were outside the buffalo region there was nothing for them [to eat] but the prairie dogs. The only fault they could find with prairie dogs was that they were too small and very hard to get. [Rangers] always tried to keep a little flour on hand to thicken soup [and] prairie dogs, being very fat, made good soup, but this was not very satisfying; after a meal of it one became hungry again in two or three hours. Rangers would boil a prairie dog or two, the more dogs in the kettle the better, and with a little flour, make quite a pot of soup."

From interviews conducted over several years by J. Evetts Haley, published in *Southwest Review,* 1925

Lost Texas

Notla

How do these things keep happening? Here – in deepest southeast Ochiltree County – is another example of reverse thinking. Notla, a name that does not sound like much, comes from reversing the name of a wholesale grocery firm which operated a store there about 1900 – the Alton Grocery Company. There should have been a better way of naming places than reversing words.

Pull Tight

This name didn't last long for the farming settlement, but it indicated how parsimonious and obstinate early citizens were. Just before the century's turn, in soliciting a post office, government officials refused to accept "Pull Tight" as a permanent name and suggested instead – for reasons now forgotten – "Tundra." It was a strange name (meaning a treeless arctic area) for the Van Zandt County piney woods region of East Texas, but it stuck.

Col. John Watkin and his [wagon] train were caught in a driving rain between Laredo and Uvalde. Camping out, the Colonel found that a roll of bills in his pocket was wet and placed them before the camp fire to dry. While the party was eating supper, a jenny [female donkey] on which they carried their packs very innocently protruded her tongue and took in her throat $785 of Uncle Sam's currency. The Colonel, by mere chance happened to look that way just as the mule was swallowing his valuable rations, ran to her, put his hand down her throat, seized the greenbacks and brought them forth intact.

Uvalde Hesperian, March 14, 1885

Here's to old Texas, the land of the free
The home of the rattlesnake, horned frog and flea.
I'll sing of its riches and tell of its fame,
While starving to death on a government claim!

Traditional, but said of several western states

The term "cow-hunter"…has (or had) a peculiar significance in [Texas], where in times not very remote the "cow" was the medium of exchange, the standard of values, the one industry that overshadowed and eclipsed all others. At that time [1866] every man in Western Texas, be he merchant, mechanic, preacher, millionaire or poor white, owned…cattle and was estimated by others, and took his place in society, in exact proportion to the "cows" he owned. Not "cattle," but "cows," not a "cattleman," but a "cow-man," that was the generic term. In speaking of the individual cow, he generally called it a "cow-brute"; why "brute," I never could see the point in particular, for he never said "horse-brute," or "hog-brute," but always "cow-brute."

The complicated system of marks and brands was as unintelligible to me as the marks on an Egyptian monument, but was so plain to the native that "he who ran might read," and this literally, for as the cowman dashed over the prairie at full speed the marked ears and often obscure brand was as an open book.

The cow-man of those days led a hard and adventurous life; he was by turns hunter and Indian fighter, for his cattle roamed over a vast range, and in his pursuit of them he was likely at any time to meet with bands of hostile Indians and have to fight for his life. He was a walking (or riding) arsenal in the way of firearms, and carried his double-barreled shot gun across his lap, and his two big brass-mounted, old-fashioned dragoon pistols in his belt. The daily struggle for existence that was led by the cowman, his familiarity with danger, his constant exposure to the elements, his woodcraft, all combined to make him an ideal frontiersman, who is fast passing away. In these degenerate days of syndicates and pasture fences and cattle kings, the cow-man of twenty years ago is nearly extinct, and soon we will know him no more.

H.H. McConnell, *Five Years a Cavalryman*, 1888

W.W. Schermerhorn, an attorney of San Angelo, once a citizen of this town, while under the influence of liquor last week in the saloon of Memph Elliot, had his feet badly burned by some unprincipled party pouring alcohol in his boots and setting fire to them. The proprietor of the saloon, Memph Elliot, is charged with the crime, and the people of San Angelo are very indignant at the outrage. It is thought that amputation will be necessary in order to save his life. Judge Schermerhorn has entered suit against Elliot for $4,000, which he will have no trouble in recovering, as he has good witnesses who saw the affair.

Colorado City Clipper, April 11, 1885

"*No rendirse, muchachos!*"
("Don't surrender, boys!")

Traditional, but probably mythical, last words of Alamo commander William Travis, as he lay dying near a breach in the north wall of the Alamo

I GOT MY FIRST GLIMPSE OF THE FAR WEST WHEN I WAS BARELY 9 YEARS OLD

…and I was miserably disappointed in it, for it was nothing like I had pictured in my mind from reports that neighbors who had previously pioneered had sent back. I was fully expecting to see Indians pop out from behind every tree, and I couldn't see any use in the long, woodsy stretches of oak, hackberry, elm and cottonwood, unless they did. At that they hid bands of them, but, as luck had it – bad I called it then, but afterward I thanked my stars – we didn't scare 'em up. Prairie travel was much more to my notion, for wild game of the kind that was new to me was abundant. I remember that buffalo herds just about scared me to death, and that when I was told to hands off of 'em, it just about took my life to do it, for the idea of sending a bullet whizzing at one was extremely fascinating.

…It amuses me now to think what little frontier settlements Houston and Dallas were at that time [about 1853]. But to me they were the real thing. Fort Worth, garrisoned with soldiers, was immensely attractive, but we seldom went by there, unless we were headed for Red River or that vicinity. I reckon there was as many as two dozen houses, possibly a few more or less, besides the fort buildings, in the town. It was a sight to a green country boy to watch the soldiers drilling, and all such, and I wished I could stay and watch them indefinitely. Every time we passed through Fort Worth, I resolved that sometime – when I had a lot of money being a cowboy, that being my idea of getting rich, and being sure that it took money to make a soldier – I was going to be one.

Attributed to Bill Morgan in *Dallas Semi-Weekly Farm News*, circa late 1930

TEXANESE

Lopes and Smokes

This was an early means of estimating distance. The term springs from the fact that most travel was by horseback, and the usual casual gait was a lope. Cowboys rolled their own cigarettes, which was a tricky maneuver requiring the rider to stop the horse and "fix the makings." So a trip might be four smokes distant. In this century, in West Texas, driving their pickups, cowboys often measure distance by beers: "Big Spring's 'bout five beers direct west, and one beer left, outta Stamford," a West Texan once explained.

Hubbin' It

Doing the best you can with what you got, which is not much, but that's the way most rural Texans made it in the early years. The term comes from the metal rim on wagon wheels, which rusted and broke often, leaving the wagons "riding on the hub." In rough times, cowboys used to say they were "hubbin' hell."

Whipout

A roll of cash. It's what showy Texans, like newly-created oil millionaires, called their pocket cash when they wanted to impress someone – "That ol' Cadillac sure put a dent in my whipout." Often the whipout was all the money the showoff had in the world, but making an impression was more important than admitting he was short on finances.

Plunder Room

This is a Hill Country term that came from early German settlers. It is a room, either in or near a house, that was used for storage, and came from the German word – "plunder" – meaning "trash." It's the place, like an attic, where all of us keep our stuff that should be thrown away, but is not.

One of Texas' best-known journalists and authors and one of America's most successful travel writers, Jerry Flemmons is a thirty-two-year veteran staff member, reporter, columnist, feature writer and travel editor of the *Fort Worth Star-Telegram*. He has toured the world for more than twenty-five years, into 120 countries for more than two million air and land miles aboard jets and ships, autos and trains, mopeds, horses, camels, elephants, dog sleds dugout canoes, hot-air balloons, a blimp and one zebra.

Flemmons' stories have won most state writing awards and have been reprinted in college textbooks. As a news journalist, he has covered major international stories: the Kennedy assassination; the Jack Ruby trial; the shootings and murders from atop the University of Texas tower, where he was the only reporter to witness the carnage on the tower moments after police shot Charles Joseph Whitman. He was one of six newsmen who served as pallbearers for Lee Harvey Oswald's burial in Fort Worth. He reported from South Vietnam and other Southeast Asia war zones.

Through all his travels, Jerry Flemmons' heart remains in Texas, where he was born, raised, educated, and has kept a home base always. *Texas Siftings* speaks strongly of his Texanness and of his willingness to share Texas with the world.